Astrological 1

This is the perfect book f̲ᵒʳ̲ logical knowledge, who wants to know the best time to schedule any type of activity. It is also perfect for the wise person who wants to know *when not* to schedule something!

Have you wondered about whether you should take that trip or ask for that raise? Do you want to know when the best time is for a wedding? How about knowing in advance the times when you will be the most creative and dazzling—wouldn't that help when needing to impress the boss?

This book is really different from all of the others that have been published on transits (those planets that are actually moving around in the heavens making aspects to our natal planets). It gives the subject area first—such as creativity, relationships, health, etc.—and then tells you what transits to look for. You don't even need to know that much about astrology, because the introductory chapters are so thorough that you will be able to use this book with only an ephemeris or astrological calendar to tell you where the planets are. Everything else is explained in detail. The author explains what transits are, how they affect your daily life, how to track them, how to make decisions based on transits and much more. Then she moves on to specific areas of concern and what to look for in the planets.

Just a few of the topics covered are: accidents, business, career, communication, creativity, education, romance, finance, health, law, real estate, travel, marriage, energy, and relationships of all types.

With the information in each section, you can combine as many factors as you like to get the most positive results. If you are going on a business trip you can look at the accidents section to avoid any trouble, the travel section to find out the best date, the relationship section to see how you will get along with the other person, the business section to see if it is a good time to do business, the communication section to see if things will flow smoothly and on and on. In this way, you can choose the absolute best date for just about anything! You will be amazed at how effective this system is. Electional astrology has been used for centuries, but now it is being given in the most easily understood and practical format yet.

About Edna Copeland Ryneveld

Edna Copeland Ryneveld, who was born and raised in Texas, lives with her husband on a 160-acre farm in southwestern Missouri. In addition to raising chickens and a few head of cattle, they own and operate a health food store in the nearby town of Bolivar.

Ms. Ryneveld has taught school and worked as a secretary in California, and was employed for three and a half years as a copywriter and traffic director at a radio station in Bolivar. While working at the radio station, she at one time had her own program on astrology.

As a writer, Ms. Ryneveld has had magazine and newspaper articles, short stories, and poetry published. She was founder and president of a local writer's club and describes herself as an avid reader, with a wide range of interests. She is especially interested in astrology and has been studying it extensively for several years. Her experiences with the subject led her to write this, her first book.

To Write to the Author

We cannot guarantee that every letter written to the author can be answered, but all will be forwarded. Both the author and the publisher appreciate hearing from readers, learning of your enjoyment and benefit from this book. Llewellyn also publishes a bi-monthly news magazine with news and reviews of practical esoteric studies and articles helpful to the student, and some readers' questions and comments to the author may be answered through this magazine's columns if permission to do so is included in the original letter. The author sometimes participates in seminars and workshops, and dates and places are announced in *The Llewellyn New Times*. To write to the author, or to ask a question, write to:

Edna Copeland Ryneveld
c/o THE LLEWELLYN NEW TIMES
P.O. Box 64383-674, St. Paul, MN 55164-0383, U.S.A.

Please enclose a self-addressed, stamped envelope for reply, or $1.00 to cover costs.

THE LLEWELLYN MODERN ASTROLOGY LIBRARY

Books for the *Leading Edge* of practical and applied astrology as we move toward the culmination of the 20th century.

This is not speculative astrology, nor astrology so esoteric as to have little practical application in meeting the needs of people in these critical times. Yet, these books go far beyond the meaning of "practicality" as seen prior to the 1980's. Our needs are spiritual as well as mundane, planetary as well as particular, evolutionary as well as progressive. Astrology grows with the times, and our times make heavy demands upon Intelligence and Wisdom.

The authors are all professional astrologers drawing from their own practice and knowledge of historical persons and events, demonstrating proof of their conclusions with the horoscopes of real people in real situations.

Modern Astrology relates the individual person in the Universe in which he/she lives, not as a passive victim of alien forces, but as an active participant in an environment expanded to the breadth *and depth* of the Cosmos. We are not alone, and our responsibilities are infinite.

The horoscope is both a measure and a guide to personal movement—seeing every act undertaken, every decision made, every event, as *time dynamic*, with effects that move through the many dimensions of space and levels of consciousness in fulfillment of Will and Purpose. Every act becomes an act of Will, for we extend our awareness to consequences reaching to the ends of time and space.

This is astrology supremely important to this unique period in human history, when Pluto transits through Scorpio, and Neptune through Capricorn. The books in this series are intended to provide insight into the critical needs and the critical decisions that must be made.

These books, too, are "active agents," bringing to the reader knowledge which will liberate the higher forces inside each person to the end that we may fulfill that for which we were intended.

—Carl Llewellyn Weschcke

Llewellyn's Modern Astrology Library

Transits in Reverse

Edna Copeland Ryneveld

1989
Llewellyn Publications
St. Paul, Minnesota, 55164-0383, U.S.A.

International Standard Book Number: 0-87542-674-3
Library of Congress Catalog Number: 88-45191

First Edition, 1988
First Printing, 1988
Second Printing, 1989

Library of Congress Cataloguing-in-Publication Data
    Transits in reverse / by Edna Ryneveld.
        p. cm. — (Llewellyn's practical astrology series)
    Bibliography: p.
    ISBN 0-87542-674-3 :
    1. Horoscopes. 2. Transits—Miscellanea. I. Title. II. Series.
    BF1728.A2R96 1988
    133.5—dc 19
                                                                88-45191
                                                                CIP

Cover Painting: David Egge

Produced by Llewellyn Publications
Typography and Art property of Chester-Kent, Inc.

Published by
LLEWELLYN PUBLICATIONS
A Division of Chester-Kent, Inc.
P.O. Box 64383
St. Paul, MN 55164-0383, U.S.A.
Printed in the United States of America

Dedication

To Betty Finnegan, friend and catalyst
&
Cheryl Coen and Robert Copeland,
my indispensable critics

Contents

There is a tide in the affairs of men,
Which taken at the flood, leads on to fortune;
Omitted, all the voyages of their life
Is bound in shallows and in miseries.
—William Shakespeare
Julius Caesar, Act IV. Sc. 3

Know the flow and go with it.
—Edna Copeland Ryneveld
Transits in Reverse, No Act

Introduction

Time, Sweat and Transits

New to astrology and very inexperienced with it several years ago, I naively and enthusiastically turned to the ephemeris once to see if it might be a good time to buy a small business my husband and I had seen for sale. We were very excited about it and were almost of a mind to snap it up immediately before someone else did. I pulled out both our charts and wrote down the transits in effect for that day. Then I lugged a large book on transit interpretation down off the shelf above my desk and read the meaning of all those transits. Each one ran about three hundred words.

I found nothing. Nothing, at any rate, about buying or selling a business, investing in anything, or about finances in general.

However, I wasn't too surprised not to find anything pertinent for the very day the idea struck (remember, I was new to astrology), and went happily back to the ephemeris. This time I wrote down all the transits for the two of us for the coming week.

Again, nothing.

Then the coming month.

Nothing.

Then the next month. And the next. And the next and the next and the next.

Nothing. Nothing. Nothing.

By this time, I was getting tired and just a tad irritable. Finally, hundreds of transits and hours later, by now exhausted and very irritable, I found an apparently applicable transit—for eleven months down the road.

"To heck with it," I said and we went ahead and bought the business. (We've had it for six years now and are still thinking maybe it's a "sleeper.")

Another time, we wanted to sell some real estate, and I again sweated through a similar exercise: hours of uncertainty, looking up transits and reading through interpretations, searching, searching, searching for a reference to a specific topic. I wondered then and many times afterwards: Why isn't there a book that lists events or areas of interest and then gives transits that pertain to them, instead of the other way around?

Finding none available, I decided to write one myself, so, here it is! With this book, if you want to know about one particular thing, you can look it up instead of sitting around trying to fish it out of tons of unrelated verbiage or trying to figure it out by applying your perhaps-not-yet-acquired experience. This sort of "cookbook" astrology is often sneered at in the literature as being beneath one's dignity and intelligence. But, believe me, to a rank beginner, these types of books are worth their weight in time, sweat, and anxiety. They're like training wheels on a bicycle or the Suzuki method of teaching music—first, the novices gain confidence and pride in their ability to perform like "the grownups" and then they venture on to learn to pop wheelies or to compose symphonies.

This book is your training wheels for transits. And, as paradoxical as it might seem, you'll eventually find it easier to "go forward" with transits after having done them in reverse for a while.

One more thing. I do not claim absolute completeness for this book, though I have tried to be as thorough as possible. The traditionally-formatted astrology books I've consulted and cross-checked, plus some others you may find interesting, are listed in the Bibliography. Some are truly excellent, and I'm especially indebted to Robert Hand's *Planets in Transit* for his psychological insights.

—Edna Ryneveld
Humansville, Mo.

Chapter 1

Transit Tracking

A "transit" is astrological shorthand for a point or time during which a transiting (moving) planet makes an aspect of certain degrees to one or more of your natal planets or to an important angle. You find out where a transiting planet is at any given time by checking its position in an ephemeris, a book of planetary positions used by navigators and astrologers alike.

Any good bookstore should have ephemerides or be able to get one of several types for you. The *Llewellyn Astrological Calendar* and the *Llewellyn Daily Planetary Guide* both contain a current ephemeris. If you prefer, you could use one of the astrological services listed in their catalog, *The Llewellyn New Times**, to ascertain your transits or to have your natal chart done.

Or you could draw one up for yourself. There are many books available that teach you how, and it's not at all difficult.

Neither is finding transits, once you have your natal chart and an ephemeris in hand. Simply turn to any month in question in an ephemeris of the current year. Find the date in the left-hand column, and by reading across to the right, you'll find the transiting positions of the planets in columns headed by the symbols for each planet. (See Chapter 2 for the symbols.)

---

* See the Stay In Touch page in the back of this book for order information.

These positions are then compared with those of your natal planets to determine if there is a transiting aspect. If so, there is a transit of your natal planet. For instance, suppose your natal Jupiter is at ten degrees Scorpio, and by looking in the ephemeris for today's date, you find that Saturn is at ten degrees Virgo. Since that is exactly 60 degrees apart, you have *transiting* Saturn sextile *natal* Jupiter, or, as it's more often phrased, Saturn sextile Jupiter (assuming you or whomever you're discussing it with knows you mean transiting and not natal aspects). The transiting planet is always listed first.

You do this with all the transiting planets, checking them against each of the natal planets, up to 180 degrees in either direction. Then, if you're not an experienced professional who knows all the pertinent information in your bones, you turn to a book on transits and read an interpretation for each one you've found.

This is fine if you just want to know, in general, what may be coming up for you. It's an excellent way to be prepared to handle any possible problems or to take advantage of any approaching opportunities. However, if at the moment you're concerned with your love life, your relationship with your boss, or whether or not you should hock your socks and invest in real estate, reading through the information for all those transits can be frustrating and time-consuming. And even then, you might not find what you were looking for.

How to Use This Book

With this book, all you do is turn to the chapter you're interested in, where you'll find the transiting planet always listed before the natal planet. Then you either:

1) scan down the transits listed and compare them with your list of current transits to see if you have any of that category in effect at the moment; or

2) select an appropriate transit from the chapter and scan through the ephemeris to see when it will be in effect for you.

Suppose, for example, you are huddling around the fire on a cold, blustery night in January dreaming of your summer vacation. Not wishing to repeat last year's fiasco (during which nothing went right, there were delays on every hand, and you came home feeling more tense than when you left), you turn to the chapter on travel in this book.

Looking quickly through the brief descriptions, you find several that indicate a propitious time to take a vacation. You make note of those and turn to your ephemeris for next June, July, and August. Soon you find you have two of the favorable transits in effect next summer, one in early June and one in late July.

Eagerly, you check all your transits in effect for the targeted time in June and in July. Since there are a couple of possibly unfavorable ones also indicated for the first time slot, you decide, with a great deal of confidence and relief, to take your vacation in the latter part of July. How can you miss? You'll have Venus in the first house (you're in the vacationing mood), Mars in the ninth (travel will be pleasant), Venus trine Mercury (a good time to start a vacation), and no adverse transits in sight!

Cross-Checking

No transit is an island, however. You should check all possible cross references to what you're looking for, i.e., Physical Energy to Health, Communications to Business and Relationships, Accidents to Travel and so on.

Suppose, for example, you are a salesperson planning to take a business trip in the near future. Whether or not you find anything in the travel section pertaining to business travel (or any travel) during the time you'll be able to take the trip, you should check other sections as well. Look into Relationships (how you'll relate to customers or colleagues), Business (a good time to make an impression, take risks, forge ahead, or to hold back and listen?), Self (self-confidence, assertiveness), Accidents, Communications, and anything else you think pertinent. If most or all of these areas are favorable and there are no heavy-handed adverse transits in effect at the time, your sales trip should work out well whether you found any mention of travel or not.

Equivocating? Me?

In this and other astrology books, you'll notice the liberal use of modifying words like "may," "tendency," "probably," "perhaps," "could," "possibly," and so on. Many people seize this astrological propensity to detract from the discipline. Actually, these words are utilized because, even though the energy of the transit is available and the conditions for its implementation are right (much like a tornado watch instead of a warning), you, in your infinite wisdom and consummate use of free will, may (!) choose not to actualize them. Or, they may simply be minor transits in relation to other transit energies in effect at the same time. Or, it may just not be the proper time in your life for them to mean much. A particular transit at age 17 or 21 or 42 will manifest—or be actualized by you—in completely different ways. The use of these qualifiers indicates astrology's incredible flexibility and universal application rather than any so-called inherent wishy-washiness.

By the same token, nothing is written in concrete. Yogananda, one of the great yogis of all time, used to "go against the stars" on purpose just to prove that he could:

> Occasionally I told astrologers to select my worst periods, according to planetary indications, and I would still accomplish whatever task I set myself. It is true that my success at such times has been preceded by extraordinary difficulties. But my conviction has always been justified: faith in divine protection, and right use of man's God-given will, are forces more formidable than are influences flowing from the heavens.

Paramahansa Yogananda
Autobiography of a Yogi

And so can you.

Chapter 2

Stalking Symbols, Gamboling with Glyphs, and Descending on Degrees

The daily trek of the planets across the heavens, "around" the Earth, is plotted on a circular diagram called a *chart*, *birth chart*, *natal chart*, or *horoscope*. This naturally entails an apparent journey of 360 degrees. The relationship between a transiting planet's position and a natal planet's position is described by the number of degrees on the circle between them. Over the centuries certain degrees of distance, or *aspects*, have been found consistently important and are used by astrologers almost to the exclusion of all others. These are:

Aspect Name	Degrees of Separation	Symbol
Conjunction	0	♂
Sextile	60	✳
Square	90	☐
Trine	120	△
Opposition	180	♂

Like the effect of different types of music on a pair of dancers, each aspect contributes a unique set of constraints and opportunities to its planetary consorts. Planets in conjunction, either in natal or in transiting aspect, for instance, will have a different reaction to each other (and you to them) than the same planets in any other aspect. It is these differing relationships which are detailed, by category, in this book.

Glyphs

The origin, development, and meaning of the glyphs for the signs of the zodiac and the planets is a fascinating and illuminating study in itself. For our purposes now, however, it's enough to know the symbols and be able to use them. Their use will save you time and space.

SIGN	GLYPH	PLANET	GLYPH
Aries	♈	Sun	☉
Taurus	♉	Mercury	☿
Gemini	♊	Moon	☽
Cancer	♋	Earth	⊕
Leo	♌	Venus	♀
Virgo	♍	Mars	♂
Libra	♎	Jupiter	♃
Scorpio	♏	Saturn	♄
Sagittarius	♐	Uranus	♅
Capricorn	♑	Neptune	♆
Aquarius	♒	Pluto	♇ or ♀
Pisces	♓		

Knowing the symbols and glyphs for the aspects, planets and signs, then, you can write Saturn trine Sun in Sagittarius as ♄ △ ☉ in ♐.

Where the Planets Are

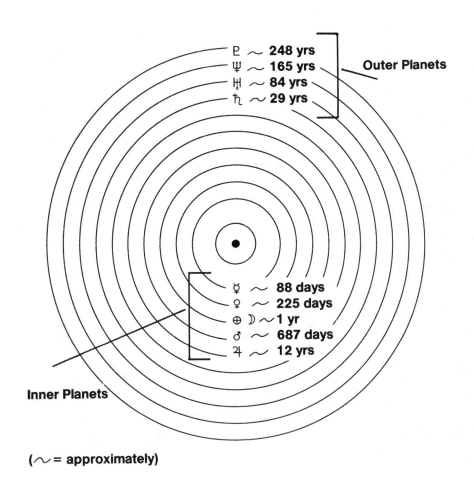

Outer Planets

♇ ~ 248 yrs	
♆ ~ 165 yrs	
♅ ~ 84 yrs	
♄ ~ 29 yrs	

☿ ~ 88 days	
♀ ~ 225 days	
⊕ ☽ ~ 1 yr	
♂ ~ 687 days	
♃ ~ 12 yrs	

Inner Planets

(~ = approximately)

ACTUAL SOLAR SYSTEM
(Heliocentric)

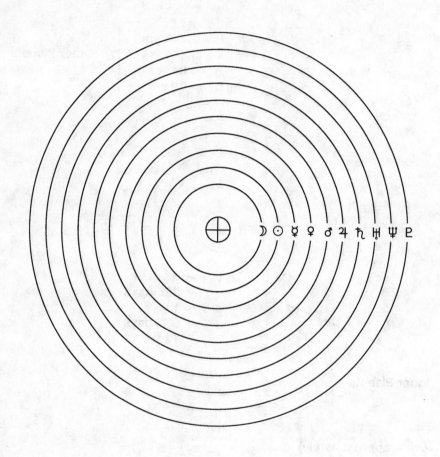

ASTROLOGICAL (Geocentric) VIEW

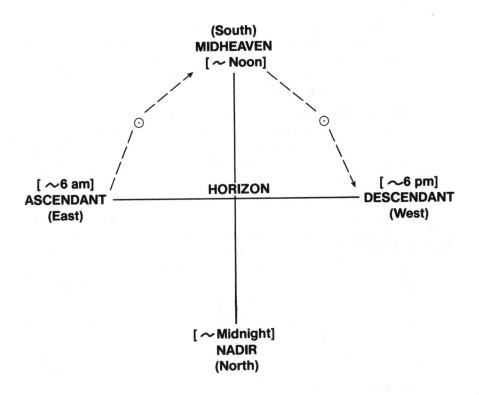

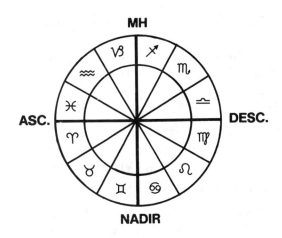

9

Ascendant, Descendant, Midheaven, Nadir

In addition to the signs, houses, and planets, there are four other important points of the horoscope. In your birth chart, the *Ascendant* is the point on the horizon (in the East, naturally) where the Sun rose on the day of your birth. Directly opposite the Ascendant is the point on the horizon (of Earth, viewed from Earth) where the Sun set. This point is called the *Descendant*.

Visualize a line connecting these two points, and then a line vertically intersecting it at its midpoint, forming a +. The top of the vertical line, symbolizing the Sun's daily zenith, is called the *Midheaven*, or *Medium Coeli*. Its opposite point (on the other side of the Earth) is the *Nadir*, or *Imum Coeli*. The + thus formed is often referred to as the *Cross of Matter*, symbolizing Earth (or the material plane to some), while the outer circle of a horoscope diagram represents the universe, symbolizing infinity (or the spiritual plane). (See chart on page 9.)

These points are also called the *Four Angles*, and they lend extra strength and importance to any planet within eight or ten degrees of them. The angles are intense channels of energy, and they magnify the significance and inherent characteristics of nearby planets, much as a nearby TV transmitter enhances your set's reception.

Of the Four Angles, astrologers pay particular attention to transits to the Ascendant and Midheaven, and you'll find such transits often referred to in many sections of this book.

Multiplicities

The signs of the zodiac are divided into two groups known as *quadruplicities* and *triplicities*. (Curiously, there are three quadruplicities and four triplicities.) The quadruplicities are the *Cardinal, Fixed*, and *Mutable* signs, as follows:

Cardinal: Aries, Cancer, Libra, and Capricorn
Fixed: Taurus, Leo, Scorpio, and Aquarius
Mutable: Gemini, Virgo, Sagittarius, and Pisces.

The triplicities are the elements *Fire, Air, Water*, and *Earth:*

Fire: Aries, Leo, and Sagittarius
Air: Gemini, Libra, and Aquarius
Water: Cancer, Scorpio, and Pisces
Earth: Taurus, Virgo, and Capricorn.

I'm telling you all this because you can expect certain and distinct categories of events or experiences to occur when a planet transits through a particular classification of sign. According to Frances Sakoian and Louis Acker in their book, *Transits Simplified* (see Bibliography), a planet transiting a:

Cardinal sign is "likely to bring about immediate crisis situations";

Fixed sign means "entrenched conditions can be encountered or overwhelming change could occur";

Mutable sign means that "irritations and stimulations from the past could influence the nature of the transit";

Fire sign indicates "issues will concern personal authority, leadership, and growth. Events will be handled in a positive, outgoing manner";

Earth sign signifies that "practical affairs of life will be emphasized and dealt with as the individual is confronted with them";

Air sign means "intellectual and social issues will be emphasized, often with the individual taking the initiative";

Water sign indicates "the emotions, feelings, and intuitive impressions will play a part in the transpiring events, often with the native responding to the outside stimuli in a personal way."

This information can help you better understand the nature of your transits, if you care to use it. However, simply turning to the chapter in this book detailing the area of life you're interested in at the moment will be immensely helpful on its own.

Chapter 3

Orbs, Timing, and Decisions

When looking up your transits in the ephemeris, where do you start counting? Ten degrees before they're exact? Five? Three? Only when it's precisely exact?

The number of degrees you allow between a transiting planet's position and its exact point of aspecting a natal planet is called an *orb*. Astrologers differ on the degrees of the orbs they use, depending on the nature and size of the planets involved, on the type of aspect that is being made, and maybe even on the weather on alternate Thursdays.

Generally, the larger, slower-moving outer planets are allowed a greater orb than the speedier inner planets. I like to think of orbs as spheres of influence emanating from the planets, much like the coverage area of radio broadcasting transmitters. A 50,000-watt transmitter can cover a larger area than its 2500-watt baby brother. Your car radio can pick up the super broadcaster from many miles away, while you might have to be within 20 miles of the smaller one to catch your favorite yodeler.

And so it is with planets. A super broadcaster such as Saturn, say, may be able to make its influence felt from as far away as ten degrees before it makes an exact aspect to a natal planet. Since Saturn moves relatively slowly, taking 28 years to complete an orbit, that ten degrees could translate into several months or even a year before it makes an exact square, trine, or other aspect. Feisty, fleet-footed Mercury, on the other hand, is a lightweight among planets whose broadcasting power would be classed in the local, low-watt range. His influence isn't usually picked up until he gets closer to making the exact transit.

There is another variable, however: the quality of your receiver. A poor receiver will get little or no reception, even from a super broadcaster, until it's practically right on top of it. That is to say, a person with little self-awareness who just plows through life like a dazed duck on a goose farm will not be sensitive enough to discern the foreshadowing of an impending transit, important or otherwise.

Arbitrary designation of different orbs for different planets by different astrological writers should be taken with a grain of brewer's yeast. Everyone's degree of sensitivity to astrological events and everything else varies. And even this does not remain constant throughout a lifetime. By being aware of yourself and observing how and when various transits affect you, you sensitize and fine-tune your "receiver." You will come to know at what distance ahead of an exact transit you become aware of its effects, depending on the size and nature of the planet, on the type of transit involved, and, yes, maybe even on the weather on alternate Thursdays.

By "become aware of its effects," I mean you'll begin to feel stirrings in your life or thoughts in the area of the transiting planet's influence. The effects will begin to "fade in," something like the Doppler Effect (named after the fellow who made the observation that a sound's frequency increases as it approaches you and fades as it gets further away from you). They'll fade in to (build up to) a crescendo and then fade out.

In practice, the subject of the number of degrees of orb (or the distance from exact transit) doesn't loom terribly large. It becomes a matter of intuitive knowledge as to whether to expect a planet's transiting influence to "kick in" six months, six days, or six minutes before it's exact in your life. Until then, you can use the point of exact aspect, as the transit will normally be stronger then anyway, or use the following as a general guideline.

Aspect	Sun, Moon	Inner	Outer
Conjunction	10°	4°	6°
Opposition	10°	6°	8°
Trine	8°	4°	6°
Square	7°	4°	5°
Sextile	4°	2°	3°

Timing

Some astrologers maintain that it's unnecessary to pay attention to the transits of the inner planets, because they move so rapidly that any influence they may have is too fleeting to be of importance. It's true that a transit by the Moon may last only a couple of hours, while a fly-by of Mercury, Venus, or Mars may last a day or two, maybe a little longer. Yet, these can be very helpful when planning your day-to-day activities—say, all else being equal (meaning no big no-no's from other transits), whether to have the gang in on Friday (favorable Venus) or whether you'd better utilize the evening by staying home alone listening to subliminal self-awareness tapes while cleaning out the garage or riding ten fast miles on your stationary bike (difficult Mars).

Still, many people prefer not to bother with the inner planetary transits, electing to let the "little things" take care of themselves while they concentrate on the major cycles or areas of development indicated by the transits of the larger, slower planets. You, too, may find keeping up with the many transits of the inner planets something of a bother. It's of interest to note, however, that everything in the universe is interconnected. Nothing is wasted or useless, whether *we* are aware of its function or not.

Many astrologers have noted that when something of importance happens, whether it be an event or personal transformation (though an important event will usually trigger a transformation and *vice versa*), there is more than one transit signifying it. An event or type of event indicated by a long-range, outer-planet transit will often occur when at least one corroborating inner planet also transits. If you never take inner-planet transits into consideration, you will, *of course*, accord them no importance—and lose a useful timing tool.

Another way to help pinpoint when an event may occur or when a transit's influence may be most intense is to notice whether the transiting planet is direct, making a station, or retrograde. From our vantage point here on Earth, the planets often appear to engage in some sleight-of-hand shenanigans. It's all optical illusion, of course, but they do, from time to time, look as if they stand still and then reverse their normal course and travel backwards along their orbits. In the ephemeris you'll find this indicated by an "R" or " ℞ " beside a planet's position for when it turns retrograde and "D" for the day it turns direct, or begins to "go forward" again. Not all ephemerides will mark an "S" for standing still—called "making a station"—but you can tell because the planet's position doesn't change for days or weeks.

When a planet makes a station over one of your natal planets, it's like someone's taking you by the shoulders and giving you a good shake. Your attention is requested. And it's during this time, especially if reinforced by another transit, that the event signified by this transiting planet will very likely occur.

A transiting planet can make a pass over a natal planet three times in succession by going retrograde: first direct, then retrograde, then direct again. Some say that an area of your life in which you need to learn lessons or make changes will be "politely" brought to your attention during the first pass. If you do nothing about it, the lesson is reinforced more strongly during the retrograde phase (especially if this includes a station). Most can't ignore the problem at this point, but if you do succeed in repressing it, the third pass really hits you on the head and forces you to change or take action in some way. If you handle the situation during the first or second transit, however, there will be no problems during the third. Some planets will even go retrograde and direct several times, possibly contacting your natal planet several more times.

Deciding Which Transit to Bank On

Occasionally, transits will present you with conflicting indications. Then you must decide which transit to "bank on." Experience and careful self-observation will eventually soften this dilemma for you. Fortunately, though, there are guidelines you can consider in the meantime.

Some transits produce more impact than others, and in formulating your plans, it would behoove you to take this into account, waiting, for instance, for a more "heavy-duty" transit to embark on something truly important to you. This was touched on a bit before in talking about more than one transit being in effect for significant events in your life.

You can see, then, that if only one transit is in effect which indicates, say, a good time for financial speculation, especially if it involves only inner planets, it would not be indication enough for you to invest your life savings and the family cow in Air Castles, Inc.

A transit by an outer planet will carry more significance by virtue of its longer duration, if nothing else. To say that the outer planets generally deal with weightier subjects than the inner planets may therefore be begging the question. It may be they just last longer. To someone whose personal focus is not mental but physical activity, a transit of Mercury, emphasizing mental pursuits, may feel as onerous as Saturn's longer-term, heavy hand at times. It may seem to that person like income tax time in July.

A transit will also be more important or intense to you if it reinforces the proclivities of the natal planet, house, and aspects over which it is passing. It will be like adding a candle to a room that already contains one, rather than lighting a single candle in the dark.

The strength of the planet being transited will also determine the relative strength of the transit. Transiting Neptune conjunct Moon in the fifth house will not be as influential as, say, Neptune conjunct natal Neptune on the Ascendant. (Because, like Boardwalk, the Ascendant is an important location, and Neptune, like Rockefeller, is more loaded than John Q. Moon.)

As mentioned in Chapter 2, transits on or near all the angles—Ascendant, Descendant, Nadir, and Midheaven—can be given extra emphasis.

The transiting aspects of conjunction and opposition are usually considered strongest, followed by squares and trines. And, as mentioned earlier, a longer transit or one which passes over a point three or more times by retrograding and then going direct again will obviously have a more profound effect than one which lasts only a few hours or days (though a shorter one can serve as a trigger to release the pent-up pressure of the longer one).

Therefore, if you're wanting to advance your education, you'd stand a better chance with Jupiter transit Mercury, especially if it makes a station, and especially in the third or ninth house, than to plunk down your several thousand dollars under a Mercury-transit-Jupiter impulse.

Your age and position in life should also be taken into account when attempting to apply a transit to yourself. An unemployed 25-year-old dockworker will not want to give as much weight to advice about expanding his capital investments as would an entrepreneur of any age.

If all this sounds about as clear as smog on a hot, still day, don't worry. As you work with your transits or those of others, you'll be amazed at how quickly you'll develop a sixth sense about it. You'll learn from experience, which is still the best teacher, and your intuition will sharpen. It's like learning to bowl or drive or fly or walk across a cow pasture. It's difficult at first because you have to remember all the moves, but soon your automatic pilot takes over, and you'll find yourself maneuvering like a professional.

Chapter 4

Accidents

Accidents do not happen. They're caused. As Einstein said in his theory of relativity, more or less, nothing is ever created or destroyed. When potentials within you are activated by a transiting planet and you try to suppress or ignore the energy thus released, it doesn't just disappear. It has to go somewhere, and it's often released in a form you absolutely cannot ignore, such as an accident or illness which forces you to do what you should have done in the first place.

Whether you can believe it or not, you subconsciously arrange for your own accidents and illnesses for your own ends, which is to say, for your own ultimate good and growth as an individual. The universe is a great and complex mechanism and you are a part of it, though you may have temporarily forgotten that upon entering this life.

Most of us fear or resist external or internal change in our lives even if we really know, deep down, that it's in our best interest in the long run. We much prefer the familiar simply because it is familiar and comfortable. So we resist or refuse to admit the truth even to ourselves.

Obviously, then, the best way to avoid traumatic incidents is to be as self-aware as possible, to be totally honest with ourselves, and to go along or work with whatever plans (energies) the universe (we) may have in mind for us.

Transit Descriptions

SUN CONJUNCT MARS

Your physical energy is running high right now, and if you don't find a way to properly handle it, it may very well be expressed as an accident or illness. Try not to act rashly under this transit, especially around sharp metal objects and machinery.

SUN SQUARE MARS

Some sort of vigorous physical activity is definitely in order for today. Your feelings of aggression need a safe outlet, or accident or illness could result. Think you have no aggressive feelings? Check again; you've probably suppressed them, in which case others with axes to grind may be pulled to you like magnets, and, sure enough, will give you a chance to work out some hostility.

SUN OPPOSITION MARS

You may very well experience feelings of hostility or aggression today, and if these are suppressed, accident or illness could result. Try to find a positive way to vent these energies, possibly through vigorous physical activity or constructively talking out problems with others.

SUN CONJUNCT URANUS

If you're reluctant to allow the Uranus energies of this transit to break you out of your ruts, you may sublimate them. But energies will out one way or another, and suppressed Uranian energies can emerge in the form of accident-proneness. Learn to express these liberating energies positively—be loose, be flexible.

SUN SQUARE URANUS

Uranus provides impetus to get you out of your old ruts and routines. If you try to ignore or suppress this energy for change, it's very likely to be expressed as an accident of some sort. Be extremely careful in all dangerous situations today. Better still, go ahead and do something different, change your routine, find out or honestly admit what's really bugging you and do something about it.

SUN OPPOSITION URANUS

As usual, suppressing Uranian energy for change and not utilizing it consciously could result in accidents.

SUN CONJUNCT PLUTO

There is no need to become paranoid, but avoiding unsavory characters and areas might be a good idea now. Violent or disturbing encounters of a rough kind *sometimes* occur under this transit.

SUN OPPOSITION PLUTO

Dangerous places, situations, and persons should be avoided during this transit if at all possible. If this isn't entirely possible, at least take all necessary precautions.

MOON SQUARE MARS

You may be emotional, irritable, and prone to acting hastily—all of which could lead to an accident. Be especially careful around sharp metal objects.

MOON OPPOSITION MARS

Be aware of all you do today, all your movements. Hasty, unthinking actions could result in an accident.

MERCURY OPPOSITION MERCURY

Pay attention to everything you do now, especially while traveling. Rash or impulsive actions could prove dangerous.

MERCURY SQUARE MARS

Arms and legs are especially vulnerable to accident while you're walking or driving now. You should be very careful during these activities if you harbor any suppressed rage, hostility, or aggressiveness. Also watch out while around any objects that could cause burns or cuts.

MERCURY OPPOSITION MARS

Avoid potentially dangerous machines or instruments if you feel yourself becoming impulsive or rash. Be careful while engaged in any possibly dangerous activity, such as driving. Burns to arms or legs are possible. Look within yourself to see if you're suppressing anger or hostility. If so, you're likely to be an accident just waiting for a chance.

If not, this transit may very well go unnoticed.

MERCURY CONJUNCT URANUS

It's best to be cautious today. Curb any inclination toward impulsive behavior. Your thinking may not be as sharp as usual, and errors that could lead to accidents might occur.

MERCURY SQUARE URANUS

Do your best to avoid any sudden, impulsive moves, especially while driving.

MARS IN FIRST HOUSE

Be particularly cautious during times that Mars transits an afflicted planet in your first house.

MARS IN FOURTH HOUSE

Be especially careful to avoid injury or fire in or around the home when or if Mars transits an afflicted planet in your fourth house.

MARS IN SIXTH HOUSE

Don't repress those frustrations you're feeling now. Work them out constructively, somehow, or they could lead to an accident. Hard, physical activity can help, as can talking out and positively working out your problems with those who are causing the frustrations.

MARS CONJUNCT SUN

Unless you're accident-prone as a rule, this transit will probably not cause you any difficulties. Your physical energy is very high, and working it off will improve your health and state of mind in any case.

MARS SQUARE MOON

Do try to be conscious of yourself and all your moves today. You'll have a tendency to behave irrationally, impulsively, and irritably. Be particularly careful in familiar surroundings. Injuries to eyes sometimes happen with this transit.

MARS CONJUNCT MERCURY

You're likely to be impatient to get wherever you're going today and possibly inclined to take risks you wouldn't normally consider.

Take your time, however, and don't speed while driving.

MARS SQUARE MERCURY

Be very careful while driving or working with machinery or sharp tools. In fact, it would be good if you could avoid all those things, especially if you feel angry or irritable.

MARS OPPOSITION MERCURY

Take extreme care in everything you do today, especially driving. Don't speed, and watch out for others who may be doing so. Also be careful in any situation that could endanger arms and feet. Legal embroilments could result from accidents today.

MARS CONJUNCT MARS

If you repress the high amount of energy generated by this transit, accidents or run-ins with people who are themselves feeling irritable and aggressive may happen to you. Let this energy out; do something strenuously physical, something that you enjoy doing.

MARS SQUARE MARS

The tremendous amount of energy you feel today may lead you to be rash and impulsive unless you can properly work it off. Take care in all you do today.

MARS CONJUNCT JUPITER

Your high level of energy and exuberance may make you so over-confident that you'll take unnecessary risks. Be doubly cautious today in any activity that could be at all dangerous.

MARS CONJUNCT SATURN

If you are feeling angry inside, this is not a good day to work with sharp tools. Do some other physically demanding work that requires concentration.

MARS CONJUNCT URANUS

This transit is known for sudden upsets of all kinds. Accidents can happen, though they are mostly due to your own rash impulsive-ness. You can avoid them by being careful, especially around machinery and sharp tools—particularly if you're harboring anger inside. Get it out and be careful.

MARS SQUARE URANUS

Persons who have resisted change in their lives until they are now forced to do something about it will be prone to accidents because of rashness and impulsiveness. This is the time to begin making changes in your life voluntarily, which will utilize all that rash energy constructively.

MARS OPPOSITION URANUS

Rash, impulsive behavior could lead to accidents now if you insist on trying to resist or suppress the energy for creative, possibly sudden, change signified by this transit.

MARS CONJUNCT PLUTO

This is no time to charge into dangerous situations or neighborhoods. Your ego is dominant now, as is your desire for power, and you're apt to attract others of the same ilk. There *could* be violent encounters.

MARS SQUARE PLUTO

Avoid potentially dangerous situations, neighborhoods, and people. The energies of this transit can be explosive.

MARS OPPOSITION PLUTO

As with other Mars/Pluto aspects, this is a time to avoid dangerous tools, situations, and places. Also avoid making others angry at you; they could become violent.

MARS OPPOSITION MIDHEAVEN

Take care in and around your home today. Domestic accidents sometimes arise under this transit.

MARS CONJUNCT ASCENDANT

Accidents sometimes happen at this time, especially if you've been holding in anger, resentment, or your energy in general. Hard physical labor or other activity is advised to dissipate these energies. Don't physically overdo, however. Be careful of sharp, metal tools.

MARS SQUARE ASCENDANT

Unless you feel reasonably certain that you have your aggressions worked out, be extremely cautious with—or avoid altogether—

dangerous tools or machinery.

MARS OPPOSITION ASCENDANT

As with all difficult Mars transits, be wary of sharp instruments and dangerous situations. This is especially true if you're feeling angry or frustrated. Hard physical work or play is a good way to handle this energy.

JUPITER TRINE SUN

You may tend to overestimate your physical abilities now. If this transit should occur with another that is associated with accidents, trouble may result.

JUPITER CONJUNCT MARS

This is not necessarily an accident-prone transit. The problem is, you'll feel so energetic and strong that you will be apt to overextend yourself or take foolish risks.

JUPITER SQUARE MARS

Your high energy, total self-confidence, exuberance, and impulsiveness could lead you to take foolish risks, which could lead to accidents. Try to calm down and be more deliberate in your actions.

JUPITER OPPOSITION MARS

You feel so energetic and exuberant today, you're sure nothing can go wrong and are apt to take foolish risks. Try to avoid this, though; you're not really as all-powerful as you feel today.

SATURN SQUARE MARS

Unnecessary risks will not pan out under this transit and could very likely lead to bone injuries. This is one time you should play it safe in any situation. Learning to properly handle anger would help.

SATURN OPPOSITION MARS

Pent-up anger or frustration may lead to accidents under this transit if you don't take preventative measures, such as being very careful and handling emotions positively.

SATURN SQUARE URANUS

If you've become too rigid and are unable to accept change in your life, the resulting tensions may manifest as an accident. You have the opportunity now to eliminate the useless, worthless, or unnecessary from your life. Why resist? A tree that bends with the wind will not be as traumatized as one that bucks the prevailing energies.

SATURN SQUARE PLUTO

Avoid dangerous situations or people. Violent incidents are sometimes indicated by this transit.

URANUS IN SIXTH HOUSE

Uranus wants to revolutionize your work, to get rid of the old ruts and routines, the worthless and unnecessary. If you rigidly insist on clinging to the old because "we've always done it this way," accident or illness may force change upon you.

URANUS CONJUNCT SUN

Change is occurring in your life, and if you attempt to resist too fiercely, accidents may result. Be very careful during this period.

URANUS SQUARE SUN

Go along with necessary changes in your life now, but be true to yourself and stick to your guns. Resisting Uranian urges toward change and freedom or trying to ignore them can lead to accident-proneness.

URANUS OPPOSITION SUN

This transit acts as an impetus toward true self-expression—being and expressing who you really are. Resisting this impulse can result in accidents.

URANUS SQUARE MOON

Sudden accidents are a possibility in or around, or even to, your home. Make a safety inspection and be careful.

URANUS CONJUNCT MERCURY

Take care while traveling. Try to curb impulsive behavior or a tendency toward rash risk-taking.

URANUS SQUARE MERCURY

You may be nervous and have a tendency to act impulsively. These conditions can lead to accidents. Be careful, and travel only as absolutely necessary.

URANUS CONJUNCT MARS

Avoid all dangerous objects associated with these two planets—machinery, firearms, sharp instruments, explosives. Also be especially careful while driving, and in fact, while in any situation that could prove potentially dangerous. Accidents are not inevitable under this transit, but, especially to the already accident-prone, they are a possibility.

URANUS SQUARE MARS

Find a positive manner in which to assert yourself today, and you'll probably experience no difficulty under this transit. Watch a tendency to act rashly.

URANUS OPPOSITION MARS

Your "damn the torpedoes" mood is likely to lead you into rash, impulsive actions that can result in accident or illness if you don't consciously try to control them. Control—not suppress totally. Yes, you have a need to be self-assertive, but doing so in a positive, controlled manner is best.

URANUS OPPOSITION MIDHEAVEN

Accidents in or around the home are a possibility. Make a safety check and take care. Your parents should be warned to be careful, too.

PLUTO SQUARE SUN

This transit will try to teach you to handle yourself and power correctly. If you don't—if you abuse power—then accident or injury, possibly an assault, may occur. Avoid dangerous areas or persons to be on the safe side.

PLUTO SQUARE MERCURY

There may be dangerous situations connected with your work, especially if it happens to include some form of transportation. Be very careful during this time.

PLUTO CONJUNCT MARS

You have tremendous energy now, and it's best to use it by doing some kind of hard work or play. Non-use of it may result in violence.

Avoid all dangerous situations, neighborhoods, and people.

PLUTO SQUARE MARS

Your high energy, impulsiveness, and possible anger and frustration may make you accident-prone at this time. Try to use and express your energy constructively and positively to avoid accidents. Be careful around machinery, sharp instruments, firearms, dangerous neighborhoods or situations.

PLUTO OPPOSITION MARS

Your ego energies are high, and if you let them run amok and go around stepping on others on your way up, you're apt to attract injuries due to accident or other people. Avoid any questionable tactics, underground elements, or dangerous situations.

PLUTO SQUARE ASCENDANT

There is a remote possibility of personal danger or violence in dangerous areas or situations. Be aware and take care. Avoid any underhanded tactics of any sort; they'll very likely backfire and cause trouble.

Chapter 5

Business/Job/Career

Whether you're a business owner or employed by others, whether you regard your work as a job or a career, you can benefit from planning for it with the transits in this chapter. Cross-checking with other, related chapters, such as Relationships (with co-workers, clients), Mental Energy (a day for details or the broad view?), Self, Travel, Accidents, Communications, and Finances, will also aid you.

Planning ahead for your success does make sense. As Charles E. Luntz wrote in *Vocational Guidance by Astrology*, "Swimming against the current is good exercise but slow progress. Enough natural obstacles are usually provided to the attainment of success that we need not go out of our way to seek artificial ones." No use going against the tide in the regatta of success when you can go with it!

Transit Descriptions

SUN IN SIXTH HOUSE

Your attention will be focused on your work, and you'll enjoy trying to improve at it. Interesting things may happen in connection with your work.

SUN IN SEVENTH HOUSE

A good time for partnerships—for working with others, not by yourself. Take notice: Are you contributing your share to the arrangement? If professional advice is needed, now is a good time to ask.

SUN IN TENTH HOUSE

You may get ahead in your job or career now and may receive some recognition or a strong vote of confidence. You'll no doubt do very well as long as you don't try to fool others into thinking you're anything you're not. Total honesty is the ticket to success now.

SUN CONJUNCT MERCURY

An excellent time to begin a new business venture. You're on top of things and won't miss much, especially if you can remember to listen to what others have to say. This is also a good day to make plans for the future and/or clear out that paperwork backlog.

SUN SEXTILE MERCURY

If you have to present your views to a group or transmit important information to anyone, this is a good day to do it, for you'll be able to make yourself perfectly clear. All kinds of communications are favored today, as are buying, selling, negotiations, or other business transactions.

SUN TRINE MERCURY

A great time to begin a business trip. It's also excellent for understanding yourself and your goals and for communicating.

SUN OPPOSITION MERCURY

You may find yourself having to do a fair amount of traveling around today and could be in almost endless communication of some sort. It's extremely important that you remain objective and listen to what others have to say—carefully. Let them know that cooperative effort is uppermost in your mind. If there are confrontations, remember—be objective and consider compromise above all else. Also, if you find you have to modify old plans or make new ones, wait awhile to implement them.

SUN CONJUNCT MARS

You'll do best working by yourself today. Others may tend to get on your nerves. A good day to start a new project, especially if it involves some degree of physical activity.

SUN SEXTILE MARS

Your energy is high and you can get a lot of work done, especially if it involves some form of physical activity and other people. You'll work well with groups today, and you may find yourself presented with an opportunity to take control, to lead, or to direct in some manner.

SUN TRINE MARS

The best use for today would be for you to work alone and on your own pet projects if you can. Review these projects and make plans for their development or execution. Some may prove more important than you now realize. You're apt to face challenges soon, so it's best to be prepared ahead of time. Decide what *you* really want to accomplish, then go for it.

SUN OPPOSITION MARS

Those projects you've been so involved with are coming to a head now, and you'll be able to assess how well you handled them. If you've been consciously aware of what you've been doing and why, you'll be on firm ground. There may be, nevertheless, confrontations that can, at least, serve to show what makes you angry. Look closely to see if what you're making a big deal over is all that important to you after all. You are not your work. Your work is not you.

SUN SEXTILE JUPITER

Because of your positive attitudes and ability to work harmoniously with others, now is a good time for working with groups or holding conferences of any sort.

SUN SQUARE JUPITER

This transit spurs you on to do more than you'd usually consider doing—which is good if you're normally cautious, but which may lead to overextension if you're usually the more adventuresome type. In any case, Jupiter is like a spirited horse; with a little discipline, it can perform wonders. This applies to everything from working to spending money.

SUN OPPOSITION JUPITER

You must guard against the urge to overextend yourself in any way. Your self-confidence and optimism could lead you astray without some caution and control.

SUN CONJUNCT SATURN

You're really in the planning and organizing mood today, and you'll do well at it as long as you refrain from trying to organize everybody else's lives unduly. Tend to your duties. Do your own work and you'll feel better later. Professional advancement of some sort may be on the menu today.

SUN SEXTILE SATURN

Today, you'll work in a disciplined, organized manner, concentrating on pertinent details. This may attract very favorable attention from important persons. A good time to seek practical advice from older, more experienced persons.

SUN SQUARE SATURN

This is one of those days you'd just as soon play hooky from work. You're feeling hemmed in by that work and duty, and it prevents you from doing what you'd really like to do. Relationships with those in authority may not be topnotch, but can be improved if you realize that it's your own choices or ideas that may be the actual restricting factors. Examine the situation. Are your assumptions really true? Think about it, be patient, and your difficulties may be resolved.

SUN TRINE SATURN

Today you'll do a good, thorough job, concentrating well on details, organization and planning. You probably won't have to do anything over.

SUN OPPOSITION NEPTUNE

This is not one of your most clear-headed and self-assertive times. Better wait until this transit is over to make any important commitments.

SUN SEXTILE PLUTO

You must work for the common good today, not for ego-gratification. Whatever you're working on, look beneath the surface. Endeavor to create order out of any chaos you find lurking about.

SUN SQUARE PLUTO

Be prepared to answer for yourself and your actions today. Authority figures may ask you to do so. If you can, no problem. If not, recognize that these are areas that need working on, possibly including your attitudes. Whatever cannot withstand testing today needs changing. Machines or situations may also break down. Now is a good time to fix them once and for all.

SUN CONJUNCT MIDHEAVEN

Concentrate on achieving your goals today. You'll be dealing with persons in power, and they may or may not be impressed with your determination. It depends on whether they think you're a threat or a valuable go-getter for the team. If you seek public attention or recognition, it may happen under this transit.

SUN SEXTILE MIDHEAVEN

Achieving success is at the top of your list today. You feel very secure and confident, and though you may not necessarily be seeking attention, your efforts may bring it to you anyway. Now is a good time to plan future steps for advancement or to accomplish those already mapped out.

SUN SQUARE MIDHEAVEN

Your ambition is running high today, and this is a good day for furthering your self-interests—to a point. Being inconsiderate or insensitive to others' goals and views will work against you. If conflicts do occur, try to remain objective and willing to change if your assumptions should prove to be incorrect.

SUN OPPOSITION MIDHEAVEN

Today you must look within to your own inner needs, preferably at home or with friends. This is not a time to vigorously charge into your job or profession, but if you have to, at least try to remain objective and as low profile as possible.

SUN SEXTILE ASCENDANT

OK, so you want to show off a bit or maybe take the lead for a change. Go ahead, but don't forget to let others know you really couldn't make it without them. Actually, this day is best spent working with others.

SUN TRINE ASCENDANT

Unless you really enjoy your work, you'd probably rather be elsewhere. A good time to take some time off. If you do like your work, you may get some recognition today.

MOON IN TENTH HOUSE

Business and professional matters are in the forefront of your life today, and you may find yourself in the limelight for a while. You'll be more intuitively aware of the emotional needs of others and of groups, so meetings or negotiations may go well. But don't try to turn a professional relationship into a personal one today.

MOON CONJUNCT SUN

This is a time when you'll be in tune with those around you. A good time for conferences or group work of any kind.

MOON TRINE SUN

You're feeling good and, consequently, work well with others. A good time for conferences.

MOON SEXTILE MOON

You're more emotionally tuned in to others than usual, and if you have to make a presentation or public appearance, this is a good time for it. Rapport will be easily established. All this will especially apply to women.

MOON SQUARE MOON

This is not one of your better days for harmonious meetings or conferences. However, if what you want is not peace, but to successfully spur others to action, now is the time. Women, especially, may upset a few of your applecarts today, but pay attention: You can learn a lot about your emotional self through conflicts with them.

MOON CONJUNCT MERCURY

Because it's likely your moods will have the upper hand over your rational mind at the moment, it would be wiser now only to gather information and make decisions later.

MOON TRINE MERCURY

Your emotional and logical facilities are well-balanced. A good time to make decisions. Communications with women may be especially beneficial.

MOON OPPOSITION MERCURY

This is not a good time to engage in negotiations or discussions needing clear logic. Your emotional and rational minds may be in conflict. And, you may be "knee-jerk" reacting, reflecting patterns and prejudices ingrained in childhood, rather than in a rational manner.

MOON TRINE VENUS

You'd really rather not be working today, unless it's to beautify your surroundings in some way.

MOON CONJUNCT MARS

Your irritability and impatience today could cause problems unless you make an effort to control yourself, in which case, you may be able to accomplish chores that are usually difficult for you. Try to stay calm and be willing to compromise if necessary.

MOON SEXTILE MARS

This is one of those times when you can work almost equally well alone or with others, though in any case you demand some degree of independence. Confident and self-reliant, you'll find others will cooperate willingly with you. If need be, you can defend your point of view and take the initiative with courage and vigor.

MOON TRINE MARS

You'll find yourself wanting to start projects, as you feel very positive, energetic, forceful and courageous, but unless there is another transit backing this one up, you're apt not to want to finish them later. A good day for leading or influencing others, though.

MOON CONJUNCT JUPITER

An excellent day to make presentations or have meetings or have any contact with groups of any kind. Your good feelings toward one and all are reciprocated.

MOON SEXTILE JUPITER

You're genuinely concerned about others and they can sense it. A good time to work with groups, especially familiar ones, to persuade them to your point of view.

MOON SEXTILE SATURN

Tackle difficult or exacting jobs now. Your thoroughness will get it done right the first time.

MOON CONJUNCT URANUS

Be careful of negotiations or decisions during the time this transit is in effect. You want to do something different; you may be impulsive, possibly rash. Take care not to do something during these few hours that you'll regret, probably right away.

MOON TRINE URANUS

You're in the mood for implementing new policies and directions, and will try to persuade others to them. To do this, though, you may have to take on a leadership position, so be sure you have enough follow-up energy, because this transit is brief. Surprises may upset your plans or routine today, but you'll probably be able to handle them all right.

MOON SQUARE NEPTUNE

Not a time for clear thinking or making important decisions. Be prepared to reevaluate events of today later.

MOON CONJUNCT MIDHEAVEN

Your emotional sensitivity today will either make you more effective before groups (being more in tune with them) or, being bothered by all this emotional input, you will want to withdraw into your own personal world. It all depends on your inner sense of confidence and security.

MOON SEXTILE MIDHEAVEN

Detail or precise work will not turn you on right now, but it's a good time to make presentations to groups or before the public in general.

MOON SQUARE MIDHEAVEN

There is apt to be some tension between your personal and your professional life, especially if you've not been handling the balance well. You need to make your priorities clear to yourself. Your moods may change rapidly today, and if your goals have been mainly professional, you're likely to feel upset or dissatisfied.

MOON TRINE MIDHEAVEN

You're not feeling so pulled in two directions at once because your personal and professional lives are more in harmony with each other. If necessary, you can persuade others to your point of view.

MOON OPPOSITION MIDHEAVEN

This is not a good time to make presentations or to be in the spotlight in any way. What you really need is time alone now to think through how you feel about things.

MOON SEXTILE ASCENDANT

Your emotions are strong and you can relate well to people on that level. A good time to deal with groups, to make presentations to them, make a sales pitch, or otherwise persuade them to your point of view.

MOON SQUARE ASCENDANT

This is not the best of all possible times for clear and rational thinking. Your judgment is likely to be based on your mood. Wait for this transit to pass before making decisions.

MOON TRINE ASCENDANT

All relationships, including with groups or the public, are benefited by this transit. A female acquaintance may be especially helpful in some way.

MOON OPPOSITION ASCENDANT

This is not an especially good time for important business negotiations or any task requiring clear thinking and reason, unless the situation requires being sensitive to the feelings of others. You're apt to be more emotional than usual.

MERCURY IN FIRST HOUSE

If you can settle down your active but clear mind and focus on the business at hand, this is a good time for negotiations.

MERCURY IN SECOND HOUSE

Unless natal planets in the second house are afflicted or transiting Mercury is afflicted while passing through this house, all should go well for you in business discussions or negotiations now.

MERCURY IN THIRD HOUSE

Use this time for research and clear communicating. Things are happening too fast for final decisions.

MERCURY IN SIXTH HOUSE

This is one of those times when all sorts of new ideas will come to you for improving efficiency in your work. This is great if you'll remember to consider the delicate egos of others when informing them of your brainstorms. This is a good time for working with details and to discuss any problems with co-workers or your employer.

MERCURY IN SEVENTH HOUSE

Unless Mercury is afflicted in or while transiting this house, now is a good time for contracts and negotiations of all sorts and for discussions with a business partner.

MERCURY IN EIGHTH HOUSE

If Mercury is unafflicted in or while transiting this house, business negotiations are favored.

MERCURY IN TENTH HOUSE

You can effectively plan for your job, career, or organization you belong to now. This might entail anything from taking classes to discussing your position with superiors. Whether this is the time to ask for a raise depends on other supporting factors in your chart. Don't get so bogged down in details, though, that you miss rewarding opportunities that may arise. You may have some dealings with the public under this transit.

MERCURY SEXTILE SUN

A very busy but fruitful day, as far as communications are concerned. Excellent for committee meetings and discussions. May have to travel more than usual as well, though probably not a long distance.

MERCURY SQUARE SUN

You'll probably have plenty of paperwork, meetings, and communications today. Try to keep your ego dampened down to avoid torrid opposition. If problems do arise, you'd best wait for a better day for communications to get your points across. Don't stick up for lost causes. You may be so busy and "wired" today that you become nervous. Try to control yourself, however, as this could lead to carelessness and poor work.

MERCURY TRINE SUN

Mental work, communications, organization, and negotiations are all favored today. You can pursue new studies or reports effectively as well.

MERCURY OPPOSITION SUN

You're eager, willing, and able to communicate today, but there may be opposition from others. Compromise may be called for, but it may not be easy to accomplish. Don't try to avoid discussions, however. What's discussed today may really help later on.

MERCURY SEXTILE MOON

If you can be totally sincere and honest in your dealings with others, this is a good time for communicating with groups and getting your ideas across.

MERCURY SQUARE MOON

Emotions and unconscious impulses may interfere with rational decisions and communications today.

MERCURY SEXTILE MERCURY

Your flair for detail today bodes well for complicated discussions and business negotiations. You'll be able to cover all bases clearly and effectively, so contracts and other agreements are very likely to work out well for you.

MERCURY SQUARE MERCURY

This will very likely be a hectic day for you, and it would be help-ful if you could work under peaceful and harmonious conditions. Communications will be brisk, and it's very important that you handle them with as much insight as you can muster. You may meet with some opposition to your ideas or projects, and the main thing to remember is to be calm and flexible. If compromise is necessary, but you can't seem to reach a satisfactory one, it would be best to put off negotiations until after this transit has passed. Very few problems may develop, however, if you are well-prepared and adaptable.

MERCURY OPPOSITION MERCURY

Your mind may be too quick today for your own good. You may overlook some details, fall into sloppy thinking or hasty decisions, and fail to take others' ideas into account. Pay close attention and con-sider with care. Work with others, even if you argue. Don't hesitate to change your mind if you're demonstrably wrong. Try to leave your-self some leeway if you have to make decisions today; they may have to be modified or changed later.

MERCURY CONJUNCT VENUS

Scientific research is especially favored today, but business and financial matters, too, will benefit from your heightened ability to see patterns that unify apparently disparate elements.

MERCURY OPPOSITION VENUS

You don't much feel like getting down to serious work today and may be more willing than usual to compromise. You may be sorry later, however, if you give in on something that's important to you.

MERCURY CONJUNCT MARS

Your mind seems extra energized today, and you'll be able to stick to mental assignments longer than usual. You'll be able to verbal-ize your ideas very well, but may also be very attached to them, and hence defensive. This could lead to conflicts, which can be avoided if you'll just stop a moment to see if anything really needs defending.

MERCURY TRINE MARS

This is a good time to speak your mind, present ideas you've been hesitant about mentioning, defend your views, give a speech, even ask for a raise. Negotiations are favored, too. You'll be willing to dare to take chances.

MERCURY OPPOSITION MARS

Be careful and cautious in your dealings today. Your supply of tactfulness is running low, and it seems as if everyone wants to start something with you. Awareness that you are the one sending out subconscious hostility signals will help you exercise control. This is obviously not one of your better days for smooth communications or negotiations.

MERCURY CONJUNCT JUPITER

Today you'll be able to see the broad view and can plan with considerable foresight. You're also more tolerant of other viewpoints and able to organize efficiently. Don't let this glorious overview cause you to overlook important details, though, and do try to remember that you really aren't infallible.

MERCURY SEXTILE JUPITER

Your self-understanding is enhanced and you know what you want. You realize that you can achieve the most by cooperating with others; hence, all business dealings and negotiations are likely to go well today.

MERCURY SQUARE JUPITER

You're positive and optimistic and can see the long-range view today, so planning abilities are enhanced—except for one thing: you're likely to overlook details. Plan carefully, therefore, and be adaptable. Tone down your self-righteous attitude with others.

MERCURY TRINE JUPITER

All business transactions, buying, and selling are favored today.

MERCURY OPPOSITION JUPITER

If you take time to take care of the fine points, all your business dealings should go well today. Just don't forget the fine print, and be willing to change if necessary. Drop any hint of arrogance you may be tempted to use in dealing with others.

MERCURY CONJUNCT SATURN

You're very cautious today, but you can also be very meticulous. Leave the broad, long-range planning till later and concentrate on the details. You'll quickly see all the flies in the ointment today, and now is a good time to dig them out. Beware of letting negative thinking cripple your confidence.

MERCURY SEXTILE SATURN

Today is a good day for details, for making any necessary changes around you. Make plans or work on projects that require a broad overview some other time.

MERCURY SQUARE SATURN

Communications may very well get mixed up today, getting either delayed or misunderstood. Negotiations and personal contacts should be postponed if possible. Tackle mental tasks that need your disciplined attention to details, but leave the making of grand plans for another day. Try to overcome negative thinking.

MERCURY TRINE SATURN

Your conservative and cautious approach will serve you well at detail work, but you may lack the broad view necessary for making long-range plans. This is a good time to seek advice from a more experienced person.

MERCURY SEXTILE URANUS

This is a good time to look at those old problems from an original perspective. This can be a time of discovery and exciting challenges.

MERCURY SQUARE URANUS

Your mind is racing so fast today you may be prone to sloppy work and thinking. Get ideas down on paper and work out the details tomorrow. Also tomorrow, double-check today's work. Avoid hasty judgments or rash statements.

MERCURY TRINE URANUS

An excellent time to tackle those old problems that have been resisting satisfactory resolution. You aren't in the mood for the old routine today, which is a good thing, because you'll be bombarded with new ideas. Get them down on paper today and worry about working out their details tomorrow. It would be best to put off important decisions till another time, too.

MERCURY OPPOSITION URANUS

Your mind is working so quickly today that errors and carelessness may creep into your work. Better double-check it tomorrow. If you must do disciplined, detailed work today, make a step-by-step outline and follow it to the letter. New ideas, new people, new experiences may challenge your thinking today. If this bothers you, perhaps you've become too rigid.

MERCURY CONJUNCT NEPTUNE

This is not a good time for legal encounters or negotiations, including contracts or agreements of all kinds. Dishonesty and confusion could enter the picture.

MERCURY SQUARE NEPTUNE

Take great care in any negotiations or dealings of any sort today. There is a danger of misrepresentation. Be totally up-front and honest yourself and absolutely clear in your communications.

MERCURY OPPOSITION NEPTUNE

Don't make any important decisions or commitments based on what you may think today. This is not a good day for logical, clear thinking. Wait a couple of days, then decide. Be wary of being misled or swindled today.

MERCURY CONJUNCT PLUTO

You can forcefully and effectively get your ideas or views across today. Most people will be convinced, but some may vigorously oppose you, especially if you seem not to care about others' feelings. You may spend the day completely concentrating on one idea or viewpoint—a good thing if that's what's required at the moment, but which can otherwise waste valuable time.

MERCURY SEXTILE PLUTO

Today you want to get at the heart of any matter, and you'll dig and search and investigate until you do. A good day to check into contracts, deals, and proposals. You're not likely to be hornswoggled on this day. Once you do find an answer, you want to persuade others to your point of view. This could make you either a good mentor or a stubborn, obnoxious know-it-all.

MERCURY CONJUNCT MIDHEAVEN

This is an excellent transit for sitting down and planning out your professional future. Also, some publicity may come your way today, or you may receive some important news.

MERCURY SEXTILE MIDHEAVEN

Now is the time for planning and thinking things out; your mind is sharp, and you're unusually in touch with your emotions. A good time for negotiating or taking care of paperwork and other details you normally put off.

MERCURY SQUARE MIDHEAVEN

A good time for implementing those plans you've been making and for clarifying your position to others. Just don't forget to listen to their ideas, too. And really consider them. Don't become obsessed with something trivial, and you'll manage to do a lot of effective work today.

MERCURY TRINE MIDHEAVEN

An excellent time for making detailed plans for your career. Follow them, and all will very likely work out well. Communications are favored, including negotiations, if you don't let your perspective become too subjective.

MERCURY OPPOSITION MIDHEAVEN

Negotiating is not particularly favored now, mainly because you're apt to let your thinking become too subjective—unless you make a concerted effort to be objective and open to the ideas and opinions of others.

MERCURY CONJUNCT ASCENDANT

Because you'll be communicating well, today is quite favorable for negotiations and business dealings of all kinds. Also good for doing routine tasks. Your mind is sharp, clear, and on the ball today.

MERCURY SEXTILE ASCENDANT

Communications, negotiations, deals, short trips, or the beginning of a long trip are all favored today, as are serious discussions.

MERCURY TRINE ASCENDANT

Communications are well-nigh perfect today. Your ability to make yourself clear to others, to listen to and appreciate their points of view, your willingness to make intelligent compromises—all favor conferences and negotiations. A five-star day for the mutually beneficial exchange of ideas. Excellent also for routine communications and getting paperwork out of the way.

MERCURY OPPOSITION ASCENDANT

A good day for very clear communicating, for negotiating settlements, or for consulting a lawyer or other expert.

VENUS IN SECOND HOUSE

Financial negotiations are favored if you can refrain from giving in to extravagance.

VENUS IN SIXTH HOUSE

Just about all aspects of your work are favored now. Things and relationships will go smoothly. You may unexpectedly gain somehow, financially or otherwise.

VENUS IN SEVENTH HOUSE

All partnerships are favored by this transit. All will go smoothly, even if you have to straighten out some difficulties. This is a good time to do so.

VENUS IN TENTH HOUSE

All runs smoothly now, mainly because you are giving out such positive vibrations. You may find yourself involved in creative or artistic matters concerning your business or job.

VENUS IN ELEVENTH HOUSE

A good time to work with groups. All will go well and amicably.

VENUS SEXTILE SUN

You'll work well with a group today. If you have to make an impression on anyone—as with the boss or in an interview—this is a good time. You may receive some sort of recognition or reward due to a good impression you've made. If you have to ask for a favor, a loan, a raise—now would be a good time.

VENUS SQUARE SUN

This is one of those days you'd probably rather be sailing or whatever you enjoy for relaxation. If you must work, you'll get along well with people, but it's not really the best time to negotiate or sign important deals. You might compromise just to avoid conflict.

VENUS TRINE SUN

You'll enjoy working with others today. Also, if you need to make a good impression, this is a good time for it.

VENUS OPPOSITION SUN

You're not in the mood to do much work and, in fact, may be downright lazy and undisciplined. A good time to take a vacation day if you can.

VENUS SEXTILE MOON

You may not feel particularly in the mood for work today, but if you must deal with the public in some way, you'll be successful if you're sincere with them.

VENUS TRINE MOON

A good day to deal with groups of people in any context. They pick up on your sincerity and respond to it.

VENUS CONJUNCT MERCURY

This is a good day for negotiations, particularly if they relate somehow to entertainment or women's products.

VENUS SEXTILE MERCURY

This is excellent for transactions of all kinds. Also for dealing with groups or making an impression on anyone.

VENUS SQUARE MERCURY

Negotiating or discussing difficult or controversial matters is not favored today. Your mind lacks discipline at the moment. Anything requiring it should be put off or checked for errors tomorrow.

VENUS TRINE MERCURY

If you lead a group, you should be able to get everyone to work together well during this time. Contract negotiations should also be beneficial.

VENUS CONJUNCT VENUS

If you need to have others cooperate or to make a good impression, this transit helps.

VENUS SEXTILE VENUS

You'd probably rather play than work today, but if you have to work, you'll do it well and cheerfully. Negotiations are favored, and you may make new contacts that will help you later. Purchases today should turn out to be very worthwhile.

VENUS SQUARE VENUS

You'd really rather not do much of anything, and what you do accomplish may be sloppy. However, if you do make the effort to produce, it may be well worth your while.

VENUS OPPOSITION VENUS

Beware your urge to buy expensive items today; you could regret it later. Don't plan on getting a lot of work done today; you really don't feel like doing any, and probably won't. Put off difficult or important negotiations until this transit has passed, or you may compromise away the store.

VENUS TRINE JUPITER

You're apt to feel lazy and content with things the way they are. This is not a good time to begin a major new project unless some other transit is charging you with the energy you need to do it. However, this *is* a good day for financial endeavors.

VENUS SEXTILE SATURN

You're in a practical frame of mind and will therefore handle most business transactions to your benefit. Especially favored are business affairs concerning art objects or anything connected with beauty.

VENUS TRINE SATURN

A good day to handle all business affairs, as you are practical, objective, conservative, and fair. Today, you are not ruled by emotions.

VENUS OPPOSITION SATURN

You may be pulled one way by duty and another by your desire to have some fun. If so, stick to duty. Good ole Saturn wouldn't let you enjoy yourself if you goofed off today anyway.

VENUS TRINE NEPTUNE

Practical activity in the real world is not particularly favored today. However, creative or inspired thinking is, which could help you solve some eminently practical problems.

VENUS CONJUNCT MIDHEAVEN

Professions having to do with beauty, entertainment, relationships, and related areas are favored today. You're feeling so friendly and sociable that good relationships with clients, customers, and associates enhance your business dealings in any field.

VENUS CONJUNCT ASCENDANT

A good day for making good first impressions. In fact, you may very well attract people and circumstances favorable to you. A business opportunity may present itself.

VENUS SQUARE ASCENDANT

You're really not in the mood to discipline yourself to work and may become careless. Also, you may tend to overspend or to spend unwisely if you are in control of any purchasing. Make an effort to be careful, though, and you can control it.

VENUS TRINE ASCENDANT

You'd really rather let duty and discipline slide today. However, this can be a good time for investing if you're usually restrained about spending. Your "luck" is up.

VENUS OPPOSITION ASCENDANT

You'll impress even those you normally have trouble with today, and all should go well with everyone. This is a great day to work with a partner; there will be no disagreements. If there are any existing problems with anyone, this is the time to resolve them.

MARS IN FIRST HOUSE

Your energy is high and you'll be able to accomplish a great deal, especially if you can work mostly on your own. You're not belligerent— just not in a mood to compromise even a little.

MARS IN THIRD HOUSE

If you can refrain from being argumentative or overly aggressive, you can not only accomplish a great deal with others but can also, if necessary, convince them that your ideas or products are sound.

MARS IN SIXTH HOUSE

You'll have considerable energy and the discipline and desire to get a lot of work done. There may be conflicts, however, if you're not getting the credit you feel you deserve, or if anyone you're supervising feels they aren't. Work alone if you can and be very careful around machinery.

MARS IN TENTH HOUSE

Your ambition is high, and you can achieve much if you don't forget the needs and interests of others. Others can feel very threatened at this time and will try to oppose you unless you can bring your purposes into sync. Working alone or at least being in charge of something would be best for you now.

MARS SEXTILE SUN

Your increased self-confidence and energy enable you to work well either with groups or alone. You'll be able to communicate your point of view with vigor. A good day for negotiations. An opportunity to demonstrate your abilities may present itself, which may be of benefit to you later.

MARS SQUARE SUN

Your high energy may lead you into disputes today. You will defend your position like a wounded tiger. Everyone, including yourself, would be better served if you could compromise at least on the less important details. Don't let your ego rule you without considering others' egos and positions. If you do, there may be even tougher opposition in about six months when transiting Mars conjuncts or opposes your Sun.

MARS TRINE SUN

Your energy and self-confidence are high. This is a good time to finish a project you've been working on for a while or to initiate another. This is a good time to make decisions, take action, and deal with those in authority over you, especially if they are men.

MARS OPPOSITION SUN

If the working relationship between you and your co-workers or partners hasn't been the best, you're likely to be in for some opposition or conflict right now. If things have been running smoothly, you still can't count those chickens yet, unless the working relationship is really good or you try to improve it.

MARS SEXTILE MOON

Long-range or important decisions or plans should be put off for now. Your thinking is likely to be more emotional than objective.

MARS CONJUNCT MERCURY

Don't take everything that's said to you personally. Keep your mind occupied and yourself out of disputes, and if you avoid high-pressure tactics, you'll be able to sell your point of view to others and make a good impression.

MARS SEXTILE MERCURY

Your energy, confidence, and positive attitude make this a good time for negotiating successfully, planning for the future, taking a business trip, getting things done, and working well and fruitfully with others.

MARS TRINE MERCURY

All sorts of mental work is favored today, including writing reports, studying, planning, and so on. It's also good for negotiating and communicating with others.

MARS CONJUNCT MARS

This is a good time for beginning new projects that you'll get the credit for. You'll know the outcome in about a year when Mars opposes Mars.

MARS SEXTILE MARS

This is a good day to impress people and successfully interact or negotiate with them. Your energy and self-confidence are high. Keep your ego under control, and you'll probably do quite well.

MARS SQUARE MARS

Now is the time to channel your energy into getting work done. Physical work not involving too much detail would be the best use of this energy.

MARS TRINE MARS

You are full of self-confidence and energy. This is a good time to assert yourself, begin or finish projects, work with others (or alone if they can't keep up with you), make presentations, further your own self-interest. Whatever you do, don't sit around and do nothing.

MARS OPPOSITION MARS

You're probably encountering opposition now, and it may just be due to the way you're coming across. Your ego is in high gear, and you're probably trying to dominate others, or suppressing this, you're dealing with others who want to dominate you. You can get a lot of successful work done now, however, if you realize that your success does not have to be the result of someone else's failure. If there is conflict, the best thing to do is get it out in the open and work it out.

MARS CONJUNCT JUPITER

This transit is favorable for beginning new projects. Confidence in your own abilities brings "luck" at this time.

MARS SEXTILE JUPITER

Unless there are powerful indications to the contrary, any business ventures or projects begun now should be successful. Dealing with authorities and handling legal affairs are facilitated now, too.

MARS TRINE JUPITER

Now is a favorable time for making decisions and furthering your own interests. Even taking risks now will probably turn out well for you, mainly due to your positive attitude, which attracts good fortune.

MARS CONJUNCT SATURN

This is not a day for risky ventures or investments. Frustrations and irritations may plague you all day. You may be angry, but not have much chance to vent it. If so, do some hard physical labor that involves a degree of concentration, as long as it doesn't require sharp instruments. Otherwise, stick to routines you could almost do in your sleep.

MARS SEXTILE SATURN

A good time for making meticulous plans and tackling work

requiring patient attention to detail.

MARS TRINE SATURN

You have the patience to work on something that calls for slow, step-by-step progress and close attention to detail, and you'll probably receive recognition for your careful work. You're concerned with practical, less-than-lofty but worthy goals now, and at this rate, you're likely to achieve them.

MARS OPPOSITION SATURN

Projects in their final stages that underwent major difficulties or defeat about six months ago may totally fail now. Others may have opposed you, but it's likely you weren't well prepared for it in the first place. Other projects will succeed. If you encounter opposition and are angry, get it out in the open and clear the air.

MARS CONJUNCT URANUS

This is no time to make long-range plans. Sudden upsets are typical under this transit, and your own rebelliousness isn't helping matters, especially with authorities. The best thing for you now would be to start a project that reflects your own individuality and that you'll get credit for. If you're angry at someone, either handle it positively or be very careful around machinery and sharp tools.

MARS CONJUNCT NEPTUNE

This is not the time to start anything new or to seek ego-gratification, nor to make important decisions, especially at the behest of someone who appeals to your idealism. Truly selfless charity work is favored now.

MARS OPPOSITION NEPTUNE

Communications with close associates or partners may be less than ideal today, and misunderstandings may occur. Someone may even try to deceive you. Make an effort to see things and people as they really are, not as you'd prefer. Don't be a braggart or try to use deceitful means yourself. Working by yourself would be best; you may successfully finish something you've been working on for some time. This is not the day to shout it to the masses, though; ego-gratification is not on the agenda today.

MARS CONJUNCT PLUTO

You may find yourself involved in a power struggle or ego conflict of some kind. Be aware of what's going on and convince others that cooperation is needed to reach both your goals. You can harness this energy constructively and can accomplish a great deal, especially if it involves a change of some sort.

MARS SEXTILE PLUTO

You may have to modify your plans to achieve your ambitions, but this will better your chances. Your success will be aided if you're clear about what you really want. This is especially so if your aims are also those of the group you work with. Don't use others as stepping stones to achievement.

MARS SQUARE PLUTO

Ego conflicts and power struggles can result from your fiercely driving ambition and attempts to tell others what to do. Try to retain your calm, don't stomp on others for personal gain, and this powerful energy can be channeled into creative change. Avoid deception, the consequences of which will emerge at your next Mars/Pluto conjunction or opposition, whichever comes first. Be wary of tangling with those in power.

MARS TRINE PLUTO

The vibrations are right for making long-range plans now, and if you can integrate your own needs with those of society as a whole, you will gain considerably yourself (paradoxically, because Pluto doesn't like for you to work for personal gain alone, but gives it if you honestly work for the whole).

MARS OPPOSITION PLUTO

Your ambitions are aroused and you're willing to work hard to achieve them. You may encounter strong opposition, however, and power struggles are a distinct possibility. Avoid using underhanded techniques (they'll backfire eventually), but should others try them on you, seek help from those around you. This is not the time to be a loner. Avoid making others angry; they could turn violent. In spite of all this, it's a good time to make positive changes in your life.

MARS CONJUNCT MIDHEAVEN

You'll want to work hard today, especially on your own projects for which you'll get the kudos. Unless you're the leader, this is not a time for working with groups. Don't do anything solely for egotistical reasons; this would create devastating opposition. Make careful plans to achieve your goals.

MARS SEXTILE MIDHEAVEN

Since you are coming across today as self-confident and assured rather than egotistical, you can gain assistance from others more easily than usual. This is a good time to plan for the future and take initiatives.

MARS SQUARE MIDHEAVEN

You're feeling the aggressive force of the Mars energy quite strongly now, which can be either helpful or detrimental. If you can direct and control this energy in a positive fashion, you can accomplish a great deal of work. Otherwise, conflicts, probably with superiors, are quite likely. It's best to work alone if you can today. If you experience any anger, don't hold it in or you're likely to take it out on someone when you get home.

MARS TRINE MIDHEAVEN

Your self-confidence and energy will help you achieve just about anything you have in mind. You take the initiative and get the job done. Others may turn to you for leadership. Your confidence in yourself makes them confident in you. Any risks you take today are pretty likely to pan out.

MARS OPPOSITION MIDHEAVEN

Things are not likely to go very well for you professionally today. You're working hard, but things just don't seem to click. This is because your energies are turned more toward the domestic arena than focused on work.

MARS CONJUNCT ASCENDANT

You may find yourself leading or directing a group under this transit. As long as you consider the feelings of others and don't try to be a dictator, things should go smoothly. Conflicts may nevertheless arise today. If so, have it out immediately. But fight fair.

MARS SEXTILE ASCENDANT

If you can have a great deal of say-so, working with a group or team will go well today—if, that is, the others can keep up with your tremendous energy. Otherwise, it's best to work alone.

MARS SQUARE ASCENDANT

Teamwork is not one of your long suits today, so work alone on one of your own projects if you can. Avoid working with dangerous tools and machines, though, unless you're absolutely sure you have your aggressions worked out.

MARS TRINE ASCENDANT

You're self-confident, more decisive, and more energetic than usual. This is a good time to exchange points of view with others and to find new avenues of expressing yourself.

JUPITER IN SIXTH HOUSE

You're probably enjoying your work now and find yourself willing to take on even more than usual. You may not receive overt recognition at this time, but you'll gain in personal satisfaction, and don't worry, others will be noticing.

JUPITER IN TENTH HOUSE

Now is the time that you may finally receive recognition for your efforts, as long as you refrain from acting egotistically or domineeringly. You may change careers, moving to a more traditional Jupiter-associated field, such as law, medicine, higher education, healing, or travel. In any case, your job may require you to travel for some reason during this transit.

JUPITER SEXTILE SUN

A good time to further your own interests with those in power, to carry out financial transactions, and to plan for the future. This is also a good time to resolve any differences you may have with someone.

JUPITER SEXTILE MOON

Women may be of benefit in your business somehow. You are positive, upbeat, and friendly today. If you have to deal with groups or with the public, you'll do very well.

JUPITER CONJUNCT MERCURY

Planning for the future, buying and selling, and decision making are all beneficial activities for today. You can see now both the whole picture and the details, though there is a tendency to gloss over the importance of the details. Avoid this trap and overextending yourself, and all should go well. Communications—given or received—will be positive and fortunate.

JUPITER SEXTILE MERCURY

You'll have to take the initiative, but now is an excellent time for planning, decision making, communicating, and resolving differences. Buying and selling, contract negotiations, transactions of any sort are favored. Your positive attitudes are the key to all this.

JUPITER SQUARE MERCURY

If you can stop long enough to listen to others' ideas and opinions, this is a good time for making decisions, planning, or negotiating. Just make sure that your details are correct and that you don't bite off more than you can chew. Reexamine your ideas and make changes if necessary.

JUPITER TRINE MERCURY

If you'll take the initiative and actively look for opportunities, all should go well. This is a good time to buy or sell, to make plans, to get your ideas across.

JUPITER OPPOSITION MERCURY

Don't overlook details, and this can be a good time to conclude or negotiate any business deals. This may be a time of culmination of plans you've had in the works for as long as six years. This is also a good time for making additional plans. Again, watch the details. It would be good to have a lawyer check over contracts before you sign them. You can see the big, overall picture now, but don't try to force your vision on others.

JUPITER SEXTILE VENUS

You'll make a good impression today. If you can muster the *umph*, this is a good time to go for that interview, ask for a raise, make that presentation. You're being very sincere, warm, friendly, and honest today, and it shows. You may attract money unexpectedly. Financial matters in general run smoothly.

JUPITER SQUARE VENUS

You're really in no mood to work and just want to socialize. Take a vacation or a day off, if you can. Or, at least, try not to get stuck with too much responsibility.

JUPITER CONJUNCT MARS

Your energy and strength seem boundless, especially in any physical activity. This is a good time to begin a new project of almost any sort, but especially if it's something that requires exquisite timing. Don't forget you have to rest once in a while.

JUPITER SEXTILE MARS

This is a good time for starting new projects and for working with others. Your energy and self-confidence are way up, and if you take advantage of the opportunities coming your way, you're very likely to be successful. Because your motives are honorable, you'll be able to influence others to follow your lead. You'll be able to come up with fair compromises. Any legal confrontations should work out in your favor.

JUPITER SQUARE MARS

Your energy, self-confidence, and exuberance are so high you may have to exercise restraint in order to get anything done and to avoid taking foolish and dangerous risks. If you can control this energy, you can accomplish a great deal. Be careful not to act arrogantly. Those in authority over you may feel threatened by your drive. Unless this is your intention, you may have to assure them you mean no harm.

JUPITER TRINE MARS

A good time to start any project, resolve a dispute with a co-worker, or settle a legal matter.

JUPITER SEXTILE JUPITER

All seems perfect and right with the world now. Negotiations go smoothly, as will legal matters. A good time to expand, if you're careful not to overextend. This is a good time to take stock and make plans.

JUPITER CONJUNCT SATURN

You'll become impatient with restrictions and break away from them if you can. This may mean a change of job; or, you may expand your business or find new freedoms within your current job structure. Either way, the change is likely to be beneficial to you in the long run.

JUPITER SEXTILE SATURN

Your need for expansion is balanced with your need for caution, and therefore, any business expansion or investment is very likely to work out well at this time. You'll be able to strive patiently toward your goals and to see how to best actualize your ideals.

JUPITER SQUARE SATURN

What you do now will have a greater than usual effect on the future, so take your time deciding on the proper course. It is important to exercise caution with your finances, no matter how impatient you are with restrictions they may impose. You may have an opportunity for a better job under this transit; the change would probably be worthwhile.

JUPITER TRINE SATURN

This is a good time to expand a business, start a new one, or open a branch office, because you're able to work slowly and well with accurate and practical foresight. If any problems arise, you'll easily overcome them or pick up the pieces and start again. This is also a good time to sort out your thinking alone.

JUPITER OPPOSITION SATURN

Feeling that you've been held back, you may want to make a significant change in your career, though you may find it difficult to let go. Or, if you're happy where you are, you may find new challenges within the current structures. Striking the balance between growth and restriction is the trick here.

JUPITER SEXTILE URANUS

Don't buy the champagne until you know for sure, but sometimes sudden financial gain or advancement occurs under this transit.

JUPITER CONJUNCT NEPTUNE

If you operate from selfish motives under this transit, you'll find yourself living in the illusion that all's right with the world when it isn't—which could result in your becoming the victim of deceit or misrepresentation. This is not a good time to take a gamble.

JUPITER CONJUNCT PLUTO

You have great drive and energy to succeed and achieve power now, and you'll work very hard to obtain it. In fact, something you've been working on may reach a successful culmination. Use this energy and power wisely, and your life can be greatly enhanced.

JUPITER SEXTILE PLUTO

You'll be seeking greater freedom to express the real you. Pursuant to that, you may be placed in a position of power. If so, do not abuse this power or use it for selfish ends; maintain high integrity and work toward the good of all. Take advantage of any changes that develop; they're likely to be good for you. Someone in authority may notice you approvingly.

JUPITER SQUARE PLUTO

You want very much to succeed now, and are willing to work hard to do so. And in fact, you may achieve great success, or you may lose it. You must make sure your ideas and ideals are really worthwhile. Don't be afraid to change your mind or direction, if necessary. In your push to succeed, you may somehow antagonize someone in authority, perhaps unintentionally. Be absolutely aboveboard in everything. Legal conflicts may arise.

JUPITER TRINE PLUTO

This can be a time of success for you, and you may be put in a position of power. Be careful, however, that you do not use your power or success for purely selfish reasons. If you do, problems can develop later.

JUPITER OPPOSITION PLUTO

You may either attain the success you've been striving for or lose it. Opposition could be strong; be careful. Be extremely sure that all you do is on the up and up, and try not to rile those in authority. Be aware, also, that your solution to any given problem may not be the only solution. Keep group goals in mind, and ask others for help if you get into trouble. If you've been doing this all along, you'll probably have few problems.

JUPITER CONJUNCT MIDHEAVEN

You haven't reached the pinnacle of success, but you're heading in the right direction. Positive results may begin happening for you now. Just don't become arrogant or self-centered, and be careful of overextension without a proper safety net.

JUPITER SEXTILE MIDHEAVEN

You may advance in your job or career, possibly even assuming a leadership position. All is going smoothly now.

JUPITER SQUARE MIDHEAVEN

Your ambition is high, and you're willing to work hard to see it fulfilled. You have more self-confidence than usual, and feel you can accomplish near wonders. And you can, if you're careful not to overestimate your abilities. Also, don't ignore other important areas of your life.

JUPITER TRINE MIDHEAVEN

If in business for yourself, an opportunity to expand may develop, and barring other significant aspects to the contrary, you can probably pull it off. If not self-employed, you may receive a promotion or raise. Others may seek your professional advice and leadership.

JUPITER CONJUNCT ASCENDANT

You may gain professional success now, as your life as a whole is broadened and expanded. Do not neglect your personal life while you're at it.

JUPITER SQUARE ASCENDANT

If you can refrain from arrogance and try not to overlook the little details that promote good relationships, this may turn out to be a very beneficial time. A fortunate opportunity, or "break," may be brought to you by a friend or acquaintance.

JUPITER OPPOSITION ASCENDANT

An excellent time for signing contracts or entering into partnerships. Benefits will be mutual. Also, now is a good time to consult a lawyer or any other professional counselor. Disputes in court now will be settled in your favor.

SATURN IN FOURTH HOUSE

In terms of your outer success, this is a time of new beginnings. You're now embarking on an upward track again. "Your star is beginning to rise." You must, however, have modest expectations for now, and be absolutely sure that your "foundation," your home and personal life, are in order. Problems shoved under the rug now will impair your success later on.

SATURN IN SIXTH HOUSE

You're going to be putting in a lot of hard work and probably not getting a lot of recognition for it. It will come, though. When Saturn enters your seventh house, you'll emerge more into the limelight. Meanwhile, you now have to prepare for it. There may be difficulties, but keep at it. It's rather like training for the Olympics. It's hard now, but it will pay off.

SATURN IN SEVENTH HOUSE

Co-workers and associates are apt to be more demanding than usual. You may be getting more recognition now, and this could cause some inter-office difficulties. You'll have to prove that you can do what you say you can. If you've been developing your self-knowledge and inner awareness during the last 14 years, your career is now definitely on the rise. You'll find yourself more in the spotlight.

SATURN IN TENTH HOUSE

This can be a culmination, a peak in your career. A reward, if you will, for all the preparation you've been doing for many years. If you haven't taken any unethical shortcuts or stepped on others on your way up, this can be a very rewarding time indeed. Or it can be just the opposite if you've left bad blood behind you as you climbed to the top, if you have not prepared well, or if there are badly afflicted planets in your tenth house. The latter can be overcome, however, if the two former conditions do not apply. Don't neglect your personal life. Any problems not settled or worked out when Saturn was in the fourth house may show up now, putting a bit of a damper on your success.

SATURN IN ELEVENTH HOUSE

You've had your chance to shine as an individual star; now you must use that sparkling personality and ability to work with others. Become a team player now and you'll be amply rewarded. Also, the ideals and goals you've been trying to implement should come to fruition now, if you've prepared and worked well for them. Otherwise, accept your losses and prepare to start over.

SATURN CONJUNCT SUN

Persevere awhile longer on projects you've been working on for some time. You must work hard to bring them to completion, whether that be success or failure. Don't take on any new responsibilities or projects until you finish these others.

SATURN SEXTILE SUN

You will have to work hard during this time, but you'll have many opportunities to succeed. You can work patiently, carefully, and with discipline now—a good time to take on those hairy projects you may have been putting off. Live up to your responsibilities and commitments. Now is a time of preparation and shoring up of your inner and outer resources for the future.

SATURN SQUARE SUN

It may appear that persons in authority are throwing obstacles in your path from every angle. If you're sure you're on the right track, just hang in there and keep plugging along. Wait until your energy level is higher to vigorously resist. Projects you began about seven years ago are reaching a crisis now. Set those that aren't working adrift, and concentrate on areas that are definitely panning out.

SATURN TRINE SUN

Things are rolling along smoothly for you now, and you can get a lot done. Work hard and diligently, and you'll be favorably noticed by those above you. They'll be more likely to help you out, then, when difficulties present themselves in a few years.

SATURN OPPOSITION SUN

This is the end of a 29-year cycle, and there are apt to be many endings in your life. Soon there will be a time of beginnings. Meanwhile, your energies are low, and you'll probably feel discouraged. Others may oppose you or circumstances frustrate you. It's not likely you'll attain any of your goals now. Be patient and don't struggle too much. This, too, shall pass.

SATURN SQUARE MOON

You may be feeling lonely, depressed, frustrated. The problem is either your work has gained too much control over your personal life (Saturn over Moon) or vice versa. A period of readjustment is called for, and when the two portions of your life are back in balance, all will be right with your world again.

SATURN TRINE MOON

This is a time when your personal and professional lives harmoniously support each other. A good time for buying or selling personal real estate, making plans for the future, or otherwise combining the business world with the personal. Also, a good time to seek the advice of older persons, especially women.

SATURN OPPOSITION MOON

There may be domestic or work-related problems, stemming from the fact that you've neglected the one for the other. They must be brought into balance. This may be difficult for you, but you'll emerge from the fray a happier and more complete person.

SATURN SEXTILE MERCURY

Your ability to perceive and handle details is sharpened. Reorganize, restructure, or tackle transactions necessitating careful development now. Speculative ventures should not be attempted. You know what you think; your mind is made up. Be aware that this can lead to stabilization or to narrow-minded rigidity. Try to opt for the former.

SATURN TRINE MERCURY

You have the mental discipline and stick-to-it-iveness, now, to put long-term plans into effect if you can avoid becoming too inflexible in your thinking and too embroiled with every little detail. This would be a good time to start a new business or implement anything you've been thinking of doing for a while.

SATURN SEXTILE VENUS

Business relationships or partnerships are especially favored under this transit. You'll each work to see that the other's needs are met.

SATURN TRINE VENUS

Business partnerships and relationships will be mutually beneficial at this time. You'll each be considerate of the needs of the other.

SATURN SEXTILE MARS

You are able to discipline your considerable energy at this time
and focus it on difficult, precise, long-term projects that require hard
work and patience. You're able to work well with others if necessary,
and are capable of accomplishing a great deal.

SATURN TRINE MARS

You can work hard and long in a disciplined manner on projects
requiring exactness and attention to detail. Your focus is narrow, but
you can see the big picture as well.

SATURN OPPOSITION MARS

You may feel frustrated at every turn. Hard, physical activity will
be helpful in handling the anger that may build up. Fighting against
the tide won't do any good at this time. Actions or projects you
initiated about 14 years ago may be culminating now, and you are
reaping their consequences—or you may have outgrown the structure they have created for you. Think back, and the difficulty may
become apparent and thus solvable.

SATURN CONJUNCT JUPITER

This may be a time of restlessness, possibly to the point of changing jobs, for some people. On the other hand, if you are relatively
happy with your employment, you may simply settle in and do some
really hard work.

SATURN SEXTILE JUPITER

At this time you are capable of handling both the big picture and
the details needed to bring it about. A good time for planning for
future success. Here is opportunity; you have to supply the drive.

SATURN SQUARE JUPITER

Hindrances may seem to be coming out of the woodwork. Activities or projects you began about seven years ago are being tested, and
anything that is obviously in bad trouble should be dropped, or else it
will be challenged even more thoroughly in another seven years. You

may feel like chucking it all and changing jobs, but it's best to let this transit pass before making any definite decisions.

SATURN TRINE JUPITER

A time to plan, to consolidate your resources, to work hard, to invest for the future. You have the foresight now, and you'll be needing this solid foundation under you before too long. Consult someone older or in authority.

SATURN OPPOSITION JUPITER

Think out everything carefully and be prepared for challenges to your plans, projects, or ideas. Check to see that you're still heading in the right direction to achieve your goals. This is no time for expansion, and in fact, you may find yourself in difficulty due to overextension recently. Solidify and stabilize now. Don't begin new projects.

SATURN SEXTILE SATURN

You can work well with others now, and you may find yourself steadily approaching your goals. Changes or new directions that occurred when Saturn last squared or conjuncted your natal Saturn are now routine in your life. Work patiently now to build for the future.

SATURN TRINE SATURN

All runs like clockwork now. Your experience and calm self-assurance will be appreciated.

SATURN OPPOSITION SATURN

If you have been on the right path during the last seven to fourteen years, working steadily along to reach your goals, you'll reach them now. You'll experience the satisfaction of success and reap the rewards of all your hard work. If you experience difficulties with your work, co-workers, or employers now, however, it's a sign that you are not in the right job. Don't despair. Look for what you should be doing and jump in.

SATURN CONJUNCT URANUS

Tensions may have been building up for some time, but now they suddenly become unbearable. If this happens, you may suddenly change jobs with no warning. You're seeking change, excitement, freedom, new horizons. Or, you may harness the energy of this transit and take on difficult projects that require great effort and patient, hard work.

SATURN SQUARE URANUS

Unbearable tensions may impel you to suddenly leave your job or be fired if you're unable to accept or willingly institute constructive change in your life. If you can consciously make changes, this can be an exciting time. If you've become too rigid and are afraid of change, however, this can be a very tense and frustrating period.

SATURN TRINE URANUS

Your ability to incorporate new concepts or projects without disruption into existing structure and routine will impress those in authority. Make an effort, however, to avoid falling into routines or ruts that will be difficult to climb out of during the more difficult transits of Saturn and Uranus.

SATURN SEXTILE PLUTO

You can and probably will work very hard now. Your work will be effective, and those in power will take note. They may very well reward you in some way.

SATURN SQUARE PLUTO

You may find yourself confronted with obstacles right and left. It's best not to struggle against them like a fish in a net, but to take stock and eliminate those things or areas of your life that are not working. Try to remain calm and detached and conserve your resources, financial or physical.

SATURN TRINE PLUTO

Your energies are controlled and concentrated, allowing you to work hard and effectively. At the same time, you're able to reach a deeper understanding of yourself. The two combined make you almost unbeatable and you can advance in your ambitions. Others will respect you and want to work with you.

SATURN OPPOSITION PLUTO

Efforts begun 14 years ago will culminate, either positively or negatively, at this time. If successful, you still cannot relax, for there may be those who oppose or want to depose you. Be conciliatory but firm. If things are not working out as hoped, don't struggle fruitlessly against overwhelming odds. Cut your losses and start anew. Beware of overwork, or you could undermine your health.

SATURN CONJUNCT MIDHEAVEN

This can be a high point of success in your career and personal life. If you've prepared carefully and with integrity over the past 14 years, all will "suddenly" bear fruit. You'll be at this peak for several years. Responsibilities will also develop that you should tackle bravely and not try to shirk. If you have not prepared with honesty and integrity, or if you try to avoid responsibilities, you may lose all you've worked so hard to gain. The older you are, the more important this time will be for you.

SATURN SEXTILE MIDHEAVEN

This may very well be a time of achievement and advancement if you work at it—which you probably will, because you'll have plenty of energy and ambition. You may find it best to work alone now, if you can. Take a look at your goals and make sure they're really what you want, not what others want for you; or whether they are goals to which you just feel obligated in some fashion.

SATURN SQUARE MIDHEAVEN

You may find yourself facing opposition, including your own doubts that you are pursuing the right course. If you do decide you're on the wrong road, it's better to change careers or goals now rather than later, when it will be even more difficult.

SATURN TRINE MIDHEAVEN

You feel confident of your course of action and your goals, and you really want to make it on your own, to "do it your way." This is a good time to do that and to develop good work habits that will stand you in good stead in the future. Don't, however, fall into rigidity in any area.

SATURN OPPOSITION MIDHEAVEN

You've just gone through a period of around five to eight years when it seemed as if you were on hold, as if you could get nowhere, no matter what. Actually it was a time of preparation and now your "star" is beginning to rise toward a pinnacle of success, which will be reached in about 14 years. Now, with Saturn in your fourth house, you should concentrate on making sure your personal and domestic lives are in order, and that they will thus be a support as you turn more and more toward personal success in the years to come. What you do now is very important for your future.

SATURN CONJUNCT ASCENDANT

This can be a very busy, but productive, time. You'll be finishing off projects and will focus almost entirely on getting it done. This is not a good time to begin new projects.

SATURN TRINE ASCENDANT

At this time you're a good, steady, hard worker. You want simply to get ahead and learn all you can.

SATURN OPPOSITION ASCENDANT

Now begins the recognition you've been working for all these years. Be careful and make sure all your actions meet your ethical standards. If you do engage in any underhandedness, you'll experience extreme difficulty in a few years.

URANUS IN SECOND HOUSE

Some people change jobs under this transit, sometimes suddenly, especially if the work has become dull and stifling.

URANUS IN SIXTH HOUSE

There will be changes in your work or changes in your attitude regarding your work. You may change jobs or, better still, discover innovative new approaches to your work, whether that involves new technology, new methods, or new attitudes. Don't try to resist change or suppress the need for it. If you don't do it consciously, Uranus, through illness or accident, will force you to change.

URANUS IN TENTH HOUSE

There are very likely to be sudden changes in your job or profession, either positive or negative. Whatever the change, it's not too wise to try to resist or suppress these Uranian energies. The changes Uranus wants us to make are for our own long-term good.

URANUS SEXTILE SUN

Sudden opportunities may come now. You're discovering you have more control over your life and greater potential than you ever thought. Go for it!

URANUS SQUARE MERCURY

Things may be happening so fast that you become confused and possibly nervous. Avoid making important decisions until you can be calmer and more rational—unless dealing with technological fields, though you should be cautious here, too. Be open and flexible and avoid being authoritarian, even if you are right about something.

URANUS TRINE MERCURY

An excellent time to announce or begin a new policy or product.

URANUS OPPOSITION MERCURY

You'll be extremely busy, with things happening rapidly right and left. Try not to let them get out of hand, though, or you could become mentally exhausted. Try to remain calm and flexible, taking things one at a time. This is not a good time for negotiations or important decisions affecting the future. It's better not to travel now, too.

URANUS CONJUNCT SATURN

If your work has been restricting your ultimate growth, whether you're consciously aware of it or not, it will be subject to sudden, perhaps explosive, change now. Do not resist or suppress this energy. You'll be better for the change in the long run.

URANUS SEXTILE SATURN

Now is the time to make constructive changes within the system or organization. You're able to accomplish much along these lines and may be amply rewarded for your efforts.

URANUS SQUARE SATURN

You may become incredibly impatient with anything you see as restricting you in your job, whether it be circumstances in general or a person in particular. Your first impulse is to suddenly leave and chuck everything. Think it over. Find someone you can talk your frustrations out with as a safety valve, so that you can decide on the appropriate course of action more calmly and rationally.

URANUS TRINE SATURN

Now is a time when you can work effectively for creative change within the system. You work with both steadfastness and creativity, which may bring you a promotion or other reward for your efforts.

URANUS OPPOSITION SATURN

Sudden, upsetting events may occur. It's Uranus throwing you a curve ball to show you that you really don't have everything all figured out and that you can still grow. Tensions hidden for a long time may choose to emerge now. Don't suppress these tensions; handle them as positively as you can—or they'll harm your health.

URANUS SQUARE NEPTUNE

Be careful of being deluded in some financial area by almost anyone. Put off making any important or binding financial decisions under this transit. Your grasp of reality is slack.

URANUS TRINE PLUTO

A favorable time for finances and for making constructive and innovative changes in your business.

URANUS CONJUNCT MIDHEAVEN

There'll be sudden changes in your public image or professional life, one way or another. If you're happy with the way things have been going, all is likely to continue as such or be enhanced. If not, your fortunes are apt to turn the other way, clearing away all that is hampering your growth in this area so that you can try again in another direction.

URANUS SEXTILE MIDHEAVEN

There may be unexpected advances in your profession or job, or you may decide to take a better one. You'll be employing innovative techniques in your work to your benefit. You'll be seeking more freedom within your professional boundaries.

URANUS SQUARE MIDHEAVEN

There may be a sudden change in jobs, or upsets in your present one. You're probably trying to break free to be yourself and pursue your true life's task. If you've been on the wrong track or are resisting changing from your secure little rut, you're probably finding yourself in an almost adolescent rebellion against authority. Otherwise, you may simply be freed from some previous restrictions, with little or no disturbance.

URANUS TRINE MIDHEAVEN

You'll be creative and innovative in your career, and sudden opportunities may arise that allow you to pursue something new and different. You may even change careers, quite possibly to, or within, scientific, technological, electronic, or occult professions.

URANUS OPPOSITION MIDHEAVEN

There may be disturbances in your business relationships. Others may feel threatened or oppose you for some reason. There are changes going on within yourself; try to be aware and open to insights and to be considerate of others, and the disruptions may be avoided or kept to a minimum.

URANUS SEXTILE ASCENDANT

Partnerships in technical or occult fields are favored at this time, as are studies in these areas.

URANUS OPPOSITION ASCENDANT

Business partnerships may undergo difficulties now. They will have to either change or terminate. Basically, one of you wants a greater say and perhaps more freedom, resisting efforts of the other to totally control the arrangement.

NEPTUNE IN SIXTH HOUSE

You may experience some confusion regarding your work. The best way to advance under this transit is not to work egotistically for your own gains alone. You must try to make your work also of benefit to others. This could mean doing your job well so it benefits all in the company and its customers, or actually doing selfless volunteer work. Beware of becoming involved in anything dishonest or underhanded.

NEPTUNE IN SEVENTH HOUSE

This can be a period of poor communications, misunderstandings, gullibility, or even misrepresentations. Make everything as clear and precise as you can, and examine everything in detail. Avoid forming new partnerships now.

NEPTUNE IN TENTH HOUSE

There may be some confusion regarding your work and your place in it. What you need to look at is not so much the job itself but your attitude toward it. You are not your job, nor is it you. Do not deceive anyone and be wary of being deceived yourself.

NEPTUNE SQUARE SUN

Your grasp of reality is not quite up to par. This is not a good time to change jobs or engage in risky speculation.

NEPTUNE CONJUNCT MERCURY

Your rational grasp of reality is in a confused state. Hold off making important decisions until this transit is over. It would be wise to do so regarding any kind of negotiations, too, but if they can't be avoided, be extremely certain that communications are clear and precise and that everyone really understands everyone else. Be aware that deceit, intentional or unintentional, with yourself or involving others, is possible.

NEPTUNE SQUARE MERCURY

Your grasp of reality is not what it should be, and you may be living in a dream world. Don't make any important decisions until this transit has passed. Be aware of the possibility of deceptions by others, and don't bother trying to pull any off yourself.

NEPTUNE OPPOSITION MERCURY

This is definitely not a good time to make important decisions or to buy or sell anything. Be extremely careful that all communications are clear and spelled out in writing.

NEPTUNE CONJUNCT MARS

This is not the time to start new projects or to try to advance yourself in any way. Particularly avoid going along with anything you know to be dishonest or underhanded. You just won't be able to pull any of this off now.

NEPTUNE OPPOSITION MARS

Be especially alert for any kind of scam, and for goodness sakes, don't try to commit any yourself. They just wouldn't go at this time, and you'd very likely end up in serious trouble.

NEPTUNE CONJUNCT JUPITER
This is not a good time for investing. Wishful thinking is apt to get the better of your reason at the moment.

NEPTUNE SQUARE JUPITER
Avoid get-rich-quick schemes, risky investments or speculation of any sort now. Those rose-colored glasses are hindering your judgment at the moment.

NEPTUNE CONJUNCT MIDHEAVEN
You may suddenly feel confused and sense that you've been heading in the wrong direction all this time. Possibly so, but don't bet on it. Wait until this transit is over to make any permanent decisions or commitments. Whatever happens, just wait and observe until this transit is over.

NEPTUNE SEXTILE MIDHEAVEN
This transit is advantageous for public relations and for any business related to the arts.

NEPTUNE TRINE MIDHEAVEN
You may change professions to one in which caring for others is the main focus. Don't totally neglect your own needs, though, or you won't be able to help others as well as you'd like.

NEPTUNE OPPOSITION MIDHEAVEN
There may be upheavals in your professional life now that leave you confused. If any areas show signs of coming to an end, let them go. It's time to start a new cycle, an excellent time to stop and take stock.

NEPTUNE SQUARE ASCENDANT
You are not seeing yourself and others as you actually are. This is not a good time for any sort of negotiations.

PLUTO IN SIXTH HOUSE
There are apt to be tremendous changes in your work or job. You may even change jobs frequently to find your "niche." Or, you may

simply revamp and improve your way of working in your current occupation.

PLUTO IN SEVENTH HOUSE

Partnerships are apt to go through periods of crisis or difficulty on their way to being radically transformed during this transit, which lasts several years. Some partnerships may end. This is not a particularly good time to begin a new one.

PLUTO IN TENTH HOUSE

Your drive to succeed is greatly intensified. And you probably will succeed if you've discovered who you are and know where you want to go. If, that is, you don't resort to unethical, ruthless tactics. On the other hand, if you're still in the dark about yourself and your direction, you'll now have the ability to find out, though you may undergo quite a lot of job or career changes to do so. In either case, your efforts will be worth it.

PLUTO SEXTILE SUN

Opportunities may come through influential or powerful people. Keep your eyes open and cultivate friendships among this group. It's best, by the way, to work with groups or in cooperative ventures at this time.

PLUTO SQUARE SUN

This is very likely to be a time of power struggles, probably with someone in authority. Either you are ruthlessly trying to attain it or they are. Either way, you must resist. Do not step on others to realize your ambitions, and don't let others step on you. Don't forget there is such a thing as mutual compromise.

PLUTO TRINE SUN

There may be advancement for you now. At any rate, your effectiveness is certainly increased. Relationships with those in authority are good.

PLUTO OPPOSITION SUN

Your ambition is in high gear and, unless you're very careful, you may arouse some very powerful opposition. Power struggles may ensue. Absolutely do not attempt to dominate anyone for any reason.

And if they're attempting to run roughshod over you, resist. Whatever your course of action, make sure your inner motives are only the best and not selfish or egotistical.

PLUTO SEXTILE MOON
Financial gain is a possibility at this time. Keep your eyes and ears open.

PLUTO SQUARE MOON
Caution in financial matters is recommended during this transit. You don't have to hibernate; just be careful.

PLUTO OPPOSITION MOON
This transit is not particularly favorable for financial dealings or negotiations. Wait until it has passed for important decisions in these areas.

PLUTO SQUARE MERCURY
Be especially careful of dangerous situations in or around your work, particularly if they happen to include some form of transportation. Also, don't try to ram your ideas down the throats of others.

PLUTO TRINE MERCURY
This is a good time for making plans or writing up contracts and financial deals.

PLUTO OPPOSITION MERCURY
This is not a very good time for business negotiations. Communications are likely to be very poor, leading to misunderstandings or conflicts.

PLUTO TRINE VENUS
This is a favorable time for business ventures concerning the arts and luxury items, and for partnerships in general.

PLUTO OPPOSITION VENUS
Caution is advised in all dealings at the moment. There may be conflicts over finances. You should also be aware that unethical business practices are a possibility.

PLUTO CONJUNCT MARS

You may succeed now or face tremendous strife and tribulation, after which you may then succeed. Either way, you'll have incredible energy and you must use it. Do not attempt to dominate or run roughshod over others. You'll be most successful if you use the power of this transit for the good of all, not just for your own gratification.

PLUTO SEXTILE MARS

This transit favors taking on grand projects and getting them done. A good time to build or rebuild—anything from buildings to corporate organizational structures. You'll have tremendous energy, and you'll succeed best if you use it with groups for the good of all.

PLUTO SQUARE MARS

You may be impatient, egotistical, frustrated, angered, aggressive—or victim of same from someone else. You'll have great energy and can work hard, perhaps too hard for your own good if you don't watch it. Do try to be patient, considerate, and cooperative; and work with others for a common goal. If things come down to a fight, be sure you have supporters.

PLUTO TRINE MARS

You'll be able to work very hard and efficiently now. You may be given a position of power and will be able to make considerable progress.

PLUTO OPPOSITION MARS

Your ego energies and need to succeed are high, and if you can avoid using these twin drives to step on others on your way up, you can succeed and accomplish a great deal. Do not suppress this energy, but do control it. There may be ego conflicts and power struggles. Try to work with others toward a common goal, and you'll be even more likely to succeed. Avoid any questionable practices or underground elements.

PLUTO CONJUNCT JUPITER

This transit generally smiles on financial matters, whether they be corporate, joint, tax, or insurance. Legal actions also usually work out well.

PLUTO SEXTILE JUPITER

This is a generally beneficial time for business and professional areas, including any necessary legal actions. It's also great for working with or instructing groups. Opportunities for advancement are possible.

PLUTO SQUARE JUPITER

This can be a time of optimism and personal success and achievement—if you're careful not to take on more than you can handle and don't become so arrogant that you turn people against you. Care must be taken to remain completely honest and aboveboard. Legal confrontations, even arrest, could otherwise result. There may be problems concerning finances. Pay attention to details.

PLUTO TRINE JUPITER

You'll be resourceful and creative in your profession and may receive financial benefits at this time.

PLUTO OPPOSITION JUPITER

There may be conflicts over finances under this transit. This is not a good time for litigation, however. Avoid doing anything illegal.

PLUTO CONJUNCT SATURN

There may be conflicts and power struggles. Your tenacity and power of concentration are enhanced. Should changes begin manifesting around you, don't resist too vigorously; they're probably necessary and you'll no doubt benefit in the long run.

PLUTO SEXTILE SATURN

You'll be very thorough and dependable in your work now, and you may very well be professionally advanced for it.

PLUTO TRINE SATURN

You can work with great endurance, attention to detail, patience, and discipline now, and you may well be given more power in recognition of that fact.

PLUTO OPPOSITION SATURN

There may be great changes in work, whether you actually change jobs or not. Let them happen. If something isn't working for you, let it go.

PLUTO TRINE URANUS

An excellent time for scientific or technological work. It's also favorable for corporate or joint finances. You may come up with innovative solutions to old problems.

PLUTO CONJUNCT MIDHEAVEN

At this time you will be concerned with whether your career choice is correct, whether you're heading in the right direction, and if you're going about it in the right way. If you feel you're in the wrong field, you're very likely to change sometime during these two years, either voluntarily or otherwise. If you haven't been going about achieving your goals in the right way, you'll either fail or have to make proper changes. Pluto will be ruthless to make sure you're playing according to Hoyle, one way or another.

PLUTO SEXTILE MIDHEAVEN

There may be changes in your career or job, either due to altered goals, new opportunities within your job, or changing jobs or career altogether. If you need help or support from others, this is a good time to seek it.

PLUTO TRINE MIDHEAVEN

You may gain power at this time, either from authorities or from within. In either case, you must not misuse it. You may also have greater insight into your work and its purpose. Include others in this, and you'll all have the opportunity to become more effective. With Pluto, one must always work toward the common good.

Chapter 6

Communications

Without effective communication, we relate to this or any other plane with grave difficulty. Communication is one of the most important aspects of our lives. It's therefore truly amazing the degree to which we take it for granted or ignore it altogether.

Yet knowledge and awareness of how and when to use it can be a powerful tool in your career and in all relationships, from formal to intimate. When disagreements are likely to arise, when to forcefully put forth your ideas, when to keep your mouth shut, when to consider compromise—all this and more can be gleaned from your transits and can guide you in doing your best communicating.

Transit Descriptions

SUN IN THIRD HOUSE
A good time to tell others how you feel about a subject, but don't forget to listen to them, too. Be clear about what you think before trying to get it across.

SUN CONJUNCT MERCURY
Communications will be in high gear all day for you. You'll engage in all sorts of verbal and written exchanges. This is a good day for clearing out paperwork. If you can control your inclination to do all the talking, it's also a good day for getting your view across.

SUN SEXTILE MERCURY
All kinds of communication are favored today. You can communicate well and precisely. If there is something you've either wanted or needed to tell someone, now is the time. It's also a good day for communicating with yourself.

SUN SQUARE MERCURY
This may be a time of testing for your thinking and ideas. Communications will be coming to you rapidly from all sides, and you need to pay close attention to the subtleties at work, as well as the actual words, in order to read or listen between the lines. You'll be able to communicate clearly. Just remember to listen to what others have to say as well.

SUN TRINE MERCURY
A good time for communications. You're able to make yourself perfectly clear, and you are also interested in hearing what others have to say.

SUN OPPOSITION MERCURY
Seemingly endless communications may fill your day, but it would behoove you to do most of the listening. If you can do this, you'll learn a great deal; if not, there may be conflicts. Assure others

you're not a threat, and be willing to compromise. If this is not feasible, remain objective and, again, listen to what others are saying.

SUN OPPOSITION SATURN

Even though you don't feel like it, go ahead and make an effort to communicate, to do something constructive and rewarding, and don't let things get you down. The worst thing to do would be to pull into your shell like a frightened turtle.

MOON IN THIRD HOUSE

You'll be involved in much communicating now, and if you can maintain some measure of emotional control, it can be enlightening. Communications with women are likely to predominate. Try to avoid "knee-jerk" responses.

MOON CONJUNCT MERCURY

You'll have an easier time than usual in expressing your emotions, especially with women. Don't let yourself get lost in small talk, though, lest you forget important issues.

MOON SEXTILE MERCURY

This is a period filled with communications of all sorts. It's a good time to communicate with those you have deep feelings for—if you can overcome the inertia that sometimes occurs under this transit—because you'll be communicating your feelings easily. You'll brighten their day. Or yours, if you're the one needing a sympathetic listener.

MOON SQUARE MERCURY

In view of the fact that your objectivity is at a low ebb, this is not a particularly good day for clear-cut communicating. You're in a time of change, emotionally. Some of your opinions may be changing, too. Be honest with others about any changes that take place.

MOON TRINE MERCURY

You are very much aware of your feelings, but not to the detriment of your logical reasoning powers. This is a good time to share your feelings of love and affection with friends and family. You may be of emotional assistance to others today, and communications with women will be especially beneficial.

MOON CONJUNCT NEPTUNE

Your thoughts are fuzzy, making communication difficult. Misinterpretations and misunderstandings can easily occur. You tune in to feelings but can't express them well.

MERCURY IN FIRST HOUSE

You'll communicate effectively under this transit, if you can keep your mind from jumping too quickly from topic to topic so that you don't confuse others.

MERCURY IN THIRD HOUSE

This is an excellent time for clear communication, and you'll probably be doing more of it than usual.

MERCURY IN FIFTH HOUSE

Now is a good time for communicating your feelings and ideas to others. Remember to listen, too, and you'll make the most of this transit.

MERCURY IN SEVENTH HOUSE

Unless Mercury is afflicted either in or while transiting this house, this is an excellent time for communications of all sorts, particularly with marital or business partners.

MERCURY IN NINTH HOUSE

Communications, particularly of a philosophical nature, are favored now. You'll likely find yourself in abstract discussions of all sorts and will love every minute of it.

MERCURY CONJUNCT SUN

There will be much communicating in your life today, most of which you'll originate. You feel you must communicate, and you can do so very well now. This is a good time to impress others, if you can remember to stop and listen once in a while, too.

MERCURY SEXTILE SUN

This will be a busy day for communicating. You may even receive an important message. If you've something to say to someone, now is an excellent time to speak your piece. You'll communicate well with groups, as well as with individuals.

MERCURY SQUARE SUN

There will be more communicating for you than usual. Don't operate from an egotistical base, though; and if others do, simply wait for a better time to promote your views. On the other hand, be willing to relinquish any obviously poor ideas of your own.

MERCURY TRINE SUN

This is a good time for communicating and working to complete piled-up paperwork or phone calls. Group discussions and negotiations are favored as well.

MERCURY OPPOSITION SUN

Communications may be clear and open today but possibly discordant. A neutral arbitrator may have to be brought in to help. Perhaps you should just discuss today, and try to come to a final agreement later.

MERCURY CONJUNCT MOON

A good time to communicate with those who have something in common with you, such as family and close friends. You communicate well on an emotional level now, and you're very much in touch with your feelings. Leave problems or circumstances requiring pure logic for another time.

MERCURY SEXTILE MOON

You're tuned in to your own and others' feelings today and can therefore communicate very well on this level, both with yourself and others. A good day for introspection.

MERCURY SQUARE MOON

A good day to express your emotions, but since unconscious impulses and past habits may surface, you may run into communication difficulties. Ask yourself all day if what you feel and think is what you *really* feel and think, or simply doctrine or propaganda you've picked up and never really thought about.

MERCURY TRINE MOON

An excellent time to improve communications with women, but all persons will enjoy talking with you today. You're emotionally tuned in, and others recognize your sincerity.

MERCURY OPPOSITION MOON

While emotions should be expressed, not repressed, they may nevertheless get in the way of clear communication today. You may become so emotionally stirred up, you'll say something you'll later wish you hadn't. Logical thinking is not a strong suit today; better wait to make important decisions.

MERCURY CONJUNCT MERCURY

Today you can easily discuss things you'd normally find formidable. Don't let this opportunity be wasted in small talk. You'll have to make an effort to discuss topics of significance to you.

MERCURY SEXTILE MERCURY

All forms of communication will go well today, particularly complicated subjects involving attention to detail.

MERCURY SQUARE MERCURY

There will be much communicating going on today, and the main thing for you to remember is to be flexible. If discussions break down and compromise appears impossible, wait until this transit has passed and try again.

MERCURY TRINE MERCURY

Clear and accurate thinking aids communication now. You're objective and effective in communicating.

MERCURY OPPOSITION MERCURY

Contacts and communications are likely to be fast-paced. A good time for the exchange of ideas, even if you don't agree. Be careful of jumping to conclusions—your mind may be speeding too fast to think prudently.

MERCURY CONJUNCT VENUS

You'll have a greater facility for communicating today, both intellectually and emotionally. A good time to tell someone your feelings.

MERCURY SEXTILE VENUS

You'll be able to tell someone of your feelings today, even if you normally find this difficult. You're especially in touch with your feelings of love and friendship.

MERCURY SQUARE VENUS

This is a good time to discuss and clarify your relationship with a loved one. Should areas of disagreement surface, approach them with a willingness to compromise.

MERCURY CONJUNCT MARS

You're mentally energetic and able to articulate well. Be careful, though. You're apt to get defensive and think your ideas are great just because they're yours. Or someone else may act this way toward you. Before leaping into the fray, stop and ask yourself if anything really needs defending right now. You may not take this advice, however, since you may feel like wrangling just for the intellectual fun and challenge.

MERCURY SEXTILE MARS

You may have to persuade someone to your point of view, or defend it, both of which you'll do very well. You'll no doubt enjoy every minute of it, too.

MERCURY TRINE MARS

An excellent time for expressing your thoughts, ideas, and beliefs. Others will be impressed by your confidence and competence. Ask for a raise. Defend your views before a group. Give a speech. Whatever it is, you'll do it well.

MERCURY OPPOSITION MARS

This is a day to put on the brakes and exercise caution in your dealings with others. What you'd like to do is give everyone the benefit of your thoughts in no uncertain terms, which, of course, is no way to win friends or influence anyone. Do try to use a little tact today. If you think you can handle some constructive criticism without coming unglued, this is a good time to find out what others think of you.

MERCURY OPPOSITION JUPITER

Do not indulge in arrogance today. Be willing to listen to others' points of view and remain flexible. Maintain your sense of humor and perspective.

MERCURY CONJUNCT SATURN

Communications may be difficult today; you're afraid you'll expose yourself if you speak. You're in a negative thinking mode, and to get out of it, you must consciously attempt to communicate and to accentuate the positive side of people and things.

MERCURY SQUARE SATURN

Delays and misunderstandings are likely today. This is not the best of all times for communicating, but neither should you totally withdraw into your shell. It would help to realize you're seeing only a part of the whole picture—the negative part.

MERCURY TRINE SATURN

You may feel less than outgoing today, mainly because you have little patience for trivial small talk now. You are in a serious mood, and serious discussions will be on your agenda today.

MERCURY CONJUNCT URANUS

Communications will be on a fast track today, and you'll find it all very exciting—so exciting, in fact, that your thinking could become disorganized. Check out all new ideas and insights before reaching definite decisions or conclusions.

MERCURY SEXTILE URANUS

Exciting new ideas will evolve from your conversations. Even old friends and acquaintances are apt to surprise you.

MERCURY TRINE URANUS

Communications will be stimulating and exciting today. You're more tolerant of unusual ideas or lifestyles, and you'll benefit from exposure to new and different people.

MERCURY OPPOSITION URANUS

Tact will not be your long suit today. Be aware of this and try not to alienate the whole world. You may have to eat your words later. If challenges to your thinking bother you today, it could be a sign you're becoming too rigid.

MERCURY CONJUNCT NEPTUNE

Confused thinking may hamper clear communicating today. Or

you may be so subtle that not everyone will get your drift. Also, you may be tempted to lie your way out of a verbal confrontation. If so, it's best just to keep quiet for now. Or, you may encounter someone who will try the same with you. Better not sign anything important today.

MERCURY SEXTILE NEPTUNE
You'll be amazed at the insights into people that will be yours today. Your intuition is much enhanced by this transit, and you'll be less prone to clear thinking than to dreaminess. Communications may be a bit fuzzy.

MERCURY TRINE NEPTUNE
You really don't want to talk about practicalities today. You're more sensitive to the moods of others now; a good day for sympathetic discussions.

MERCURY OPPOSITION NEPTUNE
This is not a great day for communicating. There is apt to be confusion and misunderstanding. Be as totally honest and clear as you can. Be wary of making commitments or of signing anything.

MERCURY SQUARE PLUTO
Try to curb your desire to persuade or force others into your way of thinking. You may initiate disputes over matters that are not really all that important. On the other hand, you may be faced with someone who tries to coerce *your* thinking.

MERCURY TRINE PLUTO
Communications will tend to be serious today, and you may meet someone who will greatly influence you.

MERCURY OPPOSITION PLUTO
You may be the target of some sort of propaganda or attempt at persuasion. Be alert and get involved only with something you're really interested in.

MERCURY SEXTILE MIDHEAVEN
Communications of all types are favored today. If you've been hesitant about broaching some matter with someone, now is the time to do it.

MERCURY SQUARE MIDHEAVEN

You can get your ideas and positions across very clearly today—just don't forget to listen and think about the ideas of others, too.

MERCURY CONJUNCT ASCENDANT

Communications are likely to occupy more of your time than usual today. Your mind will be sharp, and thus all your communications will be clear and productive.

MERCURY SQUARE ASCENDANT

You may be so eager and talkative today, you don't let others get a word in edgewise. Slow down and listen; you'll get more out of it. Control your racing mind and tongue, and don't waste time in intellectual jousting or small talk, nor use your cutting wit against others.

MERCURY TRINE ASCENDANT

Communications are near perfect today. You're willing to listen and learn, as well as to speak your mind. A good day to communicate almost anything by any means.

VENUS TRINE MERCURY

Today you'll find it easy to talk with people in a lighthearted manner, to tell them how you feel, and, if necessary, to work out any difficulties you may have had with them.

VENUS OPPOSITION MERCURY

Since you'll be able to talk about any problems you may be having in a relationship without succumbing to emotional outbursts, this is a good time to try ironing out those difficulties. Keep in mind, however, that a casual remark may be taken in earnest.

VENUS TRINE MARS

Today you're able to be direct without offending. Indeed, most will appreciate your frankness.

MARS CONJUNCT MERCURY

Even though you're uncommonly cranky and testy today, taking everything that's said personally, you can get your point of view across effectively and make a good impression on others if you can keep your mind occupied and yourself out of disputes. Don't be pushy.

MARS SQUARE MERCURY

Today you may provoke others with your attitude, if not your words, making communication difficult. Be careful of what you say and do. Don't waste your energy on trivialities; if, however, a matter is important, this is a good day to stand up for your rights—as long as you're sure it's not just your ego you're standing up for.

MARS TRINE MERCURY

This is an excellent time for communications. You state your views with confidence and listen to others without feeling defensive. Your mind is alert, and you understand easily.

MARS OPPOSITION NEPTUNE

Communication with a spouse, lover, or business partner may be less than ideal. Miscues, misunderstandings, anger, resentment, mistrust may occur. Avoid deceit yourself, but be aware that someone may try it on you. Make an effort to see things and people as they really are, not as you'd prefer them to be.

JUPITER IN THIRD HOUSE

An excellent time for communications, especially for frank discussions of anything that concerns you, emotionally or philosophically.

JUPITER CONJUNCT MERCURY

Communications will be positive and fortunate. This reflects your current positive attitudes and good feelings.

JUPITER SEXTILE MERCURY

This will be a busy time for communications. Someone you haven't heard from in ages may contact you. Good news may come through friends. You'll feel inclined to write letters yourself, and it's a good time to do so. You may even do some serious writing.

JUPITER SQUARE MERCURY

You can't wait to communicate what you consider some very important information. Hold it, though. You'd better double-check first and make sure all the details are correct, and that it really is, in fact, all that important. Be sure to listen to the ideas and opinions of others, and be ready to make changes in your own thinking where necessary.

JUPITER TRINE MERCURY

A good time to promote your ideas and point of view. Even if others don't agree with you, they'll appreciate your coming out with it.

SATURN CONJUNCT MERCURY

Your communications now will be more serious than usual and perhaps more difficult. You may be searching for new ways to communicate.

SATURN SQUARE MERCURY

Communications are apt to be a problem. Your viewpoints, as well as the method you use to get them across, may be challenged. Don't withdraw. Try to work through the problems. Face it—someone else may just have a point. If you let your thinking become too rigid, you'll have to face even more serious challenges in about seven years at Saturn opposition or conjunct Mercury.

SATURN OPPOSITION MERCURY

Communications may break down, even causing the breakup of some relationships, if you've allowed yourself to become too rigid and unwilling to compromise, or if you lack the confidence to defend your ideas and opinions—assuming they're good enough to defend. If they're not, you need to do some serious rethinking.

URANUS CONJUNCT MERCURY

New ideas and insights are coming to you rapidly now, and you want to share them with everybody. More than share, you may want to convert or convince them.

NEPTUNE IN THIRD HOUSE

Communications can be so confusing and unclear during this transit that serious misunderstandings could result. Be very careful to make everything as clear and precise as you can.

NEPTUNE IN SEVENTH HOUSE

Poor communications and misunderstandings are common with Neptune in this house. Make sure everything is absolutely clear and precise. Talk it out; don't hold anything in, thinking others know what you mean or want. This is not a particularly good time to consult with professionals in any field because of the above-mentioned problems, plus there is a possibility of misrepresentation.

NEPTUNE OPPOSITION SUN

Be very precise in your communications, and make sure everyone else is, too. Deceptions or misunderstandings that lead to problems are quite possible. Critically examine everyone and everything that comes your way.

NEPTUNE SQUARE MOON

Make a concerted effort to be very precise and specific in any communications today to avoid any misunderstandings.

NEPTUNE TRINE MERCURY

Your ability to communicate is incredibly enhanced under this transit. It's excellent for teaching or writing or any other form of communicating.

NEPTUNE OPPOSITION MERCURY

Misunderstandings, even deceit, are possible under this transit. Be very clear and specific in all communications or dealings with others, even to the point of bringing a lawyer in on important areas.

NEPTUNE OPPOSITION ASCENDANT

Communication in any relationship, including with professional consultants, is likely to be poor and possibly open to deception. Make sure everything is perfectly clear and open.

PLUTO TRINE SUN

You can communicate very powerfully and effectively now, and this is likely to gain you respect, if not actual reward.

PLUTO CONJUNCT MERCURY

You'll be able to communicate more effectively and on deeper levels than usual. You must not try to persuade others to your point of view for purely egotistical reasons, however, nor let others try to do that with you.

PLUTO SEXTILE MERCURY

Your interest is in deep and significant subjects now, and this will be reflected in all your communications. You could care less about the frivolous at the moment.

PLUTO OPPOSITION MERCURY

Communications may be somewhat strained, even difficult, probably because you get an idea in your head and feel that everyone should adopt it. Or, someone will try to do the same with you. This is obviously useless. Try to avoid it, though don't become so rigid that you can't even entertain the possibility of changing your mind.

Chapter 7

Creativity

We are all creative—creating, if nothing else, our own lives and situations by our thoughts and choices. Some people, though, consciously seek to apply their native talent for creating even further, bringing new inventions, new thoughts, new beauty into the lives of us all.

For these people, especially, this chapter can be helpful. You can quickly find the times best suited to the different types of creativity. You can quit berating yourself when you're not doing what *you* think you should be doing, and with a clear conscience, can concentrate on the appropriate activity and best use of your creative faculties. It's a waste of energy to revile yourself and your personal muse when you both should just take the day off and get lost in a daydream or work on the bookkeeping.

A handy way to use this chapter would be to look up your transits as much ahead as you wish, check them with this chapter, and mark on your calendar your most creative times and how best to use them.

Transit Descriptions

SUN SQUARE VENUS

Your heart most desires harmony and beauty today. Creative crafts or home beautification may appeal to you.

SUN CONJUNCT MARS

You have incredible energy today, and it can be productively channeled into creative expression. A very good day to begin new projects.

SUN SEXTILE URANUS

Intellectual creativity is enhanced today. You're alert, and will grasp concepts and ideas more rapidly than usual.

MOON CONJUNCT NEPTUNE

Your thoughts are fuzzy. You pick up on feelings but can't express them well. Use today to read poetry or fiction, to daydream, or to study *objets d'art*.

MOON TRINE NEPTUNE

Your imagination will be stimulated today and your psychic and creative abilities enhanced. Go for it.

MERCURY TRINE MERCURY

Mentally stimulating areas (such as museums), events, or conversations—in fact, almost anything—could trigger exciting new ideas today.

MERCURY CONJUNCT VENUS

You're very open to all areas of the arts today. You can artistically enjoy just about everything you see around you.

MERCURY CONJUNCT URANUS

Ideas and insights will seem to be coming at you right and left. This is an excellent time for creativity. You may find it hard to concentrate, so get your ideas down somehow; you can work on them better when their newness has worn off a bit.

MERCURY SEXTILE URANUS

This will be a day for new discoveries, a good time to approach old problems from a new perspective. New problems will be viewed as exciting challenges.

MERCURY SQUARE URANUS

Create, create, create today! Check out the details tomorrow. Ideas may come so fast you have trouble keeping up. Just worry about getting them down today.

MERCURY CONJUNCT NEPTUNE

You may be able to express concepts you have difficulty with as a rule. You can be imaginative and subtle—so much so that not everyone will understand you. Be cautious, though; too much imagination can lead to illusion. Mysterious subjects fascinate you now, and you can understand things that might have eluded you before.

MERCURY TRINE NEPTUNE

Your imagination is stimulated, and now is a good time to give in and enjoy any flights of fancy you may have. The main thing is to relax and enjoy. Tomorrow is time enough to scrutinize whatever you may dream up today.

VENUS IN FIFTH HOUSE

An excellent time for getting involved in creative projects, whether you are the creator or a spectator at a gallery or museum.

VENUS CONJUNCT SUN

Creativity or self-expression of some sort is favored today. Let it out and enjoy yourself.

VENUS TRINE SUN

Your creativity is really cooking along today, so go to it. You may surprise even yourself.

VENUS OPPOSITION SUN

Your creativity is on the ball today, but you may lack the discipline to turn all that inspiration into something excellent and concrete. Be prepared for rewrites or corrections tomorrow.

VENUS CONJUNCT MERCURY

Your creativity is stimulated, and you'll appreciate every aspect of the fine arts today.

VENUS TRINE VENUS

Your creativity and appreciation for beauty in general are enhanced today.

VENUS CONJUNCT MARS

Your artistic creativity is stimulated by this transit in whatever field your talents lie.

VENUS SEXTILE MARS

All creative endeavors are favored today, even if it's simply beautifying your home somehow. One doesn't have to be a Picasso to be creative.

VENUS OPPOSITION MARS

Your creative energies are stimulated, and this is a good time to finish one of those projects you've had in the works awhile.

VENUS SEXTILE SATURN

You'll do well in creative projects requiring great attention to detail today—calligraphy, for instance.

VENUS CONJUNCT NEPTUNE

This is a day of inspiration for you—of visualizing another reality, almost, and rendering it artistically into this one.

VENUS SEXTILE NEPTUNE

Your creative imagination is enhanced, as is your appreciation of beauty and harmony. You'll benefit by surrounding yourself with beauty, art, poetry, even a beautiful landscape.

VENUS SQUARE NEPTUNE

Your creative imagination and inspiration are stimulated today. Sit down and tune in. You'll probably amaze even yourself.

VENUS TRINE NEPTUNE

Creativity that evolves from within will be stimulated today. Practical activity in the real world will not.

VENUS TRINE PLUTO

Your work will show the inner intensity you're feeling now, and it will be more powerful and impressive for it.

VENUS SEXTILE MIDHEAVEN

Creativity is stimulated today, and you really want to get into it, too.

VENUS TRINE MIDHEAVEN

An excellent time for creativity, and you'll probably crank out the work today. You'll be more appreciative of beauty, too.

MARS IN FIFTH HOUSE

You feel positively impelled to express yourself. This transit is better for active expression, such as sculpting or dance, than for hatching out The Great American Novel. Mars hates to sit still.

MARS TRINE MERCURY

You're alert and able to understand easily. This is a good time for study and research, stimulating conversation, writing, planning, reading—all sorts of mental activity to stimulate your creative juices and lay the groundwork for your projects.

MARS CONJUNCT VENUS

Your creativity is aroused very strongly, but you don't want to sit around and be mental about it. This transit stimulates the need to be physically creative, such as in the performing arts, sculpting, painting large murals, or anything else that is both strenuous and creative.

MARS SEXTILE VENUS

Artistic endeavors are favored now, especially if you can share the experience.

MARS TRINE VENUS

Though this transit will not in itself bring creative inspiration, the energy needed to do the work will be supplied and can be directed toward creative endeavors.

MARS OPPOSITION VENUS

You can singularly express your true self through your creative work today with unusual energy and vigor.

MARS CONJUNCT MARS

A good time for beginning new projects that you'll get recognition for. You'll know the outcome in about a year, when Mars opposes Mars.

MARS CONJUNCT JUPITER

A good time to begin new projects. Your energy and self-confidence are high now.

MARS SEXTILE JUPITER

Projects begun now are very likely to be successful.

MARS SEXTILE SATURN

A great transit for sculptors, as it favors working with metal or stone—anything requiring patient attention to detail and delayed gratification.

MARS TRINE SATURN

Work requiring attention to details and patient, careful progress—such as working in metal or stone or doing precise artwork or writing—is favored today.

MARS SEXTILE URANUS

You can break out of old ruts today. You'll be open to new thought and insights, and your thinking will be more original. Get going on something new and different.

JUPITER IN FIFTH HOUSE

You'll produce more and may find yourself positively inspired. You may even earn more than usual. This is an excellent time for creativity in any endeavor.

JUPITER IN NINTH HOUSE

This is an excellent time for writing. The ninth house is connected with publishing and publishers.

JUPITER TRINE SUN

You can accomplish a great deal today if you can overcome the tendency just to sit back and enjoy this pleasant transit. You can reach out to new heights and horizons if you try.

JUPITER SEXTILE MERCURY

If Jupiter makes a station near your Mercury, you can get some serious writing done. Even if it doesn't, this is a good time for writing of all types—including letters.

JUPITER TRINE MARS

Your urge to create is very strong. This may include a desire to have children. Now's a good time to start any creative project.

SATURN TRINE MERCURY

This is not a good time to rely on creative inspiration to see you through, but it's excellent for doing any kind of mental work requiring discipline and stick-to-itiveness, such as research.

SATURN SEXTILE VENUS

You are in a very practical state of mind. Creative projects or crafts that have a practical purpose or that require exacting, detailed work are favored now.

SATURN SQUARE VENUS

Your creativity is not a soaring eagle right now. Something about your work may be dissatisfying you; you may have to make changes to bring it more in line with a true expression of yourself.

SATURN TRINE VENUS

You can now bring great discipline, if not inspiration, to your creative projects, and you'll be inclined to work on practical, useful enterprises.

SATURN OPPOSITION VENUS

This is not likely to be one of your more inspirationally creative periods. You and your creativity are going through some changes. This, too, shall pass, and your creativity will come back with renewed vigor and insight.

SATURN SEXTILE MARS

Tasks that require disciplined hard work and patience, such as sculpting, carving, precise metal work, and so on, are favored now. You'll be able to accomplish a great deal, slowly, like the tortoise, one step at a time.

SATURN TRINE MARS

Work requiring disciplined energy, patience, and attention to detail is favored now.

URANUS IN FIFTH HOUSE

This is a time when you can be unusually creative, innovative, and original. Perhaps you'll use some new technology creatively.

URANUS SEXTILE MOON

An excellent time for all creative work. Your emotions are stimulated, and you're able to see things from a new and different point of view.

URANUS TRINE MERCURY

New, creative, out-of-the-rut, perhaps surprising solutions to your projects may come to you now.

URANUS SEXTILE VENUS

You'll have so many new ideas you'll hardly know what to do with them. Jot them all down and develop them later.

URANUS OPPOSITION VENUS

You'll have plenty of new ideas or opportunities coming your way now. Just get them down. You can develop them later.

URANUS SEXTILE MIDHEAVEN

Your creativity will be enhanced by your increased intuitiveness and willingness to take risks to innovate.

URANUS TRINE MIDHEAVEN

Your creativity will flow easily, and you'll be especially innovative and original.

URANUS TRINE ASCENDANT

Creativity and self-expression will flow easily now. In fact, it may be so easy that you let it slip by without doing anything. Don't waste this time.

NEPTUNE IN FIRST HOUSE

Artistic and musical inspiration are likely to be stimulated now. Let some time pass and have a hard look at what comes to you now before sending it out into the world.

NEPTUNE IN THIRD HOUSE

Your intuition, and thus your creativity, is enhanced under this transit. Go for it.

NEPTUNE IN FIFTH HOUSE

Your creativity is stimulated under this transit. New ideas or methods will come flooding in.

NEPTUNE SEXTILE SUN

Being especially psychically tuned in now and more in touch with your intuitive nature, you may be more creative than usual during this transit.

NEPTUNE TRINE SUN

An excellent time for creativity in the abstract. Worry about the practical details later.

NEPTUNE OPPOSITION SUN

Creativity may be enhanced, but better double-check whatever you do now after this transit has passed.

NEPTUNE SEXTILE MOON

You'll be highly intuitive, creative, and imaginative under this transit. Don't waste it all on daydreaming.

NEPTUNE SEXTILE MERCURY

You can be very creative and imaginative at this time, able to communicate your intuitive and spiritual insights to others.

NEPTUNE TRINE MERCURY

Your ability to create and to communicate are incredibly enhanced under this transit. It's excellent for teaching or writing or any other form of communicating. Your left brain and right brain are working together as an effective team.

NEPTUNE CONJUNCT VENUS

Your creative imagination will brim with new ideas. This will be one of your most active and stimulating times.

NEPTUNE SEXTILE VENUS

This transit is very favorable for artistic creativity, though you may not be very practical about it at this time. Perhaps you should create now and take care of the business end later.

NEPTUNE TRINE VENUS

An excellent time for creativity, especially for creating beauty for its own sake.

NEPTUNE OPPOSITION VENUS

Your creative imagination is enhanced at this time, and as long as you don't get lost in your own dream world, this can be a very valuable period for you.

NEPTUNE TRINE URANUS

Your intuitive and imaginative abilities are enhanced. A good time to seek new ideas, perhaps through meditation.

NEPTUNE SEXTILE PLUTO

Your intuitive creativity will be enhanced during this period. Don't be unduly upset or try stubbornly to hang on if it becomes clear or necessary that you change your style or method of doing things. A new cycle is trying to begin, but first the old must pass away.

NEPTUNE CONJUNCT MIDHEAVEN

You may become more professionally active in your particular art field, possibly making a significant breakthrough. Conversely, there may be a scandal under afflicted conditions.

NEPTUNE SEXTILE MIDHEAVEN

A favorable time for both the creative and the business end of art and art-related professions.

NEPTUNE SQUARE MIDHEAVEN

Artistic creativity or businesses may be at a low ebb during this time.

NEPTUNE SEXTILE ASCENDANT

Your intuitive faculties and creativity are enhanced under this transit. Try to do more than fantasize, though.

PLUTO CONJUNCT MERCURY

An excellent time for digging deep into research for some creative project you have in mind or are working on, especially something scientific or intellectual in nature.

PLUTO SEXTILE MERCURY

An excellent time for getting your research done. You can really make a good job of it now as a foundation for any project.

PLUTO TRINE MERCURY

Now is a good time for writing that concerns secret, deep, or hidden topics, such as the occult, psychology, geology, mining, and so on.

PLUTO CONJUNCT VENUS

Creative, intuitive insights may come your way, especially if you are sublimating sexual energy, which is very intense at the moment.

PLUTO SEXTILE VENUS

Your creativity will be stimulated, and what you do now will be on a deeper level than usual.

PLUTO TRINE VENUS

Your creativity is enhanced and deepened during this time, and what you do now will have a profound effect on your life for some time. You may receive the recognition you've been seeking.

PLUTO OPPOSITION VENUS

There may be creative inspiration with this transit, possibly of an intense, even obsessive nature.

PLUTO TRINE JUPITER

Your creative endeavors may become more insightful, intuitive, and innovative at this time.

PLUTO SEXTILE NEPTUNE
An excellent time for creativity in the arts and sciences. Your intuitive faculties are enhanced, particularly if you meditate.

PLUTO TRINE ASCENDANT
Your self-understanding is being broadened and deepened; hence, your creativity will be enhanced. You're not in the least concerned with superficialities now.

Chapter 8

Death

Death—our transition, our birth into another phase of life—is an important topic to us. Yet most modern astrology books skirt or ignore the subject completely. This is possibly due to the complicated nature of the matter. Anything as important as death is seldom presaged by only one or two simple indications, and so the writers may prefer to back off rather than throw a weasel into a crowded henhouse. Panic could ensue.

However, to say, as most astrologers do—that astrology is a self-growth and planning tool, that knowledge is power, that there *is* free will and we're responsible for our own lives, that forewarned is forearmed, and all the other clichés—to say all that and then withhold information is a glaring contradiction.

So, what knowledge I *have* been able to find is included here because I don't believe in ignorance, and I do trust in your spiritual maturity. Information does not come to you—or "soak in"—unless you have a need for it and are ready.

Transit Descriptions

SUN IN EIGHTH HOUSE
If there are many other supporting indications, this time can signify actual physical death. But this is not at all usual. This month-long transit, after all, occurs for each of us every year.

MOON IN EIGHTH HOUSE
If there are many other indications to support it, this transit may signal the time of a family member's death. This, of course, is not the usual effect of this transit, as it occurs once a month.

MERCURY IN EIGHTH HOUSE
The topic of your own mortality may enter your thoughts, as you are dwelling on all sorts of deep subjects now.

MERCURY OPPOSITION PLUTO
You may receive news of the death of someone you know. Naturally, this doesn't occur every time this transit does.

MARS CONJUNCT URANUS
Rash actions in dangerous situations could lead to sudden death if Mars is afflicted.

MARS SQUARE URANUS
This transit sometimes signals sudden deaths, though this is not its usual meaning. We all have this transit many times in our lives.

MARS CONJUNCT PLUTO
In times of war, this transit sometimes indicates a danger of death. At other times, it may simply mean the necessity of dealing with the belongings or property of the dead.

MARS SQUARE PLUTO
In times of war, this transit sometimes indicates danger of death, possibly due to radioactivity or gunshot.

MARS OPPOSITION PLUTO
In war situations, the possibility of death is sometimes signaled by this transit.

JUPITER IN EIGHTH HOUSE
This transit sometimes signals the receipt of an inheritance, though obviously, this can't always be so. It occurs more than once in all our lives.

SATURN IN EIGHTH HOUSE
You may find yourself contemplating mortality more often during this transit. Occasionally, this transit signifies the death of someone you know.

SATURN CONJUNCT PLUTO
This transit sometimes indicates the death of someone important to you.

URANUS IN FOURTH HOUSE
This transit sometimes indicates the death of a family member or relative, though by no means is this an inevitable manifestation.

URANUS IN EIGHTH HOUSE
There is a possibility of sudden death under this transit, if afflicted. Receiving an inheritance is also possible.

URANUS OPPOSITION SUN
Though not necessarily likely, a relationship may end due to death under this transit. Or, the symbolism may be played out as a death of a relationship for whatever reason. In any case, if a relationship does end, it's because its function has been accomplished, or it was inhibiting the true self-expression of either partner, or both.

URANUS CONJUNCT PLUTO
Possible sudden death of friends or relatives, though this is by no means an inevitable circumstance of this transit.

URANUS SQUARE PLUTO
The sudden death of someone meaningful to you is a possible manifestation of this transit, which signals radical changes in your life.

URANUS OPPOSITION PLUTO

Death of someone important, at least to you, may occur under this transit. It's all part of sweeping out the old order to make way for the new in your life. This may refer not to an actual death but to the end of some relationship.

NEPTUNE IN EIGHTH HOUSE

Your interest in life after death may deepen. If you have to deal with the property of someone who has died, there may be curious circumstances involved.

NEPTUNE CONJUNCT PLUTO

Your life is undergoing great changes. Old ideas and situations are falling away to make way for the new. This may or may not indicate physical death, the ultimate transformation, as death and rebirth can be symbolical—the old dies, the new is born.

NEPTUNE SQUARE PLUTO

The death of someone important to you, whether they are close or not, may occur under this transit. Sometimes it may be of a mysterious nature.

NEPTUNE TRINE PLUTO

It may now be that conditions are right for contact with deceased friends or relatives.

NEPTUNE OPPOSITION PLUTO

Changes in your life now *may* include the death of someone you know. This may have the effect of stimulating your potential for spiritual or intuitive awareness.

PLUTO IN FOURTH HOUSE

There are tremendous changes going on in your life, including in family relationships, and a death, divorce, or other separation may occur.

PLUTO IN EIGHTH HOUSE

A time when your thoughts will dwell on deep subjects, including death, rebirth, and transformation. These thoughts may be triggered by the death of someone you know, large-scale changes going on in your life, or simply by your philosophical bent at this time.

PLUTO CONJUNCT MOON

This transit sometimes indicates separation from family members through death.

PLUTO SQUARE MOON

This transit sometimes indicates the death of a family member. This is not an inevitable manifestation.

PLUTO OPPOSITION MERCURY

You may hear of the death of someone you know, possibly a relative, though this is not inevitable. You may become interested in the subject of life after death.

PLUTO CONJUNCT MARS

During a time of war, death may be indicated by this transit.

PLUTO SQUARE MARS

In a war situation this transit sometimes indicates death.

PLUTO CONJUNCT SATURN

The death of someone important to you may occur under this transit. Another cycle of growth is beginning. Accept it as such and let go.

PLUTO SQUARE URANUS

The unexpected death of someone important to you may be among the sweeping changes to which you must adjust at this time.

PLUTO OPPOSITION URANUS

The unexpected death of a person of consequence to you may occur under this transit.

PLUTO CONJUNCT NEPTUNE

If there are other, reinforcing indications, this transit may signify physical death, the evolving to a new level of existence.

PLUTO SQUARE PLUTO

Problems associated with death or with the goods and property of the dead may arise.

PLUTO TRINE PLUTO

A good time for meditation and for being open to the cosmos. Insight into life after death may result at this time.

PLUTO OPPOSITION MIDHEAVEN

The death of a family member is possible, but by no means inevitable, under this transit.

Chapter 9

Education

Education, in the truest sense, is never completed. We are learning unofficially at all times; our subconscious, if not our conscious mind, misses nothing. Yet there are times when we wish to pursue education in a more structured manner. These are the times when checking your transits can be beneficial, for you can discover when you'll be more productive at artistic, technical, or metaphysical endeavors, whether to concentrate on details or the broad view, even when best to begin such studies. There are not only "tides in the affairs of men" but also in the affairs of school buses.

Transit Descriptions

SUN IN NINTH HOUSE

This is an excellent time to begin a new study of some sort. Law, philosophy, travel, foreign countries, the spiritual and occult are especially indicated, but any new mental stimulation will be highly pleasing and beneficial to you now.

SUN SEXTILE MERCURY

Study of any and all kinds will go well today, because you're open, alert, and ready to receive.

SUN TRINE MERCURY

This transit is excellent for study of any kind. You're receptive, curious, and eager for knowledge.

SUN CONJUNCT JUPITER

Today you want to know about everything, even things you usually think are over your head. It's therefore a good day to dig in and really study.

SUN TRINE SATURN

Any job, project, or study requiring undivided attention to details is favored today.

SUN TRINE URANUS

This transit is great for studying any subject that broadens your knowledge of the universe. Science and the occult, including astrology, will be found exciting and interesting today, but you'll drop out if forced to learn by rote or focus on routine.

SUN SEXTILE NEPTUNE

You're more aware and sensitive to the cosmos than usual, and your ego-demands are down. A good time to study spiritual or occult matters or to meditate by yourself.

SUN TRINE NEPTUNE

Your spiritual sensitivity is heightened, and you're more aware of the subtleties around you. A good day for quiet study, contemplation, or meditation.

SUN SEXTILE PLUTO

This is a good time for studies that go beneath the superficial, surface level of things.

SUN TRINE PLUTO

Beginning any sort of study is favored today. You'll dig and investigate deeply to find out what you want and need to know.

MOON CONJUNCT MERCURY

For a short time your rational mind will be overruled by your emotions and moods. Hold off making decisions or trying to study subjects requiring pure logic. You can profitably use these few hours to gather information for later use. Be careful that you don't let the trivial overwhelm the more important.

MOON SEXTILE PLUTO

The hidden, the mysterious, the bottom line, the true meanings of relationships or life will appeal to you now, whether you manifest this interest by reading mysteries, by studying psychology, astrology, ESP, or by delving into your own subconscious.

MOON SQUARE ASCENDANT

You're moody; clear, rational thinking will not be your strong point now. It's best to hold off on tasks requiring reason and accurate judgment till later.

MERCURY IN NINTH HOUSE

An excellent transit for furthering your education in any field, but particularly in law, philosophy, and foreign languages or cultures.

MERCURY CONJUNCT MERCURY

All mental activity is highlighted under this transit. This is a good time to begin a new study or to tackle a difficult problem or puzzle. Logical reasoning is in tip-top shape today.

MERCURY SEXTILE MERCURY

Now is a good time for doing routine mental work requiring attention to details and figures. This is also a good transit under which to make plans, begin a new study or mental challenge, or just read for the fun of it.

MERCURY TRINE MERCURY

Your curiosity is kindled and you want to learn new things. Almost anything today could trigger exciting new ideas for you.

MERCURY SEXTILE JUPITER

Any studies that give you a greater understanding of the universe and your place in it—such as religions, philosophy, foreign cultures—would be good to pursue now.

MERCURY TRINE JUPITER

Your mind is clear and sharp now, and you're open to new ideas and information. This is a good time to study "thoughty" subjects, such as religion, law, philosophy, or psychology.

MERCURY SEXTILE SATURN

Precision and concentration are your strong suits today. You can tackle detailed mental tasks with ease.

MERCURY SQUARE SATURN

Intense mental work, disciplined attention to details, and work on the practical ins and outs of projects are favored today. Communications and making good impressions will be difficult, so put off seeing the dean or that formidable teacher for today if you can.

MERCURY SEXTILE URANUS

Subjects that give you new insights into the universe are favored today—subjects symbolized by Uranus, such as science, technology, math, astrology, and the like.

MERCURY TRINE URANUS

This is an excellent time to tackle a new study, especially science, math, technology, astrology, the occult.

MERCURY OPPOSITION URANUS

Your mind is quick today, and this could lead to sloppiness in your work. But if you can master this tendency somewhat, it's a good day for the study of math, science, technology, even astrology. You'll probably just survey the topic today and get down to the nitty-gritty later.

MERCURY SEXTILE NEPTUNE

This is a good time to study the occult, mysticism, metaphysics, or spiritual and religious subjects. Your sensitivity and intuition are enhanced now; be prepared to examine your insights rationally after this transit has passed, though.

MERCURY SQUARE NEPTUNE

Your sensitivity and intuition are enhanced today, and study of occult, mystical, spiritual, or metaphysical matters is favored. You must make an effort to keep in touch with the real world, though, or you could become confused or misled. If you can maintain the balance, you'll be rewarded with an even greater awareness.

MERCURY TRINE NEPTUNE

This is a good time for studying spiritual and occult subjects, as well as religion, art, music, or poetry. You're able to intuitively comprehend much more than usual. However, you're not very practical now, so be prepared to reexamine today's brilliant notion in tomorrow's light of reason.

MERCURY SEXTILE PLUTO

You want to get to the heart of things. A good time to study psychology, the occult, astrology, or any subject that gets below the surface. You'll investigate thoroughly and learn much.

MERCURY SQUARE PLUTO

You want to probe beneath the surface, so this is a good time for the study of such subjects as psychology, the occult, astrology, yoga, and so on.

MERCURY TRINE ASCENDANT

A good day for learning anything and for the productive exchange of ideas. Attend a lecture or class, or have discussions with one and all. You'll be willing and able to appreciate the ideas and viewpoints of others.

MARS TRINE MERCURY

You're mentally alert and able to understand easily now. This is a good transit for studying, planning, writing, reading, engaging in stimulating conversation—all sorts of mental activity.

MARS SEXTILE NEPTUNE

This is a good time to study occult, psychic, or spiritual matters. You may acquire insights that change your life in some way.

JUPITER IN THIRD HOUSE

An opportunity for further training or higher education may present itself under this transit.

JUPITER IN NINTH HOUSE

An excellent time to study abstract and consciousness-expanding subjects, such as philosophy, religion, and metaphysics.

JUPITER CONJUNCT MERCURY

You're willing and able to learn more at this time, whether you return to school or not, though this is a very good time to do so. You may find yourself traveling some distance in order to learn.

JUPITER TRINE MERCURY

Now is the time to begin studying something new to you, especially if it is of an abstract nature.

JUPITER SEXTILE JUPITER

This is an excellent time to expand your outlook through education of some sort, especially through consciousness-raising studies.

JUPITER TRINE JUPITER

This is an excellent time to enlarge your perspective with education, especially with self-awareness studies.

JUPITER TRINE URANUS

You'll be able to learn more quickly than usual under this transit.

JUPITER SEXTILE MIDHEAVEN

You can profitably further your education in any area now, but especially in law, medicine, or philosophy.

JUPITER TRINE ASCENDANT

You're eager to learn now, and this is a great time to take a course or return to school.

SATURN CONJUNCT MERCURY

This would be a good time to write that thesis or study and research a difficult and serious subject. Your mental focus is narrowed now, and you'll be extremely thorough.

SATURN TRINE MERCURY

You can utilize this transit for studying or learning anything that requires mental discipline. Don't look for creative inspiration at this time.

SATURN SEXTILE URANUS

Take up the study of something new and demanding. Or teach it. You don't find the new disruptive now and can patiently integrate it with what you already know.

SATURN TRINE URANUS

Beginning a long-term study of a new and difficult subject that will lead you into new and creative directions is an effective way to utilize the energies of this transit.

SATURN TRINE NEPTUNE

Now is a good time to begin studies that put you more in touch with your inner self and to incorporate what you learn into your outer life.

SATURN TRINE PLUTO

This is an excellent time for studies designed to bring more self-knowledge.

URANUS IN FIRST HOUSE

This is a propitious time to explore self-awareness subjects and techniques. You can be open to them now and will find them beneficial to you in the future.

URANUS IN THIRD HOUSE

This can be an exciting time for you. You'll be interested in all sorts of new things, and it's a good time to begin the study of astrology, science, technology, the occult, yoga, or other mind- and consciousness-expanding subjects.

URANUS IN NINTH HOUSE

This is a good time to study subjects of higher consciousness—religion, the occult, the mystical, even astrology—as well as the scientific and technological. If you keep an open, inquiring mind, you'll gain much from the experience.

URANUS CONJUNCT MERCURY

This is a good transit under which to take up the study of astrology, the occult, science, mathematics, and technology.

URANUS SEXTILE MERCURY

This is a great time to begin new studies, especially the scientific, technological, or mathematical. Astrology and other occult subjects are also favored. Your curiosity is awakened, but you'll be easily bored. Be sure you have sufficient interest to stick with it before signing up for a long, expensive course.

URANUS TRINE MERCURY

You're ready and eager to learn new skills and subjects. Technological and occult studies are especially favored. If you've been struggling to solve some sort of technological or mental problem, new ideas or approaches will occur to you now.

URANUS SEXTILE JUPITER

Educational opportunities may occur suddenly under this transit, whether they be formal educational pursuits or not.

URANUS TRINE NEPTUNE

This is a favorable time to seek higher education, as either a beginning or a returning student. Metaphysical, spiritual, or philosophical subjects will especially interest you.

NEPTUNE TRINE SATURN

Studying psychic, spiritual, or occult subjects will be of benefit now. You'll be well-grounded, able to learn and understand without getting confused or disoriented.

NEPTUNE TRINE URANUS
This is an excellent time to study the occult in general and astrology in particular.

PLUTO IN NINTH HOUSE
You're likely to have profound experiences and insights during this transit, and you'll probably be particularly interested in philosophical subjects.

PLUTO SEXTILE MERCURY
Your interest in the hidden, the deep, or the secret is enhanced, especially as it concerns the working of the intellect. Consequently, you'd greatly benefit from the study of psychology or psychiatry, metaphysics, or occult subjects. Your mind is penetrating and perceptive now.

PLUTO TRINE MERCURY
This is an excellent transit under which to study almost any subject, but especially those dealing with anything secret or hidden. Geology, mineralogy, psychology, magic, the occult—whatever it is, you'll learn it more quickly and in more depth than usual.

PLUTO SEXTILE JUPITER
This is an excellent transit under which to study or to teach healing of any kind, nutrition, philosophy, law, religion, or the occult.

PLUTO TRINE JUPITER
This is good transit under which to pursue higher education, especially in the fields of philosophy, metaphysics, law, or religion.

PLUTO CONJUNCT SATURN
As this is a favorable time for self-growth and regeneration, this would be a good time for the study of metaphysical or occult subjects.

PLUTO SEXTILE SATURN
This is a good time to study deep subjects or to seriously study the occult. Your mental discipline and concentration are enhanced now, yet your intuition is working well, too.

PLUTO SEXTILE URANUS

Commencing studies of science, astrology, theology, or the occult is favored now.

PLUTO CONJUNCT NEPTUNE

If you've been wanting to study astrology, metaphysics, the occult, or psychology in depth, now is an excellent time. Apply what you learn to your daily life, and you'll benefit enormously.

PLUTO SEXTILE NEPTUNE

This is an excellent time for in-depth studies of the occult, metaphysical, mystical, or spiritual, as well as the scientific or technological. Meditation is favored also.

Chapter 10

Energy

Energy is the prime mover, some would say the Prime Being, of the universe; and aside from the dense matter of our physical bodies, it also manifests in the human as the ability and desire to mobilize the physical body or mental capacities. As impulses or forms of energy in this universe, then, we should not be surprised that certain alignments or combinations of other forms of energy in that same universe impinge upon our own energetic ebb and flow.

And so it is. In this chapter you can discover whether you're ebbing or flowing with energy, mentally or physically, and so plan your days—and nights—to best utilize your resources.

Transit Descriptions

Mental Energy

SUN CONJUNCT MERCURY

Your mind is sharp today and easily concentrates on details—a good day to clear out that paperwork backlog.

SUN SQUARE MERCURY

If you're clear in your own mind about your ideas, you'll be able to communicate them clearly and forcefully. Your mental energy and activity is high; don't forget to slow down and listen to others.

SUN OPPOSITION MERCURY

This will be a mentally stimulating day. Try to remain objective, though, and listen to others. Assure others you're willing to work cooperatively with them; you'll be more likely to get your own ideas across.

SUN CONJUNCT MARS

This is not a good day for mental concentration. Your physical energy is so high you can hardly sit still. If forced to sit at a desk or other sedentary job, get up and do jumping jacks during your coffee break or something. If you don't utilize this energy properly, accidents, blowups, or illness could result.

SUN CONJUNCT JUPITER

You're willing now to tackle even subjects you usually consider beyond your capacities, and you may just find your capacities expanded in the process.

SUN TRINE JUPITER

Take in new events, activities, experiences of all kinds. Your mind can encompass expansive topics today that enhance your understanding of the universe as a whole.

SUN SEXTILE SATURN

Your mind is set for orderliness and concentration. You're organized and careful and can handle details with alacrity. You're interested in the concrete, not the philosophical.

SUN SQUARE SATURN

Your mental energy may be at a low ebb. You perhaps feel weighted down by circumstances. Try asking for help; you just may get it.

SUN SEXTILE URANUS

You're curious, imaginative, alert, and able to comprehend ideas rapidly during this transit.

SUN SQUARE NEPTUNE

You may feel both physically and mentally down today. Take heart. This, too, will pass. Try to see the world as it really is. Make plans and set goals later.

MERCURY IN FIRST HOUSE

Your mind is alert and active, and you can accomplish a great deal now if you can stick to one topic long enough.

MERCURY IN THIRD HOUSE

Your mind is suddenly alive and very active. This transit is excellent for any type of mental activity except making decisions. Things are happening too rapidly for that now. Use this time for research and for making sure everyone understands everyone else. You'll probably be communicating with one and all anyway.

MERCURY IN SEVENTH HOUSE

Intellectual stimulation is what you crave and you'll probably get it, especially with business partners or spouses.

MERCURY IN EIGHTH HOUSE

You'll find yourself thinking on deeper levels than usual. If you don't, it's a good idea to consciously pursue these thoughts. They may profoundly affect your life.

MERCURY CONJUNCT MARS

Your mental energy is running high right now, and you may even feel like having an intellectual duel here and there just for the fun of it. Beware of being egotistical and self-righteous about your every word and thought, though. Sorry, but you really aren't infallible.

MERCURY SEXTILE MARS

Mental and physical energy abounds today. Don't expect others to keep up with you, though. Maybe you should work by yourself.

MERCURY TRINE MARS

Mentally, you're willing to take on, and perhaps appreciate as a challenge, any hard or formidable problems you may be up against.

MERCURY SEXTILE SATURN

Precision and concentration are your mental strong points today. You can tackle detailed tasks with ease, but projects requiring a broad overview may intimidate you.

MERCURY SQUARE SATURN

Intense mental work, disciplined attention to details, and work on practical aspects of current endeavors are favored today. Making broad, sweeping plans is not.

MERCURY TRINE SATURN

A good time for serious, practical thinking. Also for seeking advice from those more experienced than you.

MERCURY OPPOSITION SATURN

Your thinking will be along serious lines today, and it's a good time for work requiring mental discipline. But don't overwork. You're fighting the "gloomies" today, and overdoing it won't help. Relax some, too.

MERCURY CONJUNCT URANUS

You'll be mentally in high gear today. It may be hard to concentrate, but you should try not to leap to unwarranted conclusions. Be prepared to check out any ideas or conclusions later. Mental work requiring originality and creativity will go well.

MERCURY TRINE URANUS

You'll feel more alert and mentally stimulated than ever. Everything and anything will be interesting and exciting. Your intuition will be keen. A good day to reapproach old, "insoluble" problems.

MERCURY OPPOSITION URANUS

Your mind will work at breakneck speed today. This may lead to careless work, irritability with others (they seem so *slow*), lack of mental discipline, and the scattering of energies. But, you'll also be able to grasp ideas and insights quickly. Double-check them tomorrow.

MERCURY CONJUNCT NEPTUNE

A large dose of sensitivity, subtlety, and imagination may lead to confused, less than rational, thinking today. Save problems requiring pure logic for later.

MERCURY SEXTILE NEPTUNE

This is more of a day for dreaminess and fantasizing than for clarity of thinking. Jobs requiring impeccable logic and reasoning would be best avoided today.

MERCURY TRINE NEPTUNE

Your thinking may be a bit undisciplined. Practical matters have little appeal. Better scrutinize tomorrow any ideas you hatch out today.

MERCURY OPPOSITION NEPTUNE

Your thinking is not of the highest rational order today. You probably feel as if you're being bombarded by more than you can handle. Actually, you're just more sensitive to all possible inputs than usual. Put off exacting, detailed tasks for a day or so.

MERCURY CONJUNCT PLUTO

Your thinking will be intense and incisive today, going to the heart of any matter. You may focus on one thing or idea all day, which is perfect for doing research.

MERCURY SEXTILE PLUTO

You'll crave mental challenges today and will want to get to the bottom of any subject. It's a good day for research, puzzles, or mysteries of any kind.

MERCURY SQUARE PLUTO

You may focus on one subject or thought to the exclusion of all others today, which is great for doing research and probing beneath obvious superficialities. Turn that searching mind inward, and you may learn a great deal about yourself.

MERCURY TRINE PLUTO

This is a good day for work requiring intense concentration. Mysteries, puzzles, and all mental challenges attract you.

MERCURY OPPOSITION PLUTO

You're in a mood to tackle difficult problems, puzzles, or mysteries. You'll be able to concentrate very well, which can be very productive, unless you become fixated on something trivial. A good time for research.

MERCURY SEXTILE MIDHEAVEN

Be it puzzles or pranks or planning for the future, you'll want to keep your mind busy today.

MERCURY TRINE MIDHEAVEN

Any work requiring attention to details will go well today. You're mentally alert and able to concentrate.

MERCURY SEXTILE ASCENDANT

Your mind is alert and eager, and just about anything that requires you to use it will interest you.

MERCURY SQUARE ASCENDANT

This is one of those times that your mind races so fast it nearly runs away with you. Idleness will drive you up the wall, and if nothing else, you'll keep your tongue going in high gear. Make an effort to slow down your mind and your tongue, listen to others, and you'll get more done today.

MERCURY TRINE ASCENDANT

You're mentally alert and curious today, a good time to broaden your mental horizons in any way you can.

MERCURY OPPOSITION ASCENDANT

You're looking for mental stimulation today, probably through talking with others.

VENUS SEXTILE MERCURY

This is a good day to take in a museum or concert—anything that will provide the mental stimulation you crave now.

VENUS SQUARE MERCURY

Mental discipline will not be your forte today. Save tasks requiring it for later, or be prepared to check your work tomorrow.

MARS IN THIRD HOUSE

This is a beneficial time for mental and intellectual tasks of all kinds. Your mental energy will be high.

MARS SEXTILE MOON

Your objectivity is mitigated by emotional considerations at this time. Hold off making decisions.

MARS CONJUNCT MERCURY

If you can keep your mind occupied and yourself out of disputes today, you can exert a great deal of mental effort.

MARS SEXTILE MERCURY

This is an excellent time for mental activity of any type. Your positive attitude helps in any endeavor.

MARS SQUARE MERCURY

You have a lot of mental energy today, but if things don't go right, you're apt to lose your temper, thereby dispersing a lot of the energy you need to work on the task at hand.

MARS TRINE MERCURY

You have a lot of mental energy today, and if you can't somehow keep your mind occupied, you'd better get out and do something physical. Do jumping jacks on your coffee break, if nothing else.

MARS OPPOSITION MERCURY

If you can work by yourself today, any kind of mental effort will go well. You'll have to apply some self-discipline, though, to keep from disseminating your energy in every direction and doing things too fast to do them properly.

JUPITER SEXTILE URANUS

This can be a stimulating time. You're interested in new and challenging ideas, and you can grasp them readily and solve problems easily because of a new perspective.

JUPITER TRINE URANUS

You'll be able to learn more rapidly than usual under this transit. Your mind is quick and alert, and you easily grasp new concepts.

SATURN CONJUNCT MERCURY

You'll tend to concentrate your mental energy rather narrowly now as you think seriously and deeply about a particular subject. Try not to let gloomy thoughts dominate; you're not seeing the whole picture if you do.

SATURN SEXTILE MERCURY

You're in a serious frame of mind now and can concentrate with a mental discipline that will enable you to get a lot of work done. This is a good time for detail work.

SATURN SQUARE MERCURY

This can be a time of challenge to your mental attitudes and ideas. If this upsets you unduly, your thinking may have become too rigid over the years. It's time for a mental overhaul.

SATURN TRINE MERCURY

Your energy is controlled now and can be sustained to do prolonged, precise, patient work, either physical or mental. Make an effort not to let your thinking become too rigid, though.

SATURN SEXTILE MARS

Your mental energy is disciplined now, and you're able to focus it on difficult, precise, long-term projects that require hard work and patience. You'll accomplish a great deal.

URANUS IN THIRD HOUSE

This can be an exciting time, with new interests, new information, new communications coming at you from all directions. You may be suddenly interested in astrology, science and technology, or the occult.

URANUS CONJUNCT MERCURY

Your mind will move quickly now and be stimulated by new ideas. Remain open, but don't make binding decisions or commitments now. If you find all the new insights and ideas upsetting, your thinking has probably become too rigid. Loosen up. Be flexible.

URANUS SEXTILE MERCURY

Your thinking and curiosity are stimulated, and you want to take in new ideas and concepts as if they were water. You'll be easily bored, though, and will want to flit from one subject to another.

URANUS TRINE MERCURY

Your mind is stimulated, and you're ready and eager to learn new subjects. If you've been trying to solve a problem, new ideas or approaches will occur to you now.

PLUTO CONJUNCT MERCURY

You'll have tremendous mental energy during this transit and the capacity to do very thorough research into any subject.

PLUTO SEXTILE MERCURY

Your mind is sharp, probing, and perceptive now—an excellent time for almost any intellectual challenge.

Physical Energy

SUN TRINE SUN

You energy level is high, and you'll be able to tackle anything with great vigor.

SUN OPPOSITION SUN

Your energies may be low; you may feel discouraged, tired, or tense. However, your self-awareness may be heightened, and you'll benefit from contacts with others.

SUN CONJUNCT VENUS

Your energy level is likely to be somewhere up near the roof today. This might be a good day to finally get that garage cleaned out.

SUN CONJUNCT MARS

You're very energetic today, and feel you have to get out and do something physical or you'll burst. And you may very well blow your stack, have an accident, or become ill if this energy is not channeled properly. Get up and run around your desk while others are at coffee break, if nothing else.

SUN SEXTILE MARS

Today it's a good idea to be as physically active as you can, especially in something that involves teamwork, such as a sport or a group project.

SUN SQUARE MARS

You will have prodigious energy and should find some sort of vigorous outlet for it and your feelings of aggressiveness. Don't keep any of this in; work it out.

SUN TRINE MARS

Physical activity will benefit you in all strata of your being today.

SUN CONJUNCT JUPITER

You'll feel so energetic and optimistic today you may want to bite off more than you can chew. Exercise a little control and this can be a very positive day.

SUN CONJUNCT SATURN

You may not be blessed with boundless energy today, but you'll have enough if you just concentrate on whatever really has to be done. You'll feel even worse if you don't do anything.

SUN SQUARE SATURN

Your energy may be at a low ebb. You feel weighted down by circumstances. Take another look at your own choices and assumptions; it may be you don't really have to do what you thought you were required to do. Asking for some help and getting it may raise your spirits and energy level, too.

SUN TRINE URANUS

You are energetic and restless. Get out and do something new and exciting!

SUN SEXTILE NEPTUNE

Your physical energy is not at its highest. Today would be well spent in meditation or contemplation to improve self-understanding.

SUN SQUARE NEPTUNE

You're at a point of low physical energy and probably just don't feel like coping at all. This is a good time to just take it easy and relax. It's OK—we all need this once in a while. If you absolutely can't do that, at least try not to tackle any herculean tasks today.

SUN TRINE PLUTO

You'll feel quite energetic today, and it's a good time to jump in and do what must be done. You'll feel good and, at the same time, gain in self-knowledge.

MOON CONJUNCT SUN

Unless your energy is depressed by a longer transit, you'll feel a surge of energy now that will carry you through the rest of the month. If another transit is lowering your energy, try to rest and recharge yourself today.

MOON TRINE SUN

This transit tends to give your spirits a boost, and sometimes it does the same for your energy.

MOON OPPOSITION SUN

You may feel quite energetic, but this may be undermined or complicated by different areas of your life pulling you in different directions. Work at resolving this tug-of-war and you can get a lot done.

MOON TRINE MARS

Your energy level is on the upswing today, and doing something that involves its use will be beneficial.

MOON TRINE PLUTO

Your reaction to others and to life in general is so emotionally intense now, you may find yourself drained of energy by the time this transit is over—but possibly more knowledgeable about your emotions.

MERCURY CONJUNCT URANUS

Nervousness could be a problem today. If so, simply try to relax till this transit is over.

VENUS SQUARE VENUS

Your energy is low, and you'd really rather not make the effort to do much of anything. However, if you can bring yourself to do something, it may very well be worthwhile.

VENUS TRINE VENUS

You don't feel like being very active, and in fact, it is a good time to rest and relax.

MARS IN FIRST HOUSE

You'll have a great deal of energy and should be able to get a lot done, especially if you can work independently.

MARS IN THIRD HOUSE

Your energy level is high today, and if you can refrain from being argumentative or belligerent, you can accomplish a great deal with others.

MARS IN FIFTH HOUSE

An excellent time to enjoy yourself in vigorous sports or other recreational activities. You want to be active but have fun, too.

MARS IN ELEVENTH HOUSE

An excellent time for cooperative physical activity, such as sports.

MARS CONJUNCT SUN

Your physical energy is high, and if you don't utilize it, you'll be intensely restless. Do plan some sort of hard physical activity today.

MARS SEXTILE SUN

Your physical energy is enhanced, and you'll be ready and able to tackle the world today.

MARS SQUARE SUN

Your energy is high, and it may involve you in disputes today. You're just not willing to back down and want to defend your position with extreme vigor. OK, but do be prepared to compromise at least on less important matters.

MARS TRINE SUN

You're very energetic and ready to work hard. It's an excellent time for sports; you're able to enjoy yourself without absolutely having to win.

MARS SEXTILE MOON

You have energy to work hard and diligently but want to apply yourself only to projects that involve you personally and emotionally.

MARS SEXTILE MERCURY

You have a lot of energy and confidence and can get much done. This leads to a positive, healthy attitude that helps you along in any endeavor.

MARS TRINE MERCURY

You have so much energy you can hardly sit still. This is an excellent time to go somewhere, especially if it involves physical activity, such as hiking, jogging, rowing, cycling, and so on.

MARS CONJUNCT MARS

Your energy is so high that unless you find a satisfying outlet for it, you'll be restless and irritable with everyone. If you totally repress this energy, accidents or run-ins with people who are themselves feeling irritable and aggressive may occur.

MARS SEXTILE MARS

Your energy level is very high and you just plain feel good. Doing something physical would be beneficial, though doing nothing won't be particularly harmful, just wasteful. Hard work or play with others would be very appropriate.

MARS SQUARE MARS

Your energy is very high, and the best way to handle it is to do physical work that doesn't require a lot of attention to detail.

MARS TRINE MARS

You are full of self-confidence and energy. You can get a lot done now, physically or mentally, though the physical is favored.

MARS OPPOSITION MARS

You have a lot of energy and can complete projects successfully, if you can curb your ego enough to work well with others, one-to-one.

MARS CONJUNCT JUPITER

You have a lot of energy and feel just great. This is a good time to tackle any physical labor you must do or to take part in vigorous sports. Physical activity will be easy for you now—even childbirth should it occur at this time.

MARS SEXTILE JUPITER

Your energy level is high and your health and well-being are enhanced under this transit. This is a great time for sports or exercises.

MARS TRINE JUPITER

A good time for all sorts of physical activity. Your energy is high and your muscles have good tone.

MARS CONJUNCT SATURN

Your energies are not so high today. It's best to stick to routines that you can almost do in your sleep. But if you feel angry inside, this is a good day for some demanding physical work that requires concentration, as long as it does not involve sharp instruments.

MARS SEXTILE SATURN

You're not reeking with high levels of energy, but you are able to sustain a steady effort for quite a while.

MARS TRINE SATURN

Your energy is controlled now and can be sustained to do prolonged, precise, patient work, either physical or mental.

MARS CONJUNCT NEPTUNE

Take good care of yourself now. Your energy is low and you can easily overdo.

MARS SEXTILE NEPTUNE

Your energy is at something of a low ebb. This is a good time to meditate or study occult subjects, or boost your energy by helping others.

MARS SQUARE NEPTUNE

Your energy level is very low, and you should take care not to overdo. Don't do more than you have to, and try to rest and relax.

MARS TRINE NEPTUNE

Your energy level is low, but not necessarily so low as to be a health threat. You just don't want to do much.

MARS SQUARE PLUTO

You'll have a lot of energy and can get quite a bit of work done if you can harness your energy constructively. The tendency is to come on like gangbusters and get into conflicts with others. Try to avoid this, as well as dangerous situations or places.

MARS OPPOSITION PLUTO

Your energies are high and you're willing to work hard for what you want. And you can succeed if you utilize them constructively and don't expend them all in ego conflicts.

MARS TRINE MIDHEAVEN

You have abundant energy right now, and it would be to your benefit to engage in some sort of hard physical work or vigorous athletics.

MARS SEXTILE ASCENDANT

Hard physical exertion is your ticket to happiness today. You'll go bananas if you have to just sit around.

MARS TRINE ASCENDANT

You have plenty of energy, and this is a very beneficial time for you to utilize it in physical activity. You'll enjoy it and be able to do it well. Great time for athletics.

JUPITER CONJUNCT MARS

You have so much energy with this transit, you can hardly contain yourself. Exertion that would normally tax you will seem easy for you now. A danger is that, as with most Jupiter transits, you'll overexert yourself without realizing it and have to pay for it tomorrow—or today if you take foolish risks. This is a good time for doing anything that does require energy and physical activity. Giving birth is one of these favored activities.

JUPITER SEXTILE MARS

Your energy is high, as is your confidence. This combination often brings or initiates success.

JUPITER SQUARE MARS

Your energy is so high you may have to consciously exercise restraint in order to get anything done and to avoid taking foolish risks.

JUPITER OPPOSITION MARS

You have so much energy today you can hardly contain yourself. Yet you must do so if you are not to overdo or act foolishly. Keep your cool and you can accomplish a great deal today.

SATURN IN SIXTH HOUSE

You're probably going to feel for a while as if you have too many irons in the fire. It's best to conserve your energy as much as you can; don't let it get too dispersed. Health problems could result otherwise.

SATURN SQUARE SUN

Your vitality is low. Try to conserve your energy for now until it picks up again. Don't give up; just persist patiently.

SATURN OPPOSITION SUN

This is the end of a 29-year cycle, and your energies are depleted. Rest and replenish your energy; take especial care of your health. This *will* pass.

SATURN CONJUNCT MARS

You have tremendous energy and want to go gung ho in all directions. Your efforts are apt to be hindered and limited, however, unless you can focus your energies and attention on a single objective. If you can do that, you can accomplish a great deal.

SATURN SEXTILE MARS

You are able to discipline your considerable energy at this time and focus it on difficult, precise, long-term projects that require hard work and patience. Thus, you are capable of accomplishing a great deal.

SATURN OPPOSITION MARS

Energetic physical activity can help you handle the frustration or anger you may tap under this transit.

SATURN TRINE PLUTO

Your energies are controlled and concentrated, allowing you to work hard and effectively.

URANUS SEXTILE MARS

You'll be more energetic than usual and will be willing to work very hard at anything you set your mind to. You may not want to do some things, though. Freedom is on your mind now, not self-discipline.

NEPTUNE SQUARE SUN

A time of low energy and resistance. Take care of yourself very well now.

NEPTUNE OPPOSITION SUN

Your vitality is at a low point now, as is your resistance to illness. Take good care of yourself, and don't go on any crazy diets for any reason.

NEPTUNE CONJUNCT MARS

Your energy is at a low ebb. This is not the time to make any excessive physical demands on yourself. Take care and rest well.

NEPTUNE SQUARE MARS

Your energy is apt to be quite low at this time. It's best to take it as easy as you can and certainly to avoid overdoing any physical activity.

NEPTUNE OPPOSITION MARS

Your energy is low and you may not feel like doing much of anything. Take care of your health, and don't start anything requiring a great deal of effort.

PLUTO TRINE SUN

You are in fine fettle now, and it's an excellent time to begin a physical fitness regimen.

PLUTO CONJUNCT MARS

Your energy is very high and it's important—indeed, imperative—that you utilize it. Hard, physical work is advised, especially for the benefit of others. Misuse of this energy (for the control of others) or non-use could result in danger that could be violent.

PLUTO SEXTILE MARS

All sorts of strenuous physical exertions are favored. You'll feel great, as if you could go on and on. A good time to build or rebuild, anything from barns to bodies.

PLUTO SQUARE MARS

Your energy is very high, and if not channeled properly, may cause accidents or other difficulties. Get plenty of exercise and rest.

PLUTO TRINE MARS

You'll feel a tremendous new surge of energy and will be able to work long and hard at whatever you want to do. An excellent time to begin a body-building program.

Chapter 11

Finances

They're not insured by the FDIC, but the planets can be important to your financial health. Naturally, it would be helpful to know in advance of any financial venture—be it shopping for school clothes or buying the shopping center itself—which planetary influence you could bank on.

Some transits are favorable for seeking loans, asking for raises, negotiating contracts, buying art objects, or wild speculating. Investing a few moments checking this chapter, in conjunction with the chapters on Business, Home, Law, Real Estate, and even Self, will return handsome dividends. When in the course of human events it becomes necessary to make a major purchase, then, you won't have to mortgage your serenity.

Transit Descriptions

SUN IN EIGHTH HOUSE
You may find yourself more concerned than usual with finances at this time of year, particularly joint or corporate finances.

SUN CONJUNCT VENUS
A good time for all financial matters. You may even attract money under this transit, but you'll have to guard against overspending, even extravagance.

SUN SEXTILE VENUS
This is a good time for negotiating financial arrangements for a project already underway and for almost anything financial, really.

SUN TRINE VENUS
Your admiration and love of beauty is enhanced. This is a good time for investing in objects that will appreciate in value, shopping for clothes, or buying items to redecorate your home.

SUN CONJUNCT JUPITER
This is not a particularly good day for investing because you're apt to be overly, even foolishly, optimistic.

SUN SQUARE JUPITER
Whatever your usual spending style—cautious or adventuresome—today you'll be freer with your money. Be careful that you don't overextend yourself, especially if you normally tend toward extrvagance.

SUN OPPOSITION JUPITER
There is a tendency toward overextension today. With a little control, however, the optimism and self-confidence you're feeling can be very beneficial to you.

MOON IN SECOND HOUSE
Objectivity toward expenditures is low. You're apt to buy with

your emotions, disregarding actual need.

MOON IN FIFTH HOUSE

You're too emotional and subjective now to make wise decisions regarding financial investments or speculations. Best wait till this transit passes to engage in such matters.

MOON CONJUNCT VENUS

If you're on a tight budget, it would be best to avoid shopping until this transit passes. You'll end up spending more than you otherwise would.

MERCURY IN SECOND HOUSE

This is a good time for financial negotiations, unless natal planets in the second house are afflicted or transiting Mercury is afflicted while passing through this house.

MERCURY IN EIGHTH HOUSE

Unless Mercury is afflicted in or passing through this house, now is a good time for discussions or negotiations concerning jointly held finances.

MERCURY CONJUNCT VENUS

A good day for business and financial matters. You'll be able to discern patterns where others do not.

VENUS IN SECOND HOUSE

With the admonition in mind to be careful of extravagances you may later regret, this is an otherwise excellent time for financial negotiations or investments, especially any that have to do with the arts.

VENUS IN EIGHTH HOUSE

Without half trying, you may attract money under this transit. If you need a loan, this is a good time to go for it.

VENUS SEXTILE MERCURY

This transit is excellent for all transactions, both commercial and personal.

VENUS SQUARE VENUS

Don't go shopping today if you're trying to save money. You'll have a tendency to want to buy every pretty thing that catches your fancy.

VENUS TRINE VENUS

This is supposed to be a lucky transit, attracting people, money, or objects. But it's more than luck; it's mainly your ability to let what will happen, happen without being uptight about it.

VENUS OPPOSITION VENUS

You're feeling extravagant and self-indulgent. If you're not careful, you're apt to indulge in some expensive trinket and later wish you hadn't.

VENUS SEXTILE MARS

Investment in innovative ventures is favored, especially if other favorable transits are in effect.

VENUS CONJUNCT JUPITER

This transit is said to be financially providential; however, you must watch your self-indulgent mood, or you'll spend whatever you do receive on extravagances.

VENUS SEXTILE JUPITER

This transit smiles on financial investments, particularly those symbolized by Jupiter, such as law, medicine, higher education, or foreign matters.

VENUS SQUARE JUPITER

Self-discipline is not your strong suit today, and you're inclined to spend extravagantly. If you can restrain yourself, however, you *can* invest wisely, sensibly, and profitably under this transit.

VENUS TRINE JUPITER

Investments are favored today, especially if they are in Venus-type activities, such as the arts, entertainment, beauty, and so on.

VENUS OPPOSITION JUPITER

Don't go shopping today if you must stick to a budget. You're very apt to indulge yourself and overspend, unless you have very strong self-control.

VENUS TRINE SATURN
Today you are practical and conservative, so this would be a good day for handling business affairs or for shopping if you're on a budget.

VENUS CONJUNCT URANUS
This can be a good day for investing—*if* you take time to investigate thoroughly. The fact that something is new and exciting is hardly reason enough to put money into it. There could be gains today, or losses if you don't heed the above caveat.

VENUS SQUARE URANUS
Impulsiveness for the sake of newness is apt to rule you today, so be careful with your spending.

VENUS CONJUNCT NEPTUNE
Your sense of reality is a bit weak at the moment. Hold off on any important financial decisions for now.

VENUS CONJUNCT ASCENDANT
Keep your eyes and ears open today; an auspicious business opportunity may come knocking.

VENUS SQUARE ASCENDANT
You'll tend to be careless or unattentive or unwise with spending today. If you try, though, you can control it.

VENUS TRINE ASCENDANT
This is a good time for usually financially cautious people to go ahead and invest, because this transit tends to loosen both the person and the purse strings a bit. And this may bring "luck." Of course, if you normally go the other way, this could make you want to be very extravagant, indeed.

MARS IN SECOND HOUSE
You may be inclined to spend money impulsively to indulge your ego at this time. You may tend to gauge your self-worth by what you do or do not own.

MARS IN EIGHTH HOUSE

There may be concern and possibly conflict over jointly held finances or property, either in business or in personal life. There may be an inclination to be extravagant and wasteful, which can lead to conflicts. This is not the best of times to seek a loan.

MARS SEXTILE VENUS

This is a favorable time for all financial endeavors. Your relaxed, genuinely friendly attitude will "attract" resources.

MARS CONJUNCT JUPITER

Your high level of energy and total confidence under this transit may incline you to take risks, and you're pretty likely to succeed now if the projects or investments have any worth at all. This transit favors new beginnings.

MARS TRINE JUPITER

Your attitude is such today that any risks you take are very likely to turn out successfully. Some people call this a "lucky" transit.

MARS CONJUNCT SATURN

This is not a day for risky ventures or chancy investments. You just won't have the push, the "umph," the stamina to pull it off.

MARS TRINE NEPTUNE

You're not particularly in a materialistic, "wanting" mood right now and can make do quite happily with less.

MARS SEXTILE MIDHEAVEN

This is a good time to seek financial assistance from others. Your nonthreatening attitude and air of self-confidence will win them over more easily than usual.

JUPITER IN SECOND HOUSE

This is a good time to invest or to acquire property. If you pay attention, you may learn more about yourself and your relationship with material and spiritual resources at the same time.

JUPITER IN EIGHTH HOUSE

Barring other indications to the contrary, this would be a good time to ask for a loan. This transit also indicates sometimes that you'll receive an inheritance, but more often indicates a favorable time to form a partnership in which joint finances are utilized.

JUPITER SEXTILE SUN

You may receive some money that you hadn't expected. At any rate, investments are favored now.

JUPITER TRINE SUN

Financial matters are favored, even speculative investments if they're not too far out in left field.

JUPITER CONJUNCT MERCURY

Long-range planning, buying and selling, and decision making are beneficial activities for today. Don't overlook details, avoid over-extension, and all should go well.

JUPITER CONJUNCT VENUS

You may be tempted to buy something very expensive and elegant. At least you'll think it's elegant. You want to be surrounded by beauty. Money also sometimes comes to you under this transit.

JUPITER SEXTILE VENUS

You may attract money unexpectedly. At any rate, you're likely to want to spend money on frivolous and possibly gaudy "trinkets."

JUPITER TRINE VENUS

This transit sometimes brings you money or other resources. But don't hold your breath. The operative word is "sometimes." More probable is that you'll want to spend money, possibly for *objets d'art* or something else you consider beautiful.

JUPITER OPPOSITION VENUS

Caution is the byword here. You'll have a tendency to spend money, perhaps large amounts, to satisfy your desire for something beautiful and extravagant. If you can tread carefully, however, you may be able to make fortunate investments. Be sure to look closely at all details and angles, and be sure you're not just trying to satisfy your wish to spend.

JUPITER CONJUNCT JUPITER

Now is a good time to invest or to expand your business if you always keep in mind Jupiter's caveat: don't overextend.

JUPITER SQUARE JUPITER

The temptation is to overspend and overextend now, perhaps foolishly, and then when this transit is over, you'll find yourself coming up short. Be careful, though, and things can turn out well.

JUPITER OPPOSITION JUPITER

If you can avoid giving in to the temptation to overreach or overextend, this can be a successful time for you.

JUPITER SEXTILE SATURN

You are very prudent and cautious now. Investments you make now are likely to be successful.

JUPITER SEXTILE URANUS

There may be sudden monetary gain or opportunity now. You may feel like gambling, too, which may or may not pay off.

JUPITER TRINE URANUS

If you are generally lucky in gambling, this could be one of your luckier times.

JUPITER CONJUNCT NEPTUNE

If you operate from purely selfish motives under this transit, you'll find yourself living in an illusion that all's right with the world when it may not be. Gambling or risky investments would be ill-advised at this time.

JUPITER SEXTILE NEPTUNE

You may be inclined to gamble or make risky investments because you believe they can't fail. Don't believe it.

JUPITER SQUARE NEPTUNE

Your grasp of reality may not be at an all-time high. Make sure you get all the facts before investing or spending—and make sure they *are* facts.

JUPITER TRINE NEPTUNE

You may be operating under the influence of false optimism, so check everything out carefully before gambling or speculating.

JUPITER OPPOSITION NEPTUNE

False optimism or wishful thinking may take hold of you under this transit, and you may be tempted by projects you'd otherwise not bother with. Unless you can make wild schemes pay off as a rule, it's not wise to try it under this transit.

SATURN IN SECOND HOUSE

Your attention should be directed toward learning about and possibly reordering your value system. Being too involved with your financial situation will only distract from this and cause you problems. Just do the best you can, as economically as you can, and don't dwell on the situation.

SATURN IN FIFTH HOUSE

This is definitely no time to gamble or get into risky speculative ventures. Better be conservative for a while.

SATURN IN EIGHTH HOUSE

The focus will be on joint finances and resources from others—probably negatively, unfortunately. Be prepared for this transit ahead of time by being in as secure a financial position as you can. This is no time to count on getting a loan, for instance.

SATURN TRINE MOON

The business and the personal combine easily now—excellent for business transactions concerning your home or personal real estate. This includes construction or reconstruction, as well as buying or selling.

SATURN CONJUNCT VENUS

Your financial situation may become strained now. Try not to incur any more debt during this time. Do attempt to get your finances organized and evaluate what is or isn't important to you materially.

SATURN OPPOSITION VENUS

Finances may be strained for a while. This will force you to economize and reevaluate your attitudes toward money.

SATURN CONJUNCT JUPITER

Financial change, which may or may not be beneficial, can occur under this transit.

SATURN SQUARE JUPITER

Your financial situation and your handling of resources during the last few years will be tested. If you haven't been as prudent as you could have been, financial difficulties could arise now.

SATURN TRINE JUPITER

The time is right to organize your financial affairs and to provide for a secure future. You have the ability to plan well now, and you'll be needing this solid foundation under you before too long.

SATURN OPPOSITION JUPITER

You may find yourself in financial difficulty if you have not been careful lately. You may have overspent and are now having to pay the piper. This is no time for expansion.

SATURN CONJUNCT PLUTO

This is apt to be a time of retrenchment or financial deficiency of some kind.

SATURN SQUARE PLUTO

Conserve resources and try to make do with less during this time. Go with the flow and try not to struggle too much.

URANUS IN SECOND HOUSE

These few years can very well be a time of sudden fluctuations in your financial status, one way or another. Whatever you need to experience to grow as an individual will happen, and even if it seems upsetting at the time, the end result will be positive for you. Be flexible and willing to take advantage of opportunities as they arise.

URANUS IN FIFTH HOUSE

Speculating financially under this transit will bring either sudden gains or sudden losses. Whatever happens, it should be viewed as a chance for greater self-understanding.

URANUS IN EIGHTH HOUSE

There are likely to be sudden changes in finances, especially those held jointly. It's best not to be dependent on another's finances at this time. Sometimes this transit indicates that you'll receive an inheritance.

URANUS SQUARE JUPITER

Your optimism may know no bounds and this, of course, could lead to financial difficulty. You're more inclined to gamble and to take risks. Do try to exercise a little caution, though. There may be some financial trouble at any rate, due to previously unforeseen conditions. Or, a sudden opportunity may arise. Check it out carefully.

URANUS SQUARE NEPTUNE

Be careful of being deluded by almost anyone in some area of finance. Postpone making any important or binding decisions until this transit is over.

URANUS OPPOSITION NEPTUNE

Strange or unusual difficulties with finances of any sort may occur under this transit. Keep your eyes open and your feet on the ground.

URANUS CONJUNCT PLUTO

Your intuition and insight are enhanced, and this could make financial dealings especially profitable to you now, especially if you can be flexible and willing to accept change.

URANUS SQUARE PLUTO

Financial fluctuation is a possible manifestation of this transit, which signals radical changes in your life.

URANUS TRINE PLUTO

This is a favorable time for finances from almost any quarter, though you may be more interested in philosophical questions than in material gains at the moment.

URANUS OPPOSITION PLUTO

Unexpected fluctuation of finances may occur under this transit. Remain flexible; the old is falling away to make way for the new, and if you can ride the tide, it can be exciting.

NEPTUNE IN FIRST HOUSE

This is not a good time to invest in speculative ventures. Your grasp of reality is not up to par and you could be deluded easily.

NEPTUNE IN SECOND HOUSE

Unless you can remain detached—not particularly caring whether you win or lose—this is not a good time to gamble or to speculate. Don't let anyone talk you into moneymaking schemes; you could be duped easily under this transit.

NEPTUNE IN FIFTH HOUSE

This is no time to gamble or speculate. Neptune does not impart a firm grip on reality or the material world.

NEPTUNE IN EIGHTH HOUSE

There may be confusion, misunderstanding, even misrepresentation or fraud regarding jointly held finances. This is not a good time to borrow from a friend; a misunderstanding over money can ruin a good relationship.

NEPTUNE SQUARE SUN

Your grasp of reality is not up to par. This is definitely not a good time to engage in speculation.

NEPTUNE SEXTILE VENUS

Investing in anything related to the creative arts is favored during this transit.

NEPTUNE SQUARE VENUS

Avoid get-rich-quick schemes at this time. They're very likely to have just the opposite effect.

NEPTUNE TRINE VENUS

If you go after it, taking advantage of opportunities, good fortune may come to you at this time. The arts are especially favored.

NEPTUNE OPPOSITION VENUS

This is definitely not the time to get involved in get-rich-quick schemes. Try to keep your feet on the ground.

NEPTUNE OPPOSITION MARS

Be especially alert for any kind of scam, and don't try to pull off any yourself. It just wouldn't work at this time, and you'd very likely find yourself in serious trouble.

NEPTUNE CONJUNCT JUPITER

It's best to avoid investing now. Wishful thinking is apt to be dominating your reason at the moment.

NEPTUNE SQUARE JUPITER

Avoid get-rich-quick schemes or shaky investments now. Rose-colored glasses are hindering your foresight, insight, and judgment.

NEPTUNE OPPOSITION JUPITER

It's best not to engage in speculation or gambling at this time. Beware of overextension. Overly optimistic and idealistic thinking is clouding reality for you at the moment.

NEPTUNE SQUARE URANUS

Be wary of possible deceptions. Don't make any important decisions now.

NEPTUNE OPPOSITION URANUS

There may be unusual, perhaps sudden, difficulties with finances or taxes or inheritances. Pay attention; this is reflecting inner doubt and confusion. Be flexible.

NEPTUNE SQUARE PLUTO

Be aware that you may be subject to deceptions concerning financial matters at this time.

NEPTUNE TRINE PLUTO

You may benefit from any of a number of financial areas now, possibly including inheritance.

PLUTO IN SECOND HOUSE

There may be some financial losses or setbacks during this transit. A major restructuring of your value system is going on. As always with Pluto, there is a tearing down before new construction can begin. Let it be; you'll only prolong the first stage by trying to hang on beyond the point of reason.

PLUTO IN SEVENTH HOUSE

Lawsuits or other difficulties regarding joint or corporate finances, insurance, or other financial matters are possible. At all costs, do not engage in anything underhanded if you wish to succeed.

PLUTO IN EIGHTH HOUSE

You'll somehow become involved in joint or corporate finances, possibly regarding insurance or taxes. There may be an inheritance if there are other supporting aspects in your chart. Avoid going into debt at this time if you possibly can.

PLUTO SEXTILE MOON

Your finances may improve during this period, reflecting your being more in tune with your deeper, inner self and emotions.

PLUTO SQUARE MOON

Caution in all financial dealings is advised during this transit. This is no time for chancy ventures; you may act from subconscious motivations that have little to do with the current situation.

PLUTO OPPOSITION MOON

Business, financial, or real estate dealings are not particularly favored at this time.

PLUTO TRINE MERCURY

Now is the time to sit down, really dig into your financial situation, and do some nitty-gritty planning.

PLUTO SQUARE VENUS

There may be disagreements over handling of finances. There is even a possibility of theft or extortion. You probably need to work more on the relationships concerned and especially how you handle them, rather than on the finances *per se*.

PLUTO TRINE VENUS

This is a good time to participate in joint business ventures concerning the arts or luxury items.

PLUTO TRINE MARS

You may gain financially under this transit or be given power over someone else's finances. Or both.

PLUTO CONJUNCT JUPITER

This transit is generally favorable for corporate, joint, tax, or insurance financial matters, including legal actions.

PLUTO SQUARE JUPITER

Difficulties with finances could occur. Remain completely honest and aboveboard. Pay attention to details. Be considerate of others' needs. Litigation, even arrest, could otherwise result.

PLUTO OPPOSITION JUPITER

There may be conflict over finances under this transit. Don't do anything illegal or take any differences to litigation at this time.

PLUTO SEXTILE SATURN

You may benefit from joint or corporate money in some way during this transit.

PLUTO SQUARE SATURN

There may be problems with, or possible curtailment of, resources during this period. Don't struggle to hold on beyond reason. Let go of what is not absolutely necessary. Be flexible.

PLUTO SQUARE URANUS

Financial loss of some sort may be among the sweeping changes to which you must adjust at this time. Or you may just experience a period of financial difficulty. As usual with Uranus, being flexible will help to ease the situation.

PLUTO OPPOSITION URANUS

Financial disruptions may occur under this transit. You must remain flexible. Rigidity will only make matters worse.

PLUTO CONJUNCT NEPTUNE

Strange or unusual circumstances concerning finances may occur under this transit.

PLUTO SEXTILE MIDHEAVEN

This is a good time to seek a loan if you need it.

PLUTO SQUARE ASCENDANT

There may be lawsuits over finances, particularly joint finances of any sort. Do not fault others. Look within for your own weaknesses to correct. Do not stoop to underhanded tactics of any kind for any reason.

PLUTO OPPOSITION ASCENDANT

There is a possibility of lawsuits concerning finances under this transit. Make sure all your actions are aboveboard.

Chapter 12

Health

Like accidents, good health doesn't just happen. When we begin to take responsibility for our own lives, we realize that health can be had at will, like anything else in our reality. There are, however, proclivities, one way or another, in our daily meanderings; and certain transits can act as signposts along the way. Taking heed of them, you can know in which direction to route your attention and energies so that you may be the best you can be and get on with your appointed rounds. Unless it is your karma to have the experience of a particular physical condition—and even karma can be altered—you can be in total control of your own health. This chapter, in conjunction with Chapter 18, "Your Self, Its Status and Growth," can help keep you on track.

Transit Descriptions

SUN IN SIXTH HOUSE
You'll be more concerned with looking to your health now. Reevaluating it with an eye to improvement can be advantageous.

SUN CONJUNCT MARS
If the high degree of energy you feel today is not expressed properly through physical activity of some kind, illness can occur. With Mars this usually means fevers, inflammations, or infections.

SUN SEXTILE MARS
Your energy level is high and your health quite good. You'll really benefit from physical activity today, especially with a group.

SUN SQUARE MARS
Find some sort of vigorous outlet for the tremendous energy and feelings of aggression you'll have today. Else, accident or illness could result. If you think you don't have any aggression, be very careful; you've probably buried it beneath the surface.

SUN CONJUNCT NEPTUNE
You're much more sensitive to outside influences than usual. Allergies and adverse reactions to drugs, prescribed or otherwise, may occur. Avoid drugs and alcohol; if you need to escape, try meditation.

MOON IN SIXTH HOUSE
Your attention is likely to turn to your health, diet, and hygiene at this time. Psychosomatic illnesses are a possible manifestation also.

MOON CONJUNCT SUN
If at all possible, avoid major surgery, especially on the areas ruled by your sun sign, during this transit.

MOON CONJUNCT NEPTUNE
Drugs or alcohol could be difficult to handle now, even dangerous.

Even without them, you may feel drowsy during this transit.

MOON SQUARE NEPTUNE

This transit could signal problems with alcohol or drugs. It's best to stay away from them now. Try reading, daydreaming, movies, meditation, or other pastimes if you need to relax or escape your daily routine.

MOON OPPOSITION NEPTUNE

Be especially careful of what you take into your body now because you're very sensitive to drugs, alcohol, and allergens at the moment.

MOON TRINE PLUTO

Your reaction to others and to life in general now is so emotionally intense you may find yourself drained of energy by the time this transit is over.

MERCURY IN FIRST HOUSE

There is a possibility of nervousness under this transit. Make a conscious effort to relax, and think of something pleasant for a while.

MERCURY IN SIXTH HOUSE

You'll be more interested in health and hygiene at this time and may begin a major new health improvement program. If Mercury is afflicted in this house, you may experience health problems, probably connected with nerves or a nervous condition.

MERCURY SQUARE SUN

You may be so "wired" today that you become nervous. Try to calm yourself, however, or an accident due to carelessness could result.

MERCURY SQUARE MERCURY

Today's fast pace and your quickened mental activity may make you feel jumpy and nervous. Try to surround yourself with peace and quiet.

MERCURY CONJUNCT URANUS

Your mental activity will be speeded up today and could result in nervousness. If so, consciously relax as often as necessary and simply let this transit run its course without fretting too much about it.

MERCURY SQUARE URANUS

Your mind will be very fast-paced today, and if that is too much for your nervous system, you may become jittery. Try to relax and wait out the "storm."

MERCURY OPPOSITION NEPTUNE

Any little stress may make you nervous today. You may feel confused, on edge.

VENUS IN FOURTH HOUSE

Try to overcome the temptation to overindulge in food or drink. It won't do your digestion or weight level any good, and you'll probably feel guilty later.

VENUS IN SIXTH HOUSE

In general, your health will be good now, but it would help to avoid overindulgence in sweet or fattening foods.

VENUS CONJUNCT SUN

Your health is good, though you're not much in the mood to exert yourself physically.

VENUS SQUARE SUN

It's difficult not to indulge yourself today, but try to avoid this temptation. You'd be likely to gain weight, have indigestion, or both.

VENUS CONJUNCT MOON

Be careful of overindulgence. Digestive upsets could occur.

VENUS SQUARE MOON

Those with a tendency toward glandular problems, including menstrual abnormalities, may experience difficulty during this transit.

VENUS TRINE MERCURY

Now is a good time to relax and get rid of stress that may have been building up for some time.

MARS IN FIRST HOUSE

Be prepared to take especially good care of your health when or if

Mars transits an afflicted planet in the first house.

MARS IN FOURTH HOUSE
Indigestion due to emotional turmoil is possible. It's best not to eat when upset or overtired.

MARS IN SIXTH HOUSE
Keep physically active and try to handle any frustrations positively, rather than keeping them inside. Otherwise fevers, accidents, or infections may occur during this time.

MARS SEXTILE SUN
Your health is good or improved under this transit, and your energy is high.

MARS SEXTILE MARS
You're in good health now and will feel full of energy. This is a good time for hard physical work or athletic activity with others.

MARS SEXTILE JUPITER
Your health, energy, and well-being are enhanced under this transit.

MARS OPPOSITION JUPITER
Childbirth often takes place under this transit because the action of the pertinent muscles is favored. If overexertion is avoided, anyone's health is usually boosted during this time.

MARS OPPOSITION SATURN
The main thing now is to avoid all the stress and tension you can and relax. Stress now could be especially detrimental to you.

MARS CONJUNCT URANUS
Sudden upsets are the trademark of this transit, and if there are other transits signifying health problems, the necessity for an operation could arise now. This is by no means a usual result, though.

MARS OPPOSITION URANUS
If the energy for creative or even sudden, disruptive change signified by this transit is suppressed, health problems that may need

an operation could result. Be flexible and willing to adjust to circumstances.

MARS SQUARE NEPTUNE

You're subject to fevers, infections, and possibly allergies more than usual now. Your energy is very low. Try to rest and take care of yourself.

MARS OPPOSITION NEPTUNE

Your energies and your resistance are at a low point. Take care not to let yourself get physically depleted, or infections and fevers could move right in. Avoid alcohol and all drugs not prescribed by a doctor. You're unusually sensitive at this time.

MARS CONJUNCT ASCENDANT

Accidents or illnesses sometimes happen at this time, especially if you've been holding in anger, resentment, or your energy in general. Hard physical labor or activity would be a good way to dissipate these energies. Be careful around sharp metal tools.

MARS SQUARE ASCENDANT

Illness, such as an infection, is possible if you're repressing feelings of aggression or hostility. Even if a problem can't be settled now, it's best to go ahead and clear the air.

MARS TRINE ASCENDANT

This will be a time of positive health, of feeling good and energetic. By all means, utilize this energy now. Holding it in could be detrimental in the future.

MARS OPPOSITION ASCENDANT

Illness, such as infection or fever, can occur now, especially if you're not handling aggression or frustration properly.

JUPITER IN SIXTH HOUSE

You'll probably enjoy very good health under this transit. You may think it's *too* good when you start putting on weight. It's best to take all things in moderation now. If you've been ill, this transit will help you get well.

JUPITER TRINE SUN

You'll feel very good and confident today. It would be beneficial to engage in some sort of physical activity, especially outdoors. Just be careful not to be so confident of your abilities that you overestimate them, in which case you'll probably regret it tomorrow.

JUPITER CONJUNCT MOON

Be wary of gaining weight, and be especially careful of eating fatty foods.

JUPITER OPPOSITION MOON

It's very important to avoid all excesses today, especially eating and drinking.

JUPITER CONJUNCT VENUS

You're apt to experience the temptation to overindulge in food or drink at this time. Try to control yourself, or illness could result.

JUPITER OPPOSITION VENUS

Without careful attention to what you eat, you're very likely to gain weight now. Fatty foods, especially, may be your downfall.

JUPITER CONJUNCT MARS

You have tremendous energy and strength. This is one of the transits under which many women give birth. The only problem with this transit is that you're apt to feel so good and vigorous you'll overdo and be sorry tomorrow.

JUPITER SEXTILE MARS

Your energy will be high and your health good. A fortunate and satisfying pregnancy is usually indicated by this transit.

JUPITER TRINE MARS

Your urge to create may encompass a desire to have children. If a child is due under this transit, the birth will likely be easy.

JUPITER TRINE JUPITER

This is a time of mental and physical balance. This transit will enhance healing.

JUPITER CONJUNCT ASCENDANT

Physically and mentally, you are in good shape. You feel optimistic and confident, and your body is not likely to succumb to disease. The only thing is, you may be rather inclined to put on weight now.

SATURN IN SIXTH HOUSE

You must pay attention to your health and make sure you are in good shape. When Saturn enters the seventh house, you'll be under even heavier demands, and you have to be ready for it. Also, at that time you're likely to be more involved with the public, and you'll certainly want to be at your best.

SATURN CONJUNCT SUN

Finish whatever projects you've been working on before tackling any more. Extra work could put too much of a strain on you, particularly your circulatory system.

SATURN SEXTILE SUN

Your health is probably much improved right now, but that's no sign to relax your efforts to maintain it. In fact, you should be working to build it up for possible future crisis.

SATURN SQUARE SUN

Your energy level is low. Do everything you can to remain healthy. If you do become ill, however, reexamine your activities. Your subconscious is trying to tell you you've been heading in the wrong direction. The cardiovascular system is most at risk here.

SATURN TRINE SUN

Like Saturn sextile Sun, this is a good time to build up your health in preparation for challenges soon to come.

SATURN OPPOSITION SUN

This is the end of a 29-year cycle, and your energies are low. Take especially good care of your health now and be patient. This will pass.

SATURN CONJUNCT MERCURY

Hearing and speech disorders or nervous ailments are sometimes indicated by this transit. Depression is more likely.

SATURN SQUARE MERCURY

Problems with the lungs or speech organs may surface at this time. Take especially good care of these areas, and concentrate on clearing up or opening up your communication circuits in general.

SATURN OPPOSITION MERCURY

Problems with the lungs or speech organs may occur under this transit. Take good care of these areas and think about your communications and opinions. Have you become too rigid and unwilling to compromise?

SATURN CONJUNCT MARS

Rheumatism, arthritis, or other bone problems may flare up at this time. Take precautions against such illnesses. Avoid harboring any type of anger; let it out in as positive a manner as possible.

SATURN SQUARE MARS

Areas of possible difficulties include arthritis, rheumatism, bone injuries, blood pressure, and cardiovascular problems. These can be averted, however, with proper attitude and health-care attention. Learning to properly handle anger would be a big help.

SATURN OPPOSITION MARS

Arthritis, rheumatism, hardening of the arteries, high blood pressure, and the like are possible problems under this transit. Take measures—such as a checkup, preventative nutrition, vitamin and herbal supplements, attitude examination, and proper handling of anger and frustrations—to prevent these difficulties.

SATURN SQUARE URANUS

If you resist changes in your life and become too rigid, the resulting tension is likely to cause health problems, especially with the nervous system.

SATURN OPPOSITION URANUS

Conflict between comfortable old routines and change that is necessary for growth may cause problems with the heart or nervous system. The preventative and cure is to accept changes in your life as right and necessary for your creative growth as an individual.

SATURN CONJUNCT NEPTUNE

Be aware of and careful of your health at this time. If something feels amiss, have a checkup immediately. It may be nothing, but if something is wrong, things could get progressively worse if you put off taking care of it.

SATURN SQUARE NEPTUNE

A complete and thorough examination would be a good idea now. This transit sometimes indicates hidden disease or other health problems that are hard to detect.

SATURN OPPOSITION PLUTO

You're apt to be tempted to overwork or overextend your energies. Beware of doing so, or you'll undermine your health.

URANUS IN SIXTH HOUSE

There are changes afoot regarding your work, and if you try to resist change or suppress the need for it, Uranus is apt to take matters in hand and, through illness or accident, force change upon you.

URANUS CONJUNCT SUN

Change is occurring in your life, and if you attempt to resist it too fiercely, problems with the heart may result. If you have a proclivity for heart problems, be very careful during this period. A checkup would not be unwarranted.

URANUS SQUARE SUN

Events may be putting you through some severe tests right now to see if you can either stick to the path you've chosen or accept change if it becomes all too apparent it's the wrong path. If you try to ignore or suppress these Uranian energies, illness, probably involving the cardiovascular system, may result.

URANUS TRINE SUN

This is an excellent time to begin health improvement programs—from exercise to nutrition. Changes to improve your life are easily made now; they'll be more difficult later.

URANUS OPPOSITION SUN

You cannot forever repress the expression of your true self, and events are likely now to force that true self to crack out of its rut or shell or stifling security. Resisting this impetus will very likely result in heart problems. Take very good care of your cardiovascular system; don't "hold things in."

URANUS CONJUNCT MERCURY

If your thinking has become so rigid that you cannot accept newness, nervousness or nervous ailments may result at this time.

URANUS SQUARE MERCURY

Things are happening so rapidly now, you may find yourself more tense than usual. If you have a propensity for nervous difficulties, they may emerge at this time.

URANUS OPPOSITION MERCURY

The pace of your life is so rapid and exciting now, there is a danger that you'll let it get out of hand, which could lead to mental or nervous exhaustion. Try to remain calm, take things one at a time, stay flexible, and pay attention to good nutrition.

URANUS CONJUNCT MARS

Do not attempt to suppress the energies of these planets. You are struggling to assert yourself as an individual, and you are not going to—nor should you—stand for any interference that prevents you from doing it. Attempting to deny this process could lead to the necessity for sudden surgery.

URANUS OPPOSITION MARS

Do not suppress these energies urging you toward change. Holding them in is likely to lead to illness.

URANUS CONJUNCT SATURN

Any area of your life that has been restricting your ultimate growth, whether you're consciously aware of it or not, will be subject to sudden, perhaps explosive, change at this time. Do not resist or suppress this energy. Doing so could lead to extreme tension and its attendant physical problems, including cardiovascular disease.

URANUS SQUARE SATURN

Tensions you may be feeling between your need for personal

freedom and your need for restricting, though safely familiar, structure can aggravate any existing health problems. Dealing with, not ignoring, these tensions will help. Sometimes just talking them over with a good friend is an immense relief and a possibly enlightening experience.

URANUS OPPOSITION SATURN

Don't keep any tensions generated by sudden upsetting events inside yourself for any reason during this transit—they'll harm your health.

URANUS CONJUNCT NEPTUNE

Be extremely careful of taking any drugs under the influence of this transit, even prescribed drugs. Also, if you find yourself sleepier or more tired than usual, have a checkup to find out why.

URANUS OPPOSITION NEPTUNE

Difficulties from drugs of any sort could arise. Be especially careful when dealing with them.

NEPTUNE IN FIFTH HOUSE

Be careful of overindulgence in food, drink, or drugs if this house is afflicted. Take precautions against unwanted pregnancies as well.

NEPTUNE IN SIXTH HOUSE

Take very good care of your health now. You're unusually sensitive to toxins in the form of alcohol, drugs, and pollutants. Pay attention to the effects of any diet or nutritional regimen you may undertake. Discontinue them at the first sign of any problems. You may be more susceptible to illnesses and infections now, too.

NEPTUNE CONJUNCT SUN

Some people will experience fatigue, confusion, or depression under this transit. Everyone should be very wary of drugs—prescribed or not—and alcohol now. Also, avoid physically overdoing.

NEPTUNE SQUARE SUN

This can be a time of low vitality and low resistance. Avoid overextension of yourself, poor health practices, and drugs.

NEPTUNE OPPOSITION SUN

Your vitality is at a low point now, as is your resistance to illness. Take good care of yourself, and don't go on any crazy diets or take drugs for any reason.

NEPTUNE CONJUNCT MOON

You may be subject to fluid retention at this time. Avoid alcohol and drugs, especially if you're prone to problems in this area already. An eye checkup may be useful.

NEPTUNE SQUARE MOON

Be very careful of anything you put into your body at this time. It's extremely sensitive now and may develop an undesirable dependence. You may have digestive upsets even with ordinary foods.

NEPTUNE OPPOSITION MOON

Your body is very sensitive to any kind of drugs or unnatural substances of any sort at this time, so take care. You may experience some digestive problems anyway.

NEPTUNE SQUARE MERCURY

Health problems are likely to center on the nervous system at this time, ranging from unnecessary worry to some types of paralysis. Do not take any mind-altering drugs under this transit.

NEPTUNE OPPOSITION MERCURY

Nervous disorders may arise under this transit. They may be psychosomatic or have an actual physical cause and should be checked out by a good doctor.

NEPTUNE CONJUNCT MARS

Avoid overexertion, exposure to illness, drugs of any kind, and alcohol. Infections are possible under this transit, so take very good care of yourself. Nutritionally bolstering your immune system would also help.

NEPTUNE SQUARE MARS

Infections are a possibility under this transit. Try to take it easy, and don't overexert yourself or let yourself be exposed to illness.

NEPTUNE OPPOSITION MARS

Difficult infections or other debilitating conditions are possible under this transit, so take very good care of yourself. Your energy and resistance are low. Don't overexert yourself. Avoid drugs. Be very careful even with prescribed drugs.

NEPTUNE CONJUNCT SATURN

This transit sometimes signifies the onset of long-term illness, the symptoms of which may not occur for some time. Having a physical checkup is advised now, if you haven't had one lately.

NEPTUNE SQUARE SATURN

Better have a checkup if you haven't had one lately. This transit sometimes indicates the beginning of a slow-moving health problem.

NEPTUNE SQUARE URANUS

Avoid trying to escape the new insights or realities that may be manifesting for your growth now by turning to drugs or alcohol. Face change head on, and let yourself grow.

NEPTUNE OPPOSITION URANUS

Be careful of drugs and alcohol. Avoiding them totally would be best, but if you must take prescribed drugs, be alert to any adverse side effects. Consult your doctor immediately should any occur.

NEPTUNE SQUARE NEPTUNE

Look to your health and try not to overindulge in food or drink. This is not a good time for drugs or alcohol.

PLUTO IN SIXTH HOUSE

This transit can signal either a complete physical breakdown or a total regeneration, depending upon whether you neglect your health or whether you care for and attempt to improve it.

PLUTO SQUARE SUN

If you resist handling the energies of this transit, which wants to test your ability to handle yourself in a power-struggle situation, you may experience serious health problems that cause you to come to a grinding halt, forcing you to begin a program of physical rehabilitation.

PLUTO TRINE SUN

You are physically strong and in good condition. If you have an illness when this transit begins, it will help you to heal more readily than usual.

PLUTO OPPOSITION SUN

Take very good care of yourself now. This should include learning to handle stress in a positive manner.

PLUTO CONJUNCT MOON

This transit is often emotionally upsetting, and this can, of course, adversely affect your health. Digestive problems or other stress-related symptoms may appear.

PLUTO TRINE MOON

Rejoice! This is a very favorable time to lose weight by dieting.

PLUTO TRINE MERCURY

This is a good time to improve your health regimen—anything from diet to exercise.

PLUTO OPPOSITION MERCURY

Don't work so hard and obsessively that you have a nervous breakdown or disorder of some sort. Look to your health on all fronts, revamping your diet and exercise regimen if necessary. Also check sanitation facilities or other sources of hazardous pollution.

PLUTO SEXTILE MARS

Tremendous physical exertion is favored now. Also, this is a good time to begin a body-building or health-regeneration program. You'll feel great—as if you could go on forever.

PLUTO SQUARE MARS

Avoid overworking to the point of exhaustion. Even if you don't feel tired, take some time to relax and rest.

PLUTO TRINE MARS

You'll experience a new surge of energy and stamina. An excellent time to begin a body-building, rebuilding, or regeneration program.

PLUTO CONJUNCT SATURN

This may be a time of stress due to conflict between Pluto's wanting to get rid of the old to prepare for regeneration and Saturn's wanting to hold on. Health problems caused by stress may occur. The solution, of course, is to go ahead and let go of the old and embrace change in your life as simply another cycle of growth.

PLUTO SQUARE ASCENDANT

There is a remote possibility of personal danger or violence in dangerous areas or situations. Be aware and take care. Avoid any underhanded tactics of any sort.

Chapter 13

Home

A person's home is more than an impregnable castle of stones and mortar, or even of glass and steel. It embodies your sense of self, your sense of security, your home base from which to sally forth to slay corporate or incorporate dragons—or at least to make a living. And, as there are times to rend and sow and reap in the business world, there are also propitious times to pull up the drawbridge and read a good book, throw a wild party, clean out the garage, beautify your home, and even buy a new one. This chapter will help you to know when and how to employ your knights—and days—on the home front.

Transit Descriptions

MOON IN SECOND HOUSE

You identify with your possessions and feel very attached to them. This is obviously not a good time to clean out the garage or attic.

MOON CONJUNCT VENUS

This is an excellent time for beautifying your home or having friends over for the evening.

MOON SEXTILE VENUS

This is a good time to entertain at home. You enjoy others and your home environment today.

MOON TRINE VENUS

You're very much in the mood to spruce up the ole homestead now, and it's a good time to do it.

MOON TRINE MARS

This is a favorable time for moving or for making improvements around your home. You're energetic, for one thing, and feel in harmony with the world.

MOON CONJUNCT JUPITER

A change of residence under this transit is likely to be a good move—probably pleasant and possibly profitable.

MOON SEXTILE PLUTO

You're wanting to make changes in your home environment, even if it's only cleaning up or reorganizing.

MOON SQUARE MIDHEAVEN

Your emotions have more of the upper hand than your rational mind at the moment. This is not a particularly good time to buy a home.

MERCURY IN FOURTH HOUSE

This transit sometimes coincides with having to move because of a job change. At any rate, it's also a good time to make improvements around the house.

MERCURY TRINE MIDHEAVEN

A good time for making plans for your home or apartment. Decide what would be best to do and how to go about it. Visualize.

MERCURY OPPOSITION MIDHEAVEN

A good time to plan any necessary repairs, alterations, or upkeep of the house or apartment you live in.

VENUS IN FOURTH HOUSE

You may very well be in the mood to redecorate under this transit. If so, try to keep practical matters in mind and don't go overboard. On the whole, you'll be able to express your inner self well through your home at this time.

VENUS TRINE MOON

This is a good time to enhance the beauty of your home. You want to be surrounded by loveliness and will work to achieve it.

VENUS TRINE MIDHEAVEN

This is a great time to jump in and redecorate or beautify your surroundings in any way. Your sense of beauty and pleasure in it are heightened.

VENUS TRINE ASCENDANT

This is a good time to indulge your pleasure in beautiful things by sprucing up your own surroundings.

MARS IN FOURTH HOUSE

You may be inspired to renovate, fix up, or spruce up your home. Be very careful of injuries or fire if Mars is afflicted in this house.

MARS SEXTILE VENUS

This transit puts you in the mood for beautifying your environment. This is a good time to redecorate or renovate your home—even just to give it a good cleaning.

JUPITER CONJUNCT MOON

You realize how important your home is to you now, and you may try to improve it in some way, even if it's just giving it a good cleaning. Anyone you invite into your home now will feel comfortable and good in your surroundings. This is a favorable transit for buying a home, too.

JUPITER CONJUNCT SATURN

A change of residence is sometimes in the offing when this transit rolls around.

JUPITER SQUARE PLUTO

You want to repair or improve your home or surroundings at this time. Someone may oppose your actions, though. Be sure all your dealings are strictly aboveboard and legitimate.

JUPITER TRINE MIDHEAVEN

You may move to a larger home or make improvements on your current one under this transit.

JUPITER OPPOSITION MIDHEAVEN

You may find yourself wanting to buy a new home, improve your current one, or invest in land. What you're really looking for is a secure "home base," meaning a feeling of inner peace and strength. If you do buy a home, be sure to get exactly what you want and will be happy with, because you may find it difficult to part with later.

SATURN TRINE MOON

The business and personal combine easily now. This is a good time to buy or sell real estate (especially personal real estate), repair your existing home, organize your financial affairs, and plan for the future.

SATURN CONJUNCT JUPITER

This transit sometimes indicates a change of residence, especially if you are unhappy with your present one.

SATURN SQUARE JUPITER

You may feel restless and want to change residences. And this may be a valid thing for you to do, but it's best to let this transit pass before making any definite decisions.

SATURN CONJUNCT URANUS
You may feel a sudden urge to change residences. You are seeking change, excitement, new horizons, and this may be one way in which you do it.

URANUS IN FOURTH HOUSE
There are apt to be disruptions in your immediate surroundings—perhaps a change of residence or the need for repairs.

URANUS SEXTILE MOON
You're living through your emotions now, and you want your surroundings to be emotionally satisfying and pleasing. You may make changes in your home to bring this about.

URANUS SQUARE MOON
There may be sudden problems in the home, such as needed repairs, accidents, or something not noticed till now. This is not a good time to buy a new home.

URANUS TRINE MOON
This is an excellent time to remodel or make other changes in your home. Everything will come off with a minimum of hassle and disruption.

URANUS SQUARE VENUS
Seeking the new and exciting, you may look for beautiful and unusual decorative touches for your home. Be careful, though. Your taste tends toward the very different now, and you may not like your purchases so much after this transit is passed.

URANUS SEXTILE MIDHEAVEN
This is a favorable time to change residences or make improvements on your current home.

URANUS SQUARE MIDHEAVEN
There may be a change of residence, possibly due to circumstances beyond your control—or so you'll think.

URANUS OPPOSITION MIDHEAVEN

There may be sudden changes in and around your home, such as accidents, natural disasters, necessary repairs or renovation. Check the electrical system particularly, and make sure all safety hazards around your home are eliminated.

NEPTUNE IN FOURTH HOUSE

You may want to beautify your home to try to make it conform to your idea of what an ideal home should be. If your fourth house is afflicted, there may be difficulties with oil, gas, or water lines.

NEPTUNE SQUARE MIDHEAVEN

It might be a good idea to have your water, gas, or oil lines checked before this transit begins.

PLUTO IN FOURTH HOUSE

There may be changes in your home during this period—anything from a change of residence to repairs or remodeling.

PLUTO CONJUNCT MOON

There are likely to be changes in your residence, either through moving or through repairs.

PLUTO SEXTILE MOON

You may find yourself making changes in your home through remodeling or repairing so that it more accurately reflects your true self.

PLUTO SQUARE MOON

You may move or make repairs or improvements on your present home. You're trying to make your surroundings more "in tune" with the new, emerging you.

PLUTO TRINE MOON

Now is a good time to make repairs or other changes in your residence—or to buy a new place to live.

PLUTO OPPOSITION MOON

Check your home for structural soundness and for possible sources of pollution.

PLUTO SEXTILE MARS

This transit favors taking on grand projects and getting them done. A good time to build or rebuild.

PLUTO TRINE MARS

An excellent time for rebuilding or renovating of any kind—anything from large buildings to furniture.

PLUTO SEXTILE MIDHEAVEN

A good time to repair or renovate your home. Or, you may change residences for some reason, possibly job-related.

PLUTO SQUARE MIDHEAVEN

Your home may suddenly need repairs, or appliances connected with it may break down. Or, you may change residences altogether.

PLUTO OPPOSITION MIDHEAVEN

You may make repairs on your home or change residences. Or both.

Chapter 14

Law

Confrontations with the legal system are like accidents, ill health, or souffles—there is no guarantee they'll arise simply because there is a transit indicating they might. If confrontations *are* in the offing for you, however, some days presage the possibility of a better outcome than others; so if you have any say in the matter, you can choose a beneficial time to assail or petition the bastions of the law. If you don't have any say, you can at least be a little more prepared to do battle or be conciliatory. Who knows—you may, with Yogananda, "beat the stars" and create a perfect souffle, after all.

Of course, dealings with the law need not be confrontational. You may wish to study law, for instance, or consult a lawyer about a contract or other matter. This chapter can help you plan for these things, too.

Transit Descriptions

SUN IN SEVENTH HOUSE
Legal disputes may occur at this time. If so, consulting a lawyer is well advised.

SUN IN NINTH HOUSE
You may be involved or concerned with the law in some way now, though not necessarily in a negative manner.

SUN OPPOSITION ASCENDANT
This is a good day to consult all sorts of counselors, including lawyers.

MERCURY IN NINTH HOUSE
You may have some sort of connection with the law, but this is not necessarily negative. You may take up the study of law, for instance.

MERCURY SEXTILE JUPITER
A favorable transit for dealings with the law in any capacity.

MERCURY TRINE JUPITER
A good time to study, or to have any dealings with, the law. Your power of positive thinking helps to make it so.

MERCURY CONJUNCT NEPTUNE
This is not a good time for legal negotiations or encounters, including contracts or agreements of all kinds. Dishonesty and confusion could enter the picture, not to mention disillusion due to a very active imagination.

MERCURY OPPOSITION ASCENDANT
This transit affords an excellent opportunity for consulting a lawyer, seeking any kind of expert advice, and for negotiating contracts.

VENUS IN SEVENTH HOUSE
This is a good transit under which to settle a legal confrontation, either in or out of court.

VENUS SEXTILE JUPITER
Legal decisions today are likely to be in your favor.

MARS IN SEVENTH HOUSE
This transit sometimes indicates lawsuits, usually involving close business or marital partners. You should at least *try* to compromise.

MARS IN NINTH HOUSE
Legal conflicts are sometimes indicated by this transit. Things don't bode too well for you if there are major afflictions in this house, however.

MARS OPPOSITION MERCURY
Take extreme care to avoid accidents today. Legal embroilments could result from any that occur today.

MARS SEXTILE JUPITER
Legal affairs or any contact with authorities are likely to go well for you now.

JUPITER IN SEVENTH HOUSE
A good time to consult a lawyer, and if you have to go to court, results should be favorable to you if you don't overlook any details or try to get more than you're entitled to. Moderation, as always with Jupiter, is the key word.

JUPITER SQUARE SUN
This transit sometimes signifies conflict with the law or legal entanglements of some kind. Be willing to compromise for the benefit of all concerned.

JUPITER CONJUNCT MERCURY
This is an excellent transit for any dealings with the law. Any such encounters should turn out successfully for you, mainly because you are able to plan and prepare well.

JUPITER SEXTILE MARS

Any legal issues should work out in your favor. Should a compromise be necessary, you'll be able to find a fair one.

JUPITER TRINE MARS

This is a good time to reach an agreement in a legal dispute. The terms are apt to be in your favor.

JUPITER SEXTILE JUPITER

Any legal dealings are likely to go well at this time. A good time to reach an agreement.

JUPITER SQUARE PLUTO

Legal conflicts may surface now. Be absolutely certain all your dealings are aboveboard and legal.

JUPITER OPPOSITION PLUTO

Be sure all you do is on the up and up. This transit sometimes signifies trouble with the law.

SATURN IN NINTH HOUSE

Legal problems are sometimes indicated by this transit. This is by no means inevitable, however.

URANUS IN SEVENTH HOUSE

Legal confrontations sometimes occur during this transit, usually having to do with joint finances or partnerships, either business or personal.

URANUS IN NINTH HOUSE

It's best to avoid legal confrontations now, if you can. The outcome may suddenly go against you.

URANUS OPPOSITION ASCENDANT

You cannot predict how any legal disputes will end now, so either avoid them or get them over with as quickly as possible, and don't make waves. At the slightest pretext, the other party will really mess things up for you.

NEPTUNE IN SEVENTH HOUSE

This is not a good time to consult a lawyer or become involved in a lawsuit. Poor communications, misunderstandings, illusions, gullibility—all are likely to conspire against a positive outcome.

NEPTUNE OPPOSITION MERCURY

Absolutely do not get involved in anything you know to be on the shady side at this time. Be aware that others may try to deceive you or steal from you. Don't bother trying any such thing yourself; it won't work now. Get everything in writing.

NEPTUNE OPPOSITION ASCENDANT

Do not become involved in legal battles at this time, if you can avoid it. This is not even a good time to consult a lawyer for anything. Communications are poor now at best.

PLUTO IN SEVENTH HOUSE

Lawsuits regarding joint or corporate finances, insurance, or other financial matters are possible. At all costs, do not engage in anything underhanded if you wish to succeed.

PLUTO IN NINTH HOUSE

If afflicted, Pluto may bring difficulties with the law; however, this is not inevitable if you're careful not to ride roughshod over others without taking their rights or ideas into consideration.

PLUTO CONJUNCT JUPITER

Generally, this transit is favorable for legal activities concerning corporate, joint, tax, or insurance finances.

PLUTO SEXTILE JUPITER

This is a favorable time for any legal actions or dealings with authorities.

PLUTO SQUARE JUPITER

Legal difficulties, particularly involving finances, could arise. Be completely honest and aboveboard. Litigation, even arrest, could otherwise result. Pay attention to details. Remember the needs of others.

PLUTO OPPOSITION JUPITER

This is not a good time to have any dealings with the law. Don't do anything that might cause a run-in with it.

PLUTO SQUARE ASCENDANT

There may be lawsuits over finances, particularly joint finances of any sort. Do not stoop to use underhanded tactics of any kind for any reason. Don't blame others for your problems. Look within for your own weaknesses to correct.

PLUTO OPPOSITION ASCENDANT

Lawsuits concerning finances are a possibility under this transit. Make sure everything is aboveboard. Don't try to hide anything. Be precise in your communications.

Chapter 15

Love and Marriage

"Love," said Proust, "is space and time made directly perceptible to the heart." Indeed, a love relationship is a very special one, complicated by the interplay of the egos and libidos of those involved, a relationship in which some of the most intense karma is worked out. It can consequently be one of the most satisfying and rewarding of relationships, well worth bringing all your available inner resources to bear upon, and one with which you sometimes need all the help you can get. The sagacious use of this chapter will, it is hoped, be of assistance in making space and time perceptible to *your* heart.

Transit Descriptions

SUN IN FIRST HOUSE

Wait until this approximately month-long transit is over to solve any marital problems. You won't be so self-preoccupied that you can't see the other's point of view by then.

SUN IN FIFTH HOUSE

You may begin a new love relationship, or your sexual drive may become more stimulated in an existing relationship during this transit.

SUN IN SEVENTH HOUSE

Look closely at your partnership to be sure that you are giving as much as you are receiving. If conflicts arise, this is a good time to seek professional counsel or advice.

MOON IN FIFTH HOUSE

Your emotions are intensified now, and relationships with lovers are likely to reflect this. Your nurturing nature is also aroused, but you must guard against being overpossessive or overprotective.

MOON IN SEVENTH HOUSE

Relationships and conflicts, particularly within partnerships and especially with women, are apt to take on a more emotional tone than usual. Pay attention to what you're doing and saying, and you'll be able to learn things about yourself that you don't generally notice.

MOON IN TENTH HOUSE

This is not a good time to turn a professional relationship into a more personal one; keep it strictly business at this time. Public displays of emotion with love partners are a possibility.

MOON TRINE SUN

You feel harmonious and at peace with yourself, and this improves all your relationships, especially intimate ones.

MOON OPPOSITION SUN

There may be difficulties with the opposite sex or a brief attraction to someone who is quite unlike yourself. This may be pleasant and fun for a time, but it is not apt to be long lasting or secure.

MOON CONJUNCT MOON

You're more emotionally aware now, and women may be important in your life. However, you'd probably just as soon be by yourself at this time.

MOON CONJUNCT VENUS

You're apt to be in the mood for love today. You get along well with everyone, but a present love relationship is especially helped along. This transit sometimes pinpoints when a new relationship will begin, if there is another, more powerful transit in effect that signifies a new relationship.

MOON SEXTILE VENUS

Love relationships usually run smoothly at this time. If you've been having any trouble in your relationship, this transit will signal "time-out" and give you a chance to patch things up.

MOON SQUARE VENUS

You'll feel very loving today, and as long as you don't get too possessive, all should go very well.

MOON TRINE VENUS

This transit helps assure you that the course of true love can indeed run smoothly at times.

MOON SEXTILE MARS

You'll draw persons who are strong and courageous to you; you're attracted to them, too.

MOON OPPOSITION JUPITER

If your partner seeks to restrict you in any way, you'll rebel. Confrontations could occur. You just don't want anyone telling you what to do; if they leave you alone, you'll probably be willing to give more than your share.

MOON CONJUNCT PLUTO

Whatever you're involved in today will very likely be on a deep emotional level, one way or another. Beware of irrational possessiveness or jealously and manipulative tactics—yours or someone else's.

MOON TRINE PLUTO

A sexual relationship will be intensified now, because you're able to get to the depths of it. Your emotions and your sensitivity are heightened to the point where, today—or tonight—the two of you can really become as one.

MOON OPPOSITION PLUTO

There may be conflicts in close relationships, probably due to subconscious drives, generally buried but now emerging. One or the other of you may act jealous, possessive, or manipulative. Later, after you cool down and this transit is passed, you'll be able to learn a great deal about the both of you by reviewing what happened. Don't make any important decisions concerning your emotional life under this transit.

MERCURY IN SEVENTH HOUSE

Now is the time to work out any problems or misunderstandings with a partner, unless Mercury is afflicted in this house natally or while transiting it.

VENUS IN THIRD HOUSE

This an excellent time to communicate your feelings of love. Even if others know already, it's always nice to hear.

VENUS IN FIFTH HOUSE

You'll relate well with loved ones now. This is an excellent time to get out and have some fun with them.

VENUS IN SIXTH HOUSE

Practicality, not romance, is uppermost in your mind now. This is a good time to talk out and smooth out any misunderstandings with a loved one.

VENUS IN SEVENTH HOUSE

This transit favors all partnerships, especially partners in love.

All will go well now, even if you have some difficulty to resolve. If there are other indications in your chart, a new love interest may appear.

VENUS IN EIGHTH HOUSE

Sexual drive may be stimulated under this transit, and any relationship that is initiated under this transit will be intense. Deep, perhaps subtle, realizations about a relationship may come to you now.

VENUS IN TENTH HOUSE

You may find yourself romantically attracted to your boss or someone in authority over you. A love relationship that begins now is apt to be with such a person or with someone who is older.

VENUS IN ELEVENTH HOUSE

Your love relationship will take on a very amicable air now, and you'll feel the best of friends as well as lovers.

VENUS CONJUNCT SUN

You're in the mood for love and fun; you'll easily attract others to you today. This is a good time for entertaining or going somewhere to enjoy yourself socially.

VENUS SQUARE SUN

You feel very much like socializing today and will get along well with one and all, friends as well as lovers.

VENUS TRINE SUN

Enjoy! You feel loving and completely at ease. Just be yourself and you may find you're the life of the party—even a party of two.

VENUS OPPOSITION SUN

You are likely to be in the mood for love today. Avoid any liaison that must be discreet, though, as you're not in the right frame of mind for that. If a relationship begins under this transit, don't make any concrete commitments until you're really sure it's going to last.

VENUS CONJUNCT MOON

You're in a romantic, sentimental mood, and you want to be with a familiar someone in familiar surroundings. This is a perfect time to fix a gourmet meal and spend a quiet, candlelit evening at home.

VENUS SQUARE MOON

You may be feeling amorous, but remember to let your spouse or lover have some space.

VENUS TRINE MOON

Feelings of love are enhanced under this transit. Spend a quiet evening with someone you love.

VENUS OPPOSITION MOON

You have a strong need to give and receive love now. This is not a good time to make a permanent commitment to anyone, though. Neither is it a good time to try to iron out relationship difficulties. Your emotions are too much in control, and you're feeling just too pleasant and mellow.

VENUS CONJUNCT MERCURY

This is a good day for expressing your love to someone. You can do it easily now.

VENUS TRINE MERCURY

Tell that special someone of your love today. And, if necessary, tackle any problems that there may be in the relationship. You can do it easily and well today, getting both your love and your point across.

VENUS OPPOSITION MERCURY

Now would be a prime time to discuss any problems that may exist in a relationship. Don't be too flip and casual about what you say, though; someone may not know you're just kidding.

VENUS CONJUNCT VENUS

Take the initiative in any relationship today, and you may be pleasantly surprised at the result. Don't keep anyone in the dark about your love—tell them. If there is another, supporting transit, a new relationship might begin today.

VENUS SEXTILE VENUS

All goes smoothly today, and this transit bodes well for new romance, too.

VENUS OPPOSITION VENUS

You're feeling lazy, self-indulgent, and amorous. Go ahead. Enjoy your sensuality. All should go well, but if a problem should develop in a relationship, wait until later to try to do any serious resolving. You're likely to be willing to compromise more than necessary.

VENUS CONJUNCT MARS

Sexual desire and passion are aroused, and sex now will be mutually satisfying. You may desire a new relationship, but this transit alone is not enough to give it longevity.

VENUS SEXTILE MARS

You can give and receive love in equal portions at this time, and your energies are now attractive to the opposite sex. You're in the mood to go out and have some fun, and this would be beneficial to you.

VENUS SQUARE MARS

Your sexual energies are aroused, and this could result in either a pleasant or an unpleasant evening, depending on the current level of tensions in your relationship. A new relationship that begins now is likely to be pure sexual attraction.

VENUS TRINE MARS

Your sexual energies are aroused, but not necessarily in an aggressive manner. A new relationship that begins under this transit is likely to endure, but even if it doesn't you'll part amicably.

VENUS OPPOSITION MARS

Generally speaking, this transit magnifies the qualities of a sexual relationship: if it's good already, it'll be really good now; if it's not so good now, things will get worse. If you're not in a sexual relationship, you'll probably be attracted to, or come into conflict with, someone of the opposite sex. A relationship that begins under this transit may be based solely on physical attraction; consequently, this is not a good time to make a permanent committal.

VENUS CONJUNCT JUPITER

This is an excellent time for all relationships, including intimate ones. A new one may begin at this time, perhaps with someone very different from you. If you marry under this transit, the wedding will go well and you'll enjoy it immensely.

VENUS SEXTILE JUPITER

A new relationship that begins now will bring out your best self and prove beneficial.

VENUS OPPOSITION JUPITER

If there are other, supporting transits, a new relationship may begin now. You should be careful of being overly impressed by superficial characteristics, however.

VENUS CONJUNCT SATURN

There may be problems now, because you're having trouble communicating your feelings. Sometimes this transit signals a separation, temporary or permanent, possibly due to other responsibilities. A new relationship that begins now may be long lasting and extremely earnest.

VENUS SEXTILE SATURN

A good day to discuss and clarify your mutual expectations in a relationship. You may feel drawn to an older person, either to seek advice or to begin a love relationship. Or, you could be the older person sought by another.

VENUS SQUARE SATURN

You're apt to be coolly evaluating your relationship and its importance to you. This may lead you into a deeper understanding of yourself with respect to relationships. On the other hand, don't get too carried away into the deep; this transit often makes things seem worse than they really are.

VENUS TRINE SATURN

Relationships under this transit are stable and calm, whether they are old and familiar or new. Should a relationship begin now, there may be a substantial difference of some sort between you and your partner. Talk out any difficulties today.

VENUS CONJUNCT URANUS

Unexpected upsets could occur, either favorable or unfavorable. You're looking for excitement and are impatient with routine. Should a new relationship begin, it will probably be exciting, though it's unlikely to be too secure.

VENUS SEXTILE URANUS

You may meet a new lover today, and while it may be an excitingly new and different relationship, it may not be long lasting. If it should last, however, it may very well radically change your life. You'll have to give each other a great deal of freedom, and this in itself may be a new experience for you.

VENUS TRINE URANUS

You'll want to be with people who are different from you and your current friends. Any relationship that begins under this transit will have the Uranian traits of being exciting and different, but short-lived.

VENUS OPPOSITION URANUS

There may be unexpected occurrences in a relationship during this transit. How you view it depends upon the status of the relationship and your inherent flexibility. Uranus just loves to stamp out rigidity. Any relationship that begins under this transit will probably be unusual but short.

VENUS CONJUNCT NEPTUNE

This transit brings out your willingness to give your all for a friend or loved one. You'll be able to feel totally at one with those you love. This transit also tends to warp your sense of reality, however, so it's not a good time to make concrete decisions or commitments concerning a relationship.

VENUS SEXTILE NEPTUNE

Today you are a romantic, and if you can quit daydreaming long enough, you can feel truly at one with someone you love.

VENUS SQUARE NEPTUNE

This time can be a marvelously romantic interlude, and you'll both feel wonderful for it. Don't expect everyone to live up to *your* romantic idealism, though. In fact, relationships sometimes break up under this transit. If so, they were probably built on fantasy anyway, and a relationship that begins now probably will be. Consequently, this is not a good time to make permanent commitments. Secret love affairs may have their inception under this transit.

VENUS TRINE NEPTUNE

Either you'll be really tuned in to the needs and feelings of others, or you'll just think you are. If you consciously make the effort to be tuned in, however, you can be.

VENUS OPPOSITION NEPTUNE

You have the tendency to idealize others during this transit. Try to remember that everyone else is only human, too, so that you won't be so disappointed by the dawn of truth when this transit is over. Nor should you idealize your role in the relationship; chances are, you are *not* the only giving one in it. Also try to keep your eyes open and your wits about you. There is a possibility of deception under this transit, whether deliberate or inadvertent.

VENUS CONJUNCT PLUTO

You're sexually stimulated and looking for escape from the mundane. You may "fall in love" with someone outside your current relationship. Your feelings are intense, but this transit, as will be your infatuation, is fleeting. Jealousy or guilt or other negative emotions may complicate the picture. The best way to deal with these energies is to control and use them to become more in tune with your partner, then enjoy the ensuing fireworks.

VENUS SEXTILE PLUTO

Your sexual appetite and emotions are enhanced, deepened, intensified. You'll gain insights into your important relationships because you're going beneath the surface to find them; you're not satisfied with the superficial now. Any new relationship that begins now will probably be emotionally intense and ardent.

VENUS SQUARE PLUTO

Be willing to look deeply and honestly at your relationship. Don't resist needed change. Let your relationship change and grow, and it will be strengthened and intensified.

VENUS TRINE PLUTO

Your feelings of love and your sexual appetite are increased and enhanced today, and you'll be able to express them easily. You may gain new insight into your relationship. Any new relationship that begins today will probably be a barn-burner; it's best to let things cool down a bit before making any definite commitments, though.

VENUS OPPOSITION PLUTO

This is one of the transits associated with extramarital affairs, intense sexual energy, jealousy, emotional manipulation, and possible irrational behavior in a relationship. Subconscious tensions or motives welling up from deep within are probably the culprits. This transit is best handled by being aware of the situation and what you are doing at all times. Properly handled, these energies can produce experiences in a love relationship that can be transcending. Don't make any permanent commitments to a new relationship that begins under this transit until some time has passed.

VENUS CONJUNCT MIDHEAVEN

Today you are in love with love and with the whole world, and you want to proclaim it from the rooftops. And all goes well in relationships now. Enjoy. This is an excellent day to fall in love, tell someone you love them, get married, be with friends, have a party, socialize in any way.

VENUS SEXTILE MIDHEAVEN

All goes well today, mainly because you don't feel like disturbing the peace for any reason and are more tolerant of others. Plus, you really want to help others if you can. This is not a day to be alone—be with friends or loved ones and enjoy.

VENUS SQUARE MIDHEAVEN

You'll probably have a very pleasant and amorous time with your partner under this transit. You're in the mood to both give and receive love—an ideal situation. If, however, you have any tendency toward jealousy, selfishness, or possessiveness, *these* emotions may be enhanced, making for a difficult and unpleasant day unless you make the effort to overcome them.

VENUS CONJUNCT ASCENDANT

You feel friendly and affectionate today. A good time to enjoy any relationship and resolve difficulties. A new friend or lover may enter your life today. If so, rest assured you're making a good first impression.

VENUS SEXTILE ASCENDANT

A new love relationship may begin now, especially if there are other, supporting transits. At any rate, all goes well in any relationship now.

VENUS OPPOSITION ASCENDANT

All should go well today, but if there are any difficulties between you, this is a good day to iron them out. Take a moment to be aware of how much you mean to each other. If there are other indications supporting it, a new love relationship may begin today. If so, it will be beneficial for you.

MARS IN FIFTH HOUSE

Sexual desire and energy are intensified during this transit.

MARS IN SEVENTH HOUSE

There is a need for cooperation between close partners, but with the ego energy of Mars there is apt to be conflict instead. This can be overcome by consciously and calmly bringing difficulties into the open and making an effort to employ a true spirit of cooperation and compromise.

MARS IN EIGHTH HOUSE

Sexual desire may be enhanced during this time. There may also be increased conflict over finances jointly held.

MARS TRINE SUN

A very pleasant time for a love relationship. You're willing and eager to give as well as receive.

MARS OPPOSITION SUN

You may be irritable and just plain hard to live with due to subconscious energies that you've not been utilizing or dispersing properly. This can make any relationship rocky for the time being.

MARS SEXTILE MOON

Your emotions and desires are powerful now. Any sexual relationship will be ardently intensified.

MARS TRINE MOON

You are emotionally intense now, and this carries over into your encounters with the opposite sex. Whether it be love or hate, you'll feel it thoroughly.

MARS OPPOSITION MOON

There may very well be emotional blowups and general discord in your relationship now, especially if you are showing a distinct lack of consideration for the feelings of your partner. This will be true of any close relationship, especially with women. Look at the situation with open eyes: You can learn a great deal about yourself; others may be a reflection of your inner self at this time.

MARS CONJUNCT VENUS

Your sexual desires are strong, and if you can't satisfy them, you're apt to get very out of sorts. A new love relationship that will demand immediate or eventual consummation can be signaled if Mars makes a station or moves slowly across your natal Venus.

MARS SEXTILE VENUS

Your sexual drive is heightened, and if you're not already in a sexual relationship, you'll be looking for one. It will be an exciting and satisfying one under this transit, all else being equal.

MARS SQUARE VENUS

This transit arouses your need and desire for sexual gratification. A good relationship will be very good now. A difficult one can be improved by explicitly detailing what each wants and expects from the relationship.

MARS TRINE VENUS

Sexual activity is accentuated now, and if you're not currently involved in a sexual relationship, you'll want to be. Be aware, though, that you're liable to be attracted to almost anyone today, so be careful or you may regret it tomorrow.

MARS OPPOSITION VENUS

This transit stimulates the purely physical sexual drives, and there may be little love in the lovemaking. This can lead to feelings of exploitation and conflict. If in a nonsexually expressed relationship, you may find yourself becoming angry or irritable. All you can do is to realize the dynamics involved, try to utilize the energy creatively in some other fashion, and wait for this transit to pass; or, if appropriate, enter into sexual activity.

MARS OPPOSITION NEPTUNE

Communications may be very muddled today, leading to misunderstandings. Be as clear and precise as you can.

MARS SQUARE ASCENDANT

The course of true love is definitely not on the smooth side right now. Plus, neither of you wants to give an inch. Go ahead and have it out to relieve the tensions building up, but don't count on resolving anything just yet.

JUPITER IN FIFTH HOUSE

A sexual relationship that begins at this time will be beneficial to you. You have no need to pretend to be what you're not and can therefore have a very meaningful and rewarding relationship. Current relationships will be benefited, too.

JUPITER IN SEVENTH HOUSE

Your marriage should run smoothly now, and it may teach you something about yourself and the world at large. You may begin a relationship with, or even marry, someone from a totally different background, possibly an older person or someone from another country.

JUPITER OPPOSITION MOON

You either will feel very loving and generous with others or will turn these feelings upon yourself and be very self-indulgent and exacting of others. Your relationships, especially with women, will consequently be either wonderful or horrible. Here is a chance for self-observation and change, if necessary.

JUPITER CONJUNCT VENUS

A new love interest may enter your life at this time, and if there are no other transits to the contrary, the relationship should turn out to be pleasant and beneficial to you both. In an existing relationship, this is a good time to work out any difficulties.

JUPITER SEXTILE VENUS

You're in a flirtatious mood and, in fact, may attract a new love. In any case, you'll get along well with one and all.

JUPITER SQUARE VENUS

A new and important relationship may begin now. It will probably be very exciting and afford you an opportunity to gain insight into yourself. There is some need for self-composure and caution, though.

JUPITER TRINE VENUS

You're in a happy, sociable mood and may feel like flirting. Should a love relationship begin under this transit, you'll enjoy it very much, though it may not be long lasting.

JUPITER OPPOSITION VENUS

This can go one of two ways. Either everything will be pleasant and harmonious in a relationship or there will be tension and conflict about freedom and possessiveness. In the latter case, bring everything out into the open and try to take care of the problems now. Also, it's possible that a new relationship will begin now, which could go one of two ways.

JUPITER OPPOSITION URANUS

You want to break away from anything you think is restricting your life, whether it be a person or circumstance. There is sometimes a sudden breakup when the transit becomes exact. It may be your partner who desires more freedom; give it if you want the relationship to continue.

JUPITER TRINE ASCENDANT

A new love relationship may begin at this time, especially if it's also indicated by another transit.

JUPITER OPPOSITION ASCENDANT

Sometimes a new love will enter your life under this transit. If happily married, your marriage will be very satisfying at this time. If there has been trouble, it may be patched up now or may break up entirely, though usually on friendly terms. This is a good time to consult a marriage counselor. Basically, this is a time of self-growth through relationships.

SATURN IN FIFTH HOUSE

This may not be an untroubled time for relationships, especially if they don't allow free expression of the new you that you've been restructuring these past few years. Love affairs may be especially difficult. There may be emotional encounters that provide an opportunity for learning. Do not seek to avoid these encounters.

SATURN IN SEVENTH HOUSE

Close relationships are likely to be more demanding than usual, but problems should be faced and resolved if possible. Make sure you do not renege on any of your promises or commitments. This transit sometimes signifies the breakup of a marriage, and the source of difficulty may be your career or profession, since you may be getting more recognition in it now.

SATURN OPPOSITION SUN

This is a time of endings in your life, and it may include the end of some relationships, especially any that have been limiting to you. Be patient. A time of beginnings will come soon.

SATURN OPPOSITION MOON

This can be a very difficult and emotionally stressful time. You may feel lonely or cut off from others. Relationships may break up. There may be domestic or work-related problems, stemming from the fact that you've neglected the one for the other. You'll have to make some changes to bring the disparate portions of your life into balance. It's not likely to be easy, but it will be worth it.

SATURN CONJUNCT VENUS

This is a time of reviewing your relationships and evaluating who you really are, deciding which relationships are or are not important to you. Some may end. Others will survive and be strengthened. Sometimes a new relationship begins now as well.

SATURN SEXTILE VENUS

You institute a very practical approach to relationships now. Idealistic romanticism is not on the menu. If a relationship begins now, an age difference is likely.

SATURN SQUARE VENUS

This is a time when a relationship that is consciously or unconsciously unsatisfactory to either of you may break up. You may feel that outside circumstances have interfered, but actually, circumstances are rarely outside our control.

SATURN TRINE VENUS

You are more a realist than a starry-eyed, idealistic romanticist now. This is an excellent time to learn more about yourself and to grow through your relationships. Should a new relationship begin now, an age difference is likely. One partner may act as "teacher" in the growth process.

SATURN SQUARE JUPITER

You may feel that a relationship is restricting your freedom and want out. However, it's best to avoid making any hasty decisions under this transit. Let it pass first, then reconsider when you're calmer.

SATURN OPPOSITION JUPITER

Relationships you feel have been restricting your freedom too much may be severed at this time. Though painful, this may be to your ultimate good. Even if there is no separation, relationships may be severely tested.

SATURN CONJUNCT SATURN

If you have been in an inappropriate or unsatisfactory marriage or relationship, it will now end or undergo substantial change. It cannot endure in its present state. You may begin feeling the effects of this transit as much as a year before it becomes exact. You'll be better off in the long run if you voluntarily go along with these changes. You are entering a new and important phase of your life.

SATURN SQUARE SATURN

Inappropriate or no longer nurturing relationships may end at this time. You are undergoing a time of change and soul-searching.

SATURN OPPOSITION SATURN

If during the last square of Saturn to your natal Saturn you did not eliminate inappropriate relationships or improve those which needed it, they will very probably not survive the turmoil of this transit. Good, mature relationships now, however, will be extremely satisfying.

SATURN CONJUNCT URANUS

You're undergoing changes, seeking excitement, freedom, and new horizons. This may mean that some relationships will fall by the wayside. You may terminate a relationship suddenly, without warning. Or, you may need to radically restructure it.

SATURN SEXTILE URANUS

After the possible upheavals of about seven years ago, your relationship has stabilized. You probably feel very satisfied in it, possibly even smug.

SATURN SQUARE URANUS

You now have a golden opportunity to make creative changes in your life, to eliminate anything that is not working right for you. If this is done willingly or consciously, this can be a very exciting time. If, however, you've become too rigid and are afraid of change, this can be a very upsetting time. Relationships may end in either case, or if you're open to change, improve.

SATURN OPPOSITION URANUS

Any relationship or marriage that is resistant to change or readjustment may very likely end at this time. Calmly making positive, creative changes in it will strengthen and improve it so that the both of you are happier.

SATURN OPPOSITION ASCENDANT

Relationships may end under this transit. In any case, close relationships are likely to be severely tested—possibly because you're beginning to be recognized in other areas of your life and your partner may feel threatened. Bring any tensions out into the open and deal with them now. Don't put them off and don't attempt to ignore them.

URANUS IN FIRST HOUSE

A marriage or close relationship that cannot adjust to the new you emerging under this transit will very likely end. Basically, you are seeking new or more personal freedom—freedom to express yourself, to be the expression of yourself as you really are.

URANUS IN FIFTH HOUSE

Exciting, unusual romances may occur. You may wonder what was there, however, when the excitement wears off and daily routines must set in. In other words, don't necessarily expect these relationships to last. Also, beware of unexpected pregnancies.

URANUS IN SEVENTH HOUSE

New, unusual, short-lived romances or marriages may occur. Old relationships or marriages in difficulty may end. Even good relationships will have to undergo change and adjustment. Uranus has a way of getting rid of stale situations or routines that are not good for our best long-term interests.

URANUS IN EIGHTH HOUSE

A new and different love relationship may begin but may not last. It's best not to commit to anything permanent at this time. Even if this doesn't happen, a current relationship will have to undergo change and adjustment. You're wanting to be free of old restrictions and limitations that are no longer needed or applicable.

URANUS TRINE SUN

New relationships that begin now will be exciting and will permit you to be your true self.

URANUS OPPOSITION SUN

Relationships may end under this transit, either by death or by other separation. If so, it's because the function of the relationship has been fulfilled, or because it was inhibiting freedom of self-expression of one or both partners.

URANUS CONJUNCT MOON

Impetuous infatuations may occur under this transit. Men, especially, will fall prey to this emotionally revitalizing experience. Or changes in your intimate or home life may happen. Good or bad, they'll be sudden and surprising.

URANUS SEXTILE MOON

Your emotions are stimulated, and you can experience yourself and the world through your feelings. You give and require more emotional support and expression from all around you. If they can't give it, you'll find someone who can.

URANUS SQUARE MOON

There may be seemingly sudden problems with spouses or other close partners. Actually, tensions suppressed over the years are deciding to emerge now. If the tension has been very serious, one partner may suddenly leave. Any relationship, even a good one, is apt to require some adjustments at this time.

URANUS TRINE MOON

A relationship that begins now may bring you excitement and emotional experiences you've never before had.

URANUS CONJUNCT VENUS

You suddenly cannot stand the boredom and routine of settled-in relationships, and you'll pursue new freedom and excitement at almost any cost. Either you'll look outside the current relationship to satisfy this desire, or the existing relationship will change and develop into something new. It's best to let this transit pass before making any definite and binding decisions concerning new relationships.

URANUS SEXTILE VENUS

New and different people will enter your life now. A new love relationship may begin, and it's apt to be totally unlike any of your previous ones. If you preserve its freedom and excitement, this relationship may be long lasting.

URANUS SQUARE VENUS

You are seeking more freedom and excitement and escape from dull routine. You'll look for a relationship with someone totally different from the kind of people you usually associate with. And as long as the excitement lasts, so will the relationship, but don't count on its long-term survival. An existing, basically happy, relationship may undergo some tensions and readjustment. An unhappy marriage or relationship may break up.

URANUS TRINE VENUS

Freedom and excitement are what turn you on right now. If an existing relationship doesn't have it, now is a good time to make changes so that it does. A new love relationship may begin if you're not in one already. It will be unusual in some way, compared to previous ones, and it may very well last, preserving its interest and freedom right along.

URANUS OPPOSITION VENUS

One of you may become restless and dissatisfied with the relationship and seek to change it. Usually, more freedom is what is wanted. All tensions should be worked out now and not held back. A happy, stable relationship will be likely to survive and grow through this experience. Any new relationship that begins under this transit will probably be unusual in some way, but don't expect it to be long lasting.

URANUS OPPOSITION JUPITER

You'll want to break free of any less-than-ideal situations you've been putting up with. Or, someone may want to break free of you. Though breaking up may be unpleasant at the time, it will probably be beneficial to you in the long run.

URANUS CONJUNCT SATURN

Any relationship that has been restricting your ultimate growth, whether you're consciously aware of that fact or not, will be subject to sudden, perhaps explosive, change at this time. Do not resist or suppress this energy. You'll be better for the change in the long run.

URANUS SEXTILE SATURN

Now is a good time to make sure the structures of your life don't eventually become too rigid and confining. You can make constructive changes within your close relationships at this time. You'll be able to accomplish much and will likely be amply rewarded for your efforts.

URANUS SQUARE SATURN

Limitations that are not in your best long-term interests will become intolerable, and you'll find yourself wanting to be rid of them no matter what the consequences. Before suddenly and completely tossing all to the wind, however, it would help to talk with someone who can assist you in deciding more calmly and rationally on the appropriate course of action. The purpose here is to look closely at your life and determine where change would be appropriate and beneficial to your personal growth, not to throw over all structure willy-nilly.

URANUS OPPOSITION SATURN

Uranus may throw you a curve ball to puncture your smugness and show you that you're not a finished product yet—you can still change, grow, and mature. Sudden, upsetting events may occur that force you to reevaluate your thinking, such as a possible breakup in a relationship. Handle the tensions involved as positively as you can in order to avoid serious damage to your health.

URANUS SEXTILE MIDHEAVEN

You'll be seeking more freedom in your relationships in order to pursue your objectives unhindered. And, at this time you can make constructive changes relatively easily.

URANUS OPPOSITION MIDHEAVEN

There may be upsets in your relationships or home life, mainly because there are changes going on within yourself. Try to be aware of yourself, open to inner insights, and considerate of others; and disruptions may be avoided or kept to a minimum. Don't be afraid to face—and conquer—hidden tensions that may surface now.

URANUS CONJUNCT ASCENDANT

You'll probably be impatient with any sort of restrictions or limitations, including those that exist in an intimate relationship. One that is stable and good may experience fewer difficulties, but one or both parties may seek freedom to break out of old, expected roles. Also, you may attract totally new and different acquaintances.

URANUS SEXTILE ASCENDANT

New friendships, even marriage opportunities, may come to you now. You're ready for the new and exciting.

URANUS SQUARE ASCENDANT

Marriages or partnerships already in trouble, whether it is acknowledged or not, may not come through this disruptive transit. A good marriage will adjust and grow stronger. Any new love relationships that begin now are likely to be stimulating, though short-lived. It would be best to wait until this transit has passed before making commitments.

URANUS TRINE ASCENDANT

Tell your loved ones now how you feel about them; your capacity for self-expression is enhanced. If a new relationship begins now, it may be exciting and valuable in more ways than one, but don't count on its longevity. New friendships may form that give you sudden opportunities to do new things. They, too, may be brief.

URANUS OPPOSITION ASCENDANT

Even a good relationship is apt to be a bit rocky now, but one that has been struggling along with hidden problems or with stolid resignation is very likely to end now. Basically, one of you wants more say and perhaps more freedom within the relationship, resisting efforts of the other to totally control it. If either is too inflexible to accept change, the relationship will end.

NEPTUNE IN FIFTH HOUSE

You are more in the mood for romance than sex now, and may tend to idealize a loved one. Or you may be idealized in some way. Neither situation is to be commended; you should make an effort to see and to deal with people as they really are and treat them as equals. Don't think you can save someone from themselves or that they can save you. Also, be careful of unwanted pregnancies if this house is afflicted.

NEPTUNE IN SEVENTH HOUSE

There may be difficulties in a relationship due to poor communication, which can lead to misunderstandings. Make everything as clear and precise as you can. Don't hold anything back, thinking the other person already knows what you want or what you mean. Nor should you over-idealize the situation; try to see things as they really are. This, by the way, is not a good time to begin new partnerships.

NEPTUNE CONJUNCT MOON

Should a love relationship begin now, you may find when this transit is over that you were in love with love and not the person.

This is not the time to make permanent commitments.

NEPTUNE SQUARE MOON

There may be difficulties in relationships due to misunderstandings, so be very precise and specific in your communications and try not to take your moods and emotions too seriously at the moment. A love relationship may begin now that is totally impractical, and yet you feel unable to let it alone. This is not a wise time to make permanent commitments.

NEPTUNE TRINE MOON

A love relationship that begins now may function on a very transcendental level. It will probably be good for you in the long run, and may even make the transition to a more realistic level with little difficulty.

NEPTUNE OPPOSITION MOON

"Love is blind," may well have been a phrase invented for this transit. Be careful. Don't make any permanent commitments now. You are seeing only what you want to see.

NEPTUNE CONJUNCT VENUS

Beware of falling in love with your illusions of perfection and not the real person, otherwise you may be greatly disappointed when you "wake up" after this transit is over. It would be best not to make any permanent arrangements until this transit is well over.

NEPTUNE SEXTILE VENUS

You'll be intuitively sensitive to others—willing and able to be selfless in your devotion to them, but romanticizing or idealizing them all out of proportion to their true worth or merit. You will not greatly suffer from this, though, even if things turn out not to be what they now seem. A new love interest may begin now; possibly, even a spiritual "soul-mate" may appear.

NEPTUNE SQUARE VENUS

Your ability to wade through illusions and idealizations, possibly even deceptions, to see others as they really are will be tested. You must learn to stop deluding yourself and face yourself as you really are, first and foremost. This may be exactly what you are trying to sidestep. New loves that begin now will be part of these tests.

NEPTUNE TRINE VENUS

If a love relationship begins now, it will seem your "ideal" love, all candlelight and roses and no flaws in either of you. You'll have to work to make it last, but even after you've begun to see that not even your new love is totally perfect, this can be a very romantic relationship. You'll find the two of you are very much in tune. This is, in fact, a harmonious time in all relationships.

NEPTUNE OPPOSITION VENUS

The danger here is over-idealization of a partner, especially a new lover. This can lead to rude awakenings down the road. Don't make permanent commitments until well after this transit has passed. There may be difficulties in existing relationships, too, possibly due to poor communications, misunderstandings, even deception.

NEPTUNE CONJUNCT ASCENDANT

This is another transit to prove the adage, "love is blind." Your idealism is so aroused you may not see, or refuse to see, the faults or ploys of others. Needless to say, this is not a good time to make any permanent arrangements.

NEPTUNE SQUARE ASCENDANT

You are not seeing yourself and others realistically. Also, you may be wearing your ego like a chip on the shoulder (whether you realize it or not), which just begs Neptune to knock it off with some sort of event or experience to bring you down a peg or two. Try to just sit back and observe. If a relationship ends, try to determine what you've learned from it.

NEPTUNE TRINE ASCENDANT

You'll have much more compassion for others, but you may tend to over-idealize them, too, thinking they are wonderful and you are a nobody. This is especially true for any new love relationship that begins during this transit. Hang in there—make no permanent commitments, and reevaluate what you've learned after this transit of about one year is over.

NEPTUNE OPPOSITION ASCENDANT

The possibility of deception is in the air and communications are apt to be poor. Make sure everything is spelled out and perfectly clear and open.

PLUTO IN FIFTH HOUSE

Love affairs and existing sexual relationships are likely to be very intense. An existing one is apt to undergo tremendous change, or, if in difficulty, may end. A relationship that does come through this transit intact is probably good from now on.

PLUTO IN SEVENTH HOUSE

This is not a particularly good time to begin a marriage or other commitment, unless you are a person who absolutely needs the unsettled intensity this transit is likely to produce. All your relationships are undergoing tremendous changes—and you are changing along with them. Partnerships that are not sufficiently strong to withstand some crisis and change will probably end sometime during this transit.

PLUTO SEXTILE SUN

If you feel that any changes need to be made in a relationship, now is a time when you can do so creatively and with little trouble.

PLUTO OPPOSITION SUN

This transit often indicates power struggles in various relationships. Do not try to dominate anyone for any reason whatsoever. And, if someone tries to rule your life, resist.

PLUTO CONJUNCT MOON

There may be intense emotional encounters with friends and family, especially women. Separations may occur, possibly through death. A new cycle of life is about to begin for you, and as always with Pluto, there is first the tearing down of the old before construction of the new.

PLUTO TRINE MOON

Your emotional understanding of yourself and others is heightened. This reflects positively in your relationships. If you feel there are any changes that need to be made within a relationship, now is a good time to make them. A new relationship—not necessarily a sexual one—may begin, which will have a profound effect on your life.

PLUTO OPPOSITION MOON

There may be emotional turmoil and conflicts under this transit. Either party may be tempted to stoop to emotional stratagems to manipulate the other. Try to avoid this by insisting that each be completely honest. Otherwise, the relationship may—and probably should—end.

PLUTO CONJUNCT VENUS

Your sexual needs and desires are heightened, and if you're not in a sexual relationship at the moment, one may come now. And, whether the person is actually good for you or not, the relationship will be very intense. There may be an element of obsessiveness about a relationship that begins now. If you can find no sexual outlet at this time, you'll be either very frustrated or very creative in some way.

PLUTO SEXTILE VENUS

Your relationships will intensify and serve as a basis for insights into yourself and the meaning others have for you. Your sexual energy will be heightened at this time, and you'll learn from that, too. You'll find your capacity for love deepened; and love, both abstract and physical, can, when used correctly, expand your consciousness and help you grow. A new relationship may begin now, and it, too, will be intense.

PLUTO SQUARE VENUS

There may be tension or disruption in almost any relationship now. If so, there is a need for change within the relationship, probably reflecting needed changes within yourself as well. Be open in all communications—be completely honest. Some relationships may end under this transit; others will be strengthened. Either of you may be sorely tempted to have an affair. Don't give in—at least until this transit has been over for some time, when you'll be able to see the situation more clearly. New relationships that begin during this transit don't have good long-term records and are generally unstable.

PLUTO TRINE VENUS

You'll pleasantly learn a great deal about yourself and love under this transit. Existing relationships may change for the better and intensify. A new relationship will "sweep you off your feet," and you'll both be surprised at the intensity of feelings.

PLUTO OPPOSITION VENUS

Some profound transformations are likely to occur in a relationship now. Whether for better or worse depends on a number of things, but the main thing is to be totally honest with each other. New relationships that begin now are apt to be motivated by very powerful subconscious drives. Consequently, you may almost obsessively fall "head-over-heels" for someone who is bad for you. Or good. Sexual energies will run high.

PLUTO OPPOSITION MIDHEAVEN

There may be profound changes in your relationships now. These changes may possibly, but not necessarily, include divorce, separation, or death. They can also be positive, creative changes. The past is fading away to make way for the new. Don't resist, but use the opportunity for growth.

PLUTO CONJUNCT ASCENDANT

There may be power struggles or other difficulties in an intimate relationship now. You're undergoing a personal transformation in which aspects of yourself are emerging that you have previously kept hidden or repressed. Whether you're aware of these surfacing aspects or not, others will begin to behave differently toward you, causing you to react. Do not attempt to ignore this. Get in touch with yourself.

PLUTO SEXTILE ASCENDANT

Your relationships will become more intense and significant to you, and you'll have an opportunity to change them and, possibly, your life. Or, you may be an instrument for important change in your partner's or close friend's life. Just be sure your motives are selfless.

PLUTO SQUARE ASCENDANT

There are apt to be power struggles or other unpleasant encounters in relationships now. Those which are not on solid ground or which have fulfilled their purpose may end. If so, you'll be better off in the long run. Don't stoop to deviousness of any kind for any reason. Don't shrink from unpleasant encounters. It's best to just get them over.

PLUTO TRINE ASCENDANT

You're changing and growing, your self-understanding is deepening, and this is likely to occur within, or be partly helped by, a close relationship. It, too, is evolving and is likely to be intense.

PLUTO OPPOSITION ASCENDANT

The need for change in a close relationship will come to a head now. You must confront your difficulties and try to work them out or the relationship is likely to end. This can apply to marriage, other sexual relationships, or to close friendships.

Chapter 16

Real Estate

Being connected with the land, with the Earth, is one of humankind's fundamental, but often forgotten and neglected, needs. Some would call it a survival instinct. Just touching the Earth, being surrounded by its beauty—as in a park, a forest, a garden, or simply poking a finger into the soil of a flowerpot—is refreshing and energizing. How many offices, even, are devoid of plant life?

We humans need this connection; it's physically and psychologically important to us. The buying and selling of real estate is therefore more than an exercise in financial wizardry, whether or not we're conscious of this fact. Knowing the most propitious times to deal in this commodity, then, can be helpful to you in more ways than one. This chapter can help point you in the right direction, while the chapters on Law, Finances, and Business will also be of assistance in keeping you happily in touch with your Mother.

Transit Descriptions

SUN CONJUNCT MOON

You may be involved in transactions involving real estate, perhaps for speculation.

SUN CONJUNCT PLUTO

There is a remote chance that your residence may change as you make modifications in your lifestyle.

MERCURY IN EIGHTH HOUSE

Unless Mercury is afflicted in or while transiting this house, now is a good time for discussions concerning property, especially joint property.

MERCURY TRINE JUPITER

All business transactions, which can include the buying and selling of real estate, are favored today.

MERCURY TRINE MIDHEAVEN

This is a good day to buy or to go looking for real estate.

MERCURY OPPOSITION MIDHEAVEN

Your mind can keenly handle any negotiations regarding real estate now; it's a good time to look for or to buy property.

MARS IN FOURTH HOUSE

This house position of Mars tends to stir up all kinds of clashes, possibly including conflicts regarding real estate.

JUPITER IN FOURTH HOUSE

There may be some financial gain or other benefit through real estate for you during this transit. Or you may just thoroughly enjoy the harmony of your own home.

JUPITER IN EIGHTH HOUSE

You may find yourself involved in transactions regarding real estate at this time—possibly through or with a business partner, or concerning the distribution of an estate.

JUPITER CONJUNCT MOON

Investing in real estate, especially if it's to be a site where you'll live, would be beneficial now.

JUPITER TRINE JUPITER

This is a favorable time for buying and selling real estate, all else being equal. This is a time of opportunity in many areas, but the initiative must be yours.

JUPITER SQUARE SATURN

This is no time for expansion: finances may be difficult; there may be domestic problems. This is not a good time to invest in real estate or perhaps even to change residences.

JUPITER OPPOSITION MIDHEAVEN

You may find yourself wanting to invest in a new home or real estate. If so, take plenty of time and care to make sure it's what you can live with and be happy with for a long time. You're not going to find parting with it an easy task.

SATURN IN FOURTH HOUSE

There may be some involvement with real estate for you while Saturn is in this house. It may have something to do with your parents or with making improvements.

SATURN TRINE MOON

You're emotionally well balanced, well organized, and objective now; it's a good time to buy or sell real estate, especially if it's your home.

SATURN CONJUNCT JUPITER

This transit sometimes indicates a change of residence, especially if you're unhappy with your present one.

SATURN SQUARE JUPITER

You may feel restless and want to change your residence now. And this may be a valid thing for you to do, but it's best to let this transit pass before making any definite decisions. You'll be calmer then.

SATURN SQUARE SATURN

You may encounter problems with buildings or real estate at this time, possibly concerning your parents, authority figures, or your business. Curbing your tendency toward pessimistic thinking and accentuating the positive would probably help all around.

URANUS IN FOURTH HOUSE

A change of residence is a possibility, sometimes due to some sort of disaster if afflicted.

URANUS SQUARE MOON

This is not a good time to buy a home, unless you are forced to do so. In that case, be sure to keep both eyes open.

URANUS SEXTILE MIDHEAVEN

This transit signals a good time to change residences or make improvements on your real property.

URANUS SQUARE MIDHEAVEN

This transit sometimes coincides with an involuntary change of residence, whether through job changes, disasters, or loss of lease.

NEPTUNE OPPOSITION MERCURY

This is definitely not a good time to buy or sell. If you must, make sure every single thing is clear and spelled out in writing.

PLUTO TRINE MOON

This is a favorable time to buy a piece of real estate with the idea of building your home on it or moving into an existing structure on it. You're making positive changes in your life, and this can be one of them.

PLUTO OPPOSITION MOON

This is not a favorable time for any real estate dealings. For one thing, you're apt to be too emotional.

Chapter 17

Relationships:
Friends, Family, Professional

Relationships help define the parameters of your life and your Self. Through your relationships you can mature and live out, not just intellectually note, the definition of true, universal love. Those you meet and who become important to your growth process are friends and relatives you have known in previous lives. Welcome them back and appreciate them, both the negative and the positive; they are personifications of your karma, and you're here to assist each other along the way again. Consulting your transits regarding relationships from time to time will help you keep that in mind.

Transit Descriptions

SUN IN THIRD HOUSE

You'll find yourself having more and more communication with those around you. Make sure you're communicating effectively; don't fail to listen to their viewpoints, too.

SUN IN FIFTH HOUSE

This is a good time to be with children and to review your relationship with them. Take them out for some fun. On another level, you may meet a new love, especially if this aspect is reinforced by other transits.

SUN IN SEVENTH HOUSE

During this time of year, you would not benefit from being a loner as much as you would by working with others. Whether business or personal, partnerships should be examined now to determine your role in them. Are you giving as much as you're receiving? This is a good time to enter partnerships and to seek advice or professional counsel in any field.

SUN IN TENTH HOUSE

Your relationship with your parents may be important now, possibly having to do with business.

SUN IN ELEVENTH HOUSE

Friends and groups you're a part of will be the focus of this transit. Examine them and your relationship with them to learn more about yourself. You'll find yourself reflected in them. This is a good time to be with others on all levels, from social to strictly business.

SUN SEXTILE SUN

Relationships will be relaxed and pleasant—a good time for being with others for recreation or work.

SUN SQUARE SUN

It may seem as if someone is working against you. You should stop and realize it may not be intentional. At any rate, their actions will compel you to react by proving the validity of what you're doing. And this can be as valuable to you as to them.

SUN OPPOSITION SUN
Personal relationships and interactions of all sorts take on importance now. This is no time to retreat from contact with others.

SUN CONJUNCT MOON
Relationships will be pleasant now, particularly with women, and especially if you're not afraid of your feelings. This is a good time to discuss your relationship with a loved one.

SUN SEXTILE MOON
Relationships are relaxed and pleasant. New friends may come your way, one of which could develop into a love affair. You'll find it easier than usual to tackle any personal or relationship problems that may exist, and it's a good time to do so. You'll also enjoy having friends over for the evening.

SUN TRINE MOON
Your current calmness and equanimity is reflected in all your relationships. It's a good time to resolve any tensions. It's also beneficial to look within for more self-understanding and to help others to understand themselves. Relationships that begin today will turn out to be important to you.

SUN OPPOSITION MOON
If your inner and outer selves have been out of balance—particularly if you've been ignoring your emotional life—today may bring out serious fault lines in your relationships—especially with your spouse and family. In addition, you're likely to act in ways that may be hard to understand and certainly difficult to account for later. Take a hard, honest look within for the answers.

SUN CONJUNCT VENUS
You definitely want to be the center of attention today, and you're so vivacious and amiable you attract people to you. This sometimes includes a new love interest. This is a good time to attend or to have a party—you're apt to be the life of it. Just don't let it go to your head.

This could backfire and cause you trouble later on.

SUN SEXTILE VENUS

Spend time with friends today; all of you will enjoy it. This is a good time to make a good impression if you have to—just be yourself. An opportunity may come to you through a friend. Take time to let your friends know how much you appreciate them or to work out any problems that may exist. You'll be amply rewarded.

SUN SQUARE VENUS

You feel warm and friendly toward just about everyone today and may, in fact, attract a new love relationship. You'll be looking for love, rapport, peace, and a good time today—as long as it doesn't take too much effort. Be careful when pursuing your own pleasure not to do it in an excessive manner or in a way that would be detrimental to someone you care for. Generally, though, this is a good time to go out and enjoy yourself.

SUN TRINE VENUS

You'll very much enjoy the company of others today, and your lighthearted mood will draw others to you. There may even be a new love interest, but probably you'll just have a good time. Now is an excellent opportunity to handle and get rid of any problems you may have in a relationship.

SUN OPPOSITION VENUS

Today you'll want to be with family and friends, as you realize how much you value their love and affection. Now is a good time to talk with someone about whatever is on your mind and in your heart. If there are problems you've been ignoring in a relationship, however, you can't continue to do so today; you'll have to confront them. Pay attention to your responses; they can teach you a lot about yourself.

SUN SQUARE MARS

There may be conflicts and problems with others today. But don't "knee-jerk" react to anyone; be aware of what you're doing and why. Recognize your emotions, and you can use them positively. Should others act combatively toward you, be conscious that you may be projecting feelings that draw them to you. Vigorous physical activity will help you handle all this.

SUN OPPOSITION MARS

Relationships may be explosive today, especially close ones. Take note. What makes you irritable and angry today can teach you a lot about yourself, and you may find that whatever's bothering you is not really that big a deal. Close self-observation may show you that you're protecting your ego, not some "all-important" idea or concept.

SUN CONJUNCT JUPITER

How this transit affects your relationships depends on your basic attitudes toward others. The way you normally behave toward others will be accentuated.

SUN SEXTILE JUPITER

Your positive attitude toward everything and everyone today makes it a good time to be with friends or groups of any kind.

SUN SQUARE JUPITER

Today you should actively cultivate an attitude of compassion when dealing with others. Be willing to work with people as equals and to look at their points of view, and you should be able to successfully field any confrontations that may occur.

SUN OPPOSITION JUPITER

You'll feel so optimistic and self-confident today, you may go overboard into haughtiness. This is obviously detrimental to all relationships, but with a little restraint, this can be a good day for you, possibly giving you courage to accomplish or say things you'd normally shy away from.

SUN SQUARE SATURN

You're impatient with any restrictions today, and consequently, contacts with persons in authority may not be too smooth—unless you can realize that it's not necessarily they who are restricting you. You create your own reality. Double-check the accuracy of your preconceived notions of what you're required to do, fire up your self-discipline, and the path will soon straighten out before you.

SUN OPPOSITION SATURN

You may feel isolated, cut off from people, unable or unwilling to make the effort to communicate. To avert the depression that could engulf you, however, do force yourself to do something rewarding or constructive, and try to reach a balance in your relationships between your obligations and your own needs. This can best be accomplished by being completely frank and insisting that others do the same.

SUN CONJUNCT URANUS

You may be in a rebellious mood today, which could, quite naturally, cause problems with others—especially those in authority. You'll have to determine the fine line between acting with all-out muleheaded rashness and taking a truly self-liberating stand.

SUN SQUARE URANUS

The freedom-loving energy of Uranus makes you or those about you very impatient with restriction—yours or theirs. This could lead to disputes. Go ahead, allow yourself (or others) to break the old routine, or honestly discuss what needs changing about it and do it. You could discover something very worthwhile.

SUN OPPOSITION URANUS

Relationships—old or new, personal or business—may take an unexpected turn today. Arguments may or may not result, but in any case, you should take note of what is surprising or upsetting to you. It's trying to get you to pay attention to real needs or desires that you may have kept suppressed for a while. Simply note what it is; you can handle the practical aspects of it later.

SUN CONJUNCT NEPTUNE

Either you're so in tune with others that you're willing to help them without any thought for yourself, or you just can't handle even everyday cares and want to escape. It's hard to say which way you'll go. If you do wish to withdraw, don't turn to drugs or alcohol; you're apt to react badly at this time. Meditation would be a good substitute.

SUN SQUARE NEPTUNE

Your desire to avoid confrontations today may tempt you to take underhanded actions of some sort. They'd be likely to backfire, though; you're just not up for any really good deviousness today. But beware even if you don't fall into this trap—it may be that others try to play the same game with you.

SUN OPPOSITION NEPTUNE

Your assertiveness index is nil now, and postponing confrontations wherever possible would be your best bet. On the other hand, you may be more aware and in tune with others at this time and able to come to a profound understanding with someone. Don't make any final commitments under this transit, though.

SUN CONJUNCT PLUTO

Your encounters are apt to be intense today, for Pluto goes beneath the surface and agitates for basic change in all things. Avoid people of unsavory character.

SUN SQUARE PLUTO

Authority figures may challenge you to justify yourself and your actions. If you can't do so, recognize that you need to make some changes in your attitudes or methods or whatever. The point is, anything that cannot withstand testing now needs overhauling. This is a good time to make changes.

SUN TRINE PLUTO

If you have no ulterior motives in mind, this is a good day to impress others; you'll do so successfully.

SUN OPPOSITION PLUTO

You may be having close encounters of a difficult kind, but it will be very helpful for you to clear the air and get whatever may be the problem out into the open. These run-ins can give you insight into deeper areas of yourself. You may have to defend your position from persons in authority. Avoid being overbearing in these instances—you'll lose.

SUN SEXTILE MIDHEAVEN

You'll get along well with your superiors at work and with your family. You feel secure, calm, and confident, which benefits all your relationships.

SUN SQUARE MIDHEAVEN

You or your ambitions may come into conflict with others if you become so engrossed in your own pursuits you neglect to consider other points of view. Try to maintain your objectivity should conflicts arise, and be prepared to change your position if it turns out you are wrong.

SUN OPPOSITION MIDHEAVEN

This is a day to be with your family or close friends and also to find time for solitary introspection. You must attend to your own inner needs today. Do not ignore this. Opposition or defeat will greet you if you attempt to conquer outer worlds during this transit.

SUN CONJUNCT ASCENDANT

You feel full of vigor and vim and want to be 100 percent your self. You're in no mood for gamesmanship, and this may lead to conflict. But there is no law that says you can't be tactful and still be true to yourself—in which case you'll sail through any encounter.

SUN SEXTILE ASCENDANT

You're feeling sociable today and want to be in the limelight—at least a little. You want recognition from those close to you. But don't be afraid to let people know you need them, too.

SUN TRINE ASCENDANT

You're in a mood to have fun no matter what you're doing, and your relaxed attitude allows you to easily make a good impression on others.

MOON IN FOURTH HOUSE

Now is a good time to observe and analyze your relationships with your family. See if you're acting automatically out of habits no longer applicable. Especially notice whether you're being overly possessive and thus, perhaps, driving someone further from you.

MOON IN FIFTH HOUSE

Your emotions are intensified now, and this will be reflected in all your relationships, especially with women. Children may figure more in your life now, too, as your nurturing nature is aroused. Guard against being overpossessive or overprotective, though.

MOON IN SEVENTH HOUSE

Relationships and conflicts within relationships, especially with women, are apt to take a more emotional tone than usual. Be aware of what you're doing and saying, and you'll be able to learn things about yourself that you aren't generally aware of.

MOON IN TENTH HOUSE

Though you're more intuitively aware of the emotional needs of others, this is not a good time to turn a professional relationship into a more personal one. On another level, public emotional displays are a possibility.

MOON IN ELEVENTH HOUSE

Emotional contact or support between friends will be important to you, especially with female friends. Avoid acting jealous or over-possessive, though.

MOON CONJUNCT SUN

All goes well today, especially with the opposite sex. This goes for groups, too, so it's a good time for conferences. Your feeling of inner peace and security is reflected in all your relationships.

MOON SEXTILE SUN

You'll get along well with others today, especially with the opposite sex. A good time for making friends and really getting in contact with others emotionally. Benefits will come to you from others—perhaps from unexpected directions, but probably through friends.

MOON SQUARE SUN

If there are any problems in a relationship that you've been ignoring, they're likely to emerge now, especially in a relationship with the opposite sex. On top of which every little thing is likely to irritate you. Pay attention and take care of difficulties as they crop up.

MOON TRINE SUN

You're feeling good within yourself, and therefore get along well with one and all today.

MOON OPPOSITION SUN

You feel pulled in many directions at once. This naturally creates disharmony within you, and inner disharmony can cause difficulties in relationships. There may be problems with the opposite sex. A relationship that begins now is not too likely to last long.

MOON CONJUNCT MOON

You're more emotionally aware now, and women may be prominent in your life at this time. Usually, you'd just as soon be alone, however, and you'll seek familiar grounds for their emotional support. Your emotional intensity may cause a problem should a confrontation arise; try to hang on to your objectivity.

MOON SEXTILE MOON

Your feelings run deep at this time, and you want to be with close relatives and friends. You need emotionally intimate encounters with others today and may enjoy the company of women more than men. Conversely, however, if you have to make a public appearance, you'll do well at it.

MOON SQUARE MOON

This is not a totally harmonious period, especially in personal relationships. Try to avoid conflicts with friends and family, mainly because your perspective is all out of whack and you won't be able to get to the real root of the problems. If you need to agitate a group into action, however, this is a good time.

MOON TRINE MOON

All goes smoothly now, and you want to be surrounded by close friends and family. This is an excellent time to recharge yourself emotionally or to offer moral support to others. If you have children, they'll be especially significant to you in some way now.

MOON OPPOSITION MOON

There may be emotional conflicts during this time, which, if you can rise above your emotions and observe how they affect others, can lead to personal growth. This won't be easy now, however, as your objectivity is way below par.

MOON CONJUNCT MERCURY

Your moods will have the upper hand for a while. This is a good time to talk about your feelings with someone, especially with a woman. Don't let pleasantries or small talk keep you from the more important issues.

MOON SEXTILE MERCURY

A good time to seek a sympathetic listener for a problem if you have one. You'll be able to make others feel better, too. This is a time when you want to be with people and discuss all kinds of topics.

MOON SQUARE MERCURY

Your moods and emotions are changing almost by the minute,

and you need to express them. Go ahead and do so, just be prepared to let others do it, too. Openly acknowledge that your views and emotions are undergoing change and readjustment just now.

MOON TRINE MERCURY

You'll relate easily with others today and may be of emotional assistance to someone. You're able to equally tap both your feelings and your rationality. Talking with women will be especially beneficial today. Take the time to express your feelings to those you love.

MOON CONJUNCT VENUS

This transit favors socializing of any sort. You may also be romantically inclined with a spouse or lover.

MOON SEXTILE VENUS

You feel good and cheerful and in harmony with the world—a good time for entertaining in your home, or for going out to have a good time. It's also excellent for working things out if you've been having problems with someone close. Fight a tendency toward passivity and self-indulgence.

MOON SQUARE VENUS

You feel pleasant and sociable and very loving. Just don't pull any overpossessiveness tricks, and all will go extremely well.

MOON TRINE VENUS

Relationships are favorably influenced by this brief transit, and everyone you meet or converse with feels your glow of warmth and friendship.

MOON OPPOSITION VENUS

You want to be emotionally in touch with others today, and you don't much care whether the contact is positive or negative. It's likely to be pleasant, but in either case, you'll have the opportunity to learn about yourself.

MOON CONJUNCT MARS

You'll probably feel irritable and impatient. You'll tend to be hasty and impulsive, too, and you may attract others who are in a similar mood. The best advice under the circumstances is to try to keep your cool and stay in control of yourself, or wait for this transit to pass. Fortunately, it's brief.

MOON SEXTILE MARS

Persons who are strong and courageous will be attracted to you; you'll be attracted to them, too. In all relationships, you'll easily express your feelings.

MOON SQUARE MARS

You're feeling irritable, emotional, and impulsive, all of which could lead to run-ins with others. But you may try to skirt the real issues. Be aware of this and home in on the tough problems. Depending on your temperament, you may feel that others are going out of their way to attack you, or you may be the one lashing out. The trick in the latter case is to learn to express your emotions or hostilities reasonably, without coming across like King Kong on the Empire State Building.

MOON OPPOSITION MARS

You're in an irritable mood and may have problems at home, especially with women. Wait until this transit has passed to try to settle any problems, but then do so promptly.

MOON CONJUNCT JUPITER

You feel warm and pleasant toward everyone, and they'll in turn feel amiable toward you. Contact with women is favored with this transit, as are dealings with groups.

MOON SEXTILE JUPITER

This is a good day to be with old friends, but new ones will be welcome, too. Your warmth and genuine concern for others will come across and be reciprocated. Being around women and groups will be beneficial today.

MOON SQUARE JUPITER

Generally, you'll feel good and will be well-intentioned toward those around you. If others should start acting slightly offended or unresponsive, though, it may be that you are coming across as conceited, condescending, and know-it-all. If so, take a good look at your attitudes today. Otherwise, all should be pleasant.

MOON TRINE JUPITER

Because you feel good about yourself and are warmly affectionate toward others, people react to you in the same way. As always, you get back what you give out.

MOON OPPOSITION JUPITER

You want to be generous and giving toward people, but if they start demanding that you do so, you'll resist stubbornly. If others seek to limit or curtail your personal freedom, you'll rebel also. Arguments could ensue. Negative as all this sounds, things aren't usually all that bad under this transit as long as you're aware of what's going on.

MOON CONJUNCT SATURN

You feel that no one is offering you emotional support, whether this is true or not. Domestic problems may result. Relating to women could be tough. Don't decide questions of an emotional nature now. Really, things are looking worse than they are.

MOON SEXTILE SATURN

Mainly you want to be alone, but if you do seek company, it will be with serious conversation in mind. You're calm and reflective, sober though not depressed.

MOON SQUARE SATURN

You're having trouble relating for a while, especially with women. There may be separations, but probably not unless there is also a supporting long-range transit in effect. Don't make any drastic decisions regarding relationships at this time. You're feeling depressed and lonely, but this transit will soon pass. Honest.

MOON OPPOSITION SATURN

You feel lonely, perhaps depressed, and cut off from others, yet you seem to repel people even when they do try to help. Don't make any decisions regarding relationships during this transit; wait for it to pass, which it will swiftly do.

MOON CONJUNCT URANUS

You're feeling restless, possibly rash, impatient with the ordinary, and ache to do something "wild." If someone—heaven forbid—tries to prevent you from doing so, you may explode, creating a dispute.

This transit passes in a few hours, so just be careful not to do something you'll soon wish you hadn't.

MOON SEXTILE URANUS

You're restless and want some excitement, possibly to the point of jarring or shocking others somehow, just to get a rise out of them. You may meet a new friend, or an old one may reappear. Exciting news or opportunity may come through a friend now.

MOON SQUARE URANUS

You're feeling so doggone independent you're likely to rebel against anything anyone says just on general principles. You don't want to tolerate anyone's demands, especially emotional ones, or even perform your regular duties. Naturally all this can lead to disputes and disruptions in relationships. Beware of forming snap judgments. This is a brief transit, and conclusions reached now may seem ridiculous all too soon.

MOON TRINE URANUS

You're seeking new and different people, new and different experiences, new and different environments. With groups you may become the leader in order to push through new policies and ideas. You may make changes in your home life, which, though they may surprise your friends and family, will probably soon become the new routine.

MOON OPPOSITION URANUS

Relationships can be difficult under this transit, replete with arguments and emotional disruptions. Your conclusions are apt to be faulty, so it would be best not to make any permanent decisions about relationships now.

MOON CONJUNCT NEPTUNE

Your relationships under this transit are apt to be tricky—unclear, fuzzy, subject to misconceptions and misinterpretations. Self-delusion is a possibility. Yet, you're very sensitive to others and may tune in to their moods easily. Try to avoid negative persons for that reason.

MOON SEXTILE NEPTUNE

You're very perceptive of others' moods now. For this reason, avoid being around negative people, because you'll end up feeling lousy yourself. You may try to help others today, alone or through a group. This is a good day to be with a good friend to share insights or daydreams.

MOON TRINE NEPTUNE

You have great empathy toward others now and want to help them if you can. Try to avoid negative persons; you'll pick up their mood and feel bad yourself.

MOON OPPOSITION NEPTUNE

You aren't perceiving reality as it actually is now, and you're likely to be moody and confused. There may be misunderstandings in relationships. Don't conclude that others are picking on you until this transit passes and you can evaluate the situation more clearly.

MOON CONJUNCT PLUTO

Strong feelings, dredged up from deep within, are coming to the fore. This is a good time for self-analysis or professional therapy. Relationships with women are likely to be heavy, probably deep, possibly wonderful. Guard against the traps of jealousy and over-possessiveness.

MOON SEXTILE PLUTO

You want to get to the deep-seated feelings of any relationship. And, they are very likely to be bobbing to the surface. This is usually a good thing, as hidden or repressed emotions can ultimately be detrimental.

MOON SQUARE PLUTO

Intense emotion either from yourself or attracted from another may develop into power struggles or emotional maneuvering by one of you. The results may be neither pretty nor pleasant. On the other hand, such an encounter may provide the impetus for self-analysis, which, though you may not enjoy it, will be useful.

MOON TRINE PLUTO

You're reacting to others with great emotional intensity, and while this may exhaust you by the time this transit is over, it can also be enriching and enlightening.

MOON OPPOSITION PLUTO

Deep, hidden emotions are coming to the fore now, and encounters, especially with those close to you, may lead to conflicts. After all has settled down, you may be able to learn a great deal about the both of you by reviewing what has happened. Hold off making important emotional decisions until this transit is over.

MOON CONJUNCT MIDHEAVEN

You are emotionally sensitive to the moods of others now, and you're either going to be able to communicate well with them (especially groups), or you're going to be bothered by all this emotional input and will want to withdraw.

MOON TRINE MIDHEAVEN

You could work well with people today, persuading them to your point of view. But you may simply want to be alone or with your family and close friends for a calm, soothing time.

MOON CONJUNCT ASCENDANT

Encounters with others can be deep and enriching if you're normally at ease with your emotions, or they can be inadequate, possibly inappropriate, if you simply react on a superficial, unemotional level from habit. Women, especially, may play an important role in your life at this time.

MOON SEXTILE ASCENDANT

You want to be with others now, especially if they're close friends and relatives, and particularly if they're women. You're unusually sympathetic and sensitive. You'll do well in groups or with the public.

MOON SQUARE ASCENDANT

You're moody and will be either very sympathetic with others or totally concerned with yourself. In the latter case, it's best to go ahead and be with others, making yourself interact if necessary.

MOON TRINE ASCENDANT

Any sort of relationship is favored, but those with women may very well be beneficial to you in some way. You're more emotionally tuned-in than usual. You may be able to understand more about your relationships if you take time to observe them.

MOON OPPOSITION ASCENDANT

You're functioning on a more emotional level than usual and find it easier to express your emotions to those you're close to. And it will be important to you that your relationships give, as well as elicit, emotional support.

MERCURY IN FOURTH HOUSE

Family matters concern you now, and, indeed, this is a good time to reevaluate your domestic situation and make any necessary changes. You'll be able to communicate easily and freely now with family members to work out any problems.

MERCURY IN ELEVENTH HOUSE

This is a good time to scrutinize your ideals and goals in relationship to the groups you belong to, whether an official club, social class, or generation. Are you thinking for yourself or just parroting the views of the majority? You may meet younger persons who bring fresh ideas to your attention.

MERCURY TRINE MOON

This is an excellent time to improve relationships, especially with women, as you're emotionally sensitive and tuned-in. But everyone will enjoy talking with you today. They can tell you're on their wavelength and sincere.

MERCURY CONJUNCT MERCURY

You'll find yourself in the midst of communicating much more than usual. And if you consciously try, you can enhance almost any relationship by making the communications useful and significant.

MERCURY CONJUNCT VENUS

You'll be able to communicate your feelings readily in any relationship, and thus can come to a better understanding of one another.

MERCURY SEXTILE VENUS

You'll be able to express your feelings of love or friendship to someone, even if this is usually difficult for you.

MERCURY SQUARE VENUS

This is a good time to discuss your relationship with a loved one to be sure you both really understand each other's positions or ideas. You may find areas of disagreement you weren't aware of. Approach these with a willingness to compromise and all should go well.

MERCURY TRINE VENUS

You're congenial with everyone today and don't want to get into any hassles. Patch up any differences now. Tell friends and loved ones how you feel about them; it will be easier than usual. A good day to socialize and have a good time.

MERCURY OPPOSITION VENUS

Your relationships are likely to be pleasant today. You're willing to compromise in order to deter hassles, but don't let this get out of hand. You'll be sorry later if you've deferred to another on something that really matters to you. Tell someone you love him or her.

MERCURY CONJUNCT SATURN

Someone may leave you now, and this may affect you for quite a while. However, you should try to be aware of the positive in others as well as within yourself today. Things really aren't as bad as they seem.

MERCURY SQUARE SATURN

You're not exactly a happy little ray of sunshine and example of positive thinking today. You may feel lonely, whether it is justified or not. No matter what course of action you may consider today in regard to relationships, remember that you're seeing only the negative aspects now, which are only a part of the picture.

MERCURY TRINE SATURN

You're probably not feeling all that outgoing today and easily lose patience with small talk. This is a good time to look for the company and advice of someone older or more experienced than you. You're in the mood for some serious, practical discussion.

MERCURY OPPOSITION SATURN

Though you may entertain thoughts of breaking up a relationship, this is not a good time to go through with it. Your outlook is too negative at the moment. If you need to talk things over, do so with someone you respect as an authority.

MERCURY CONJUNCT NEPTUNE

Unclear thinking and communication could interfere with relationships. In a verbal confrontation, you may be tempted to lie your way out. This is not a good idea. Or, someone else may be dishonest with you. Don't sign anything or make decisions about relationships today.

MERCURY TRINE PLUTO

You may meet someone whose perceptions will be important to you. Conversations will be earnest and weighty today.

MERCURY OPPOSITION PLUTO

Now is the time to get to the heart of a problem, if you're having one with anyone. Don't try to be subtle. Get everything out in the open if you can. Also, be aware that someone may engage you in a power struggle or try to persuade you to do something you'd really rather not. Or you may be tempted to do the same. It's best not to.

MERCURY OPPOSITION MIDHEAVEN

The timing is right for making those family plans now—what to do for the weekend or vacation, who's to do what, when to paint the house or get Timmy those braces, and so on.

MERCURY OPPOSITION ASCENDANT

This is a good time for communicating with your spouse or partner, expressing something that has perhaps been festering below the surface—or for them to do the same with you. Also, you may have an unusual contact with a younger person. Now is a good time, too, for seeking any kind of expert or professional advice.

VENUS IN THIRD HOUSE

This is an excellent time to communicate your feelings of love to all around you, whom you probably take for granted most of the time.

VENUS IN FOURTH HOUSE

This time can be beneficially and enjoyably spent at home with your family or very close friends.

VENUS IN FIFTH HOUSE

This is an excellent time to have fun with your family or close friends. You'll get along especially well with children now. You aren't going to feel like working much anyway, so you might as well get out and have some fun if you can swing it.

VENUS IN SIXTH HOUSE

The practical workings of any relationship concern you now. This is a good time to talk out and work out any misunderstandings.

VENUS IN SEVENTH HOUSE

All relationships are highly favored now. This is a good time to settle disputes with anyone, make your position clear, or stand up for your rights.

VENUS IN NINTH HOUSE

People who are different from those you usually meet are attractive to you now, and you may learn a great deal from them.

VENUS IN ELEVENTH HOUSE

All relationships with groups, friends, acquaintances, or business associates will be very amicable now. This is a good time to negotiate or socialize.

VENUS IN TWELFTH HOUSE

If you can't be truly and wholeheartedly selfless now, as in helping, serving, or taking care of someone under this transit, don't do anything.

VENUS CONJUNCT SUN

This is a good day for love, for entertaining, or for just plain having a good time. You'll easily attract others to you.

VENUS SEXTILE SUN

You're feeling very companionable and will enjoy your friends. They'll enjoy being with you, too. This is a good time to ask for a favor, impress others, work with a group, and have a good time. You may make a new friend today, too.

VENUS SQUARE SUN

You're feeling sociable and nonassertive. This is OK, as long as you don't allow your desire for peace-at-all-costs to let you give in on something you'll later wish you hadn't.

VENUS TRINE SUN

You feel like being with your friends and having a good time. Have a party—it'll be great!

VENUS OPPOSITION SUN

This is a good day to go out and have fun with your friends or amorous attachment. Just try not to overindulge in food and drink or make any definite commitments. This is not a favorable time for relationships that demand prudence and discretion.

VENUS CONJUNCT MOON

Unless overruled by other transits, you're feeling very loving and affectionate—romantic, as opposed to sexy. You want to be with those you share something with, perhaps to reminisce. Your family will be important to you and you want to be with them, especially your mother.

VENUS SEXTILE MOON

You'll be very congenial with one and all today, especially with friends and relatives. Relationships with female relatives, especially your mother, will be good, possibly also advantageous. Fortunate breaks may come through female friends. Whether entertaining at home or dealing with the public for some reason, you'll do very well and enjoy yourself.

VENUS SQUARE MOON

Your "mothering" instincts may be triggered by this transit, and you're likely to manifest them either as warm and loving support in a close relationship or as overprotectiveness or jealousy. The former is obviously preferred. Problems with women in general or your mother in particular may occur if there are other hard aspects in effect at this time.

VENUS TRINE MOON

A banner day for relationships of all sorts. You're sincere and friendly, and others will reciprocate. Contact with women is especially satisfying. A great time to have a small party in your home or to spend a quiet evening with someone you love.

VENUS OPPOSITION MOON

You're feeling affectionate, protective, and giving. All relationships, particularly with women, will be enhanced. In a sexual relationship, remember that discretion is not always to be thrown to the wind and that this is not a good time to make a permanent commitment.

VENUS CONJUNCT MERCURY

Today even the most bashful will find it easier to express love and affection. Also, if you have to make a good impression on someone, now is a good time.

VENUS SEXTILE MERCURY

Your mood is lighthearted and sociable. Get together with friends and loved ones and have a good time. Let them know your feelings about them. It's also an auspicious time to discuss difficulties between you and another or to make a good impression on someone.

VENUS SQUARE MERCURY

Relationships should be amicable and pleasant unless there is a contradictory transit also in effect. Wait until another time to work out any problems, in any case.

VENUS TRINE MERCURY

Communications come easily to you today. It's a good time to tell someone how you feel or to work out difficulties in a relationship. You'll be able to work well with groups, too, especially if you're the leader.

VENUS OPPOSITION MERCURY

A good day to reasonably and coolly work out any problems in a relationship. Be careful with flip or casual remarks, though; someone could think you really mean them.

VENUS CONJUNCT VENUS

This is a day to get out and meet new or old friends—to enjoy one another's company, to have a party—to socialize in general. You'll make a good impression on everyone. If you need assistance or cooperation from others, ask for it today. Tell someone your feelings about them, too. You may be pleasantly surprised at the result.

VENUS SEXTILE VENUS

This transit bodes well both for new romance and for new business or personal contacts that may be helpful to you later.

VENUS SQUARE VENUS

Can you stick up for your convictions instead of compromising your individuality in a relationship? This is the area that is sometimes tested at this time. Even so, this is usually a pleasant transit.

VENUS TRINE VENUS

You'll be in a romantic mood in a love relationship, and, indeed, all relationships will be very congenial. You may even attract people who will be beneficial to you in the future.

VENUS OPPOSITION VENUS

This should be a pleasant, peaceful time. However, if you do have a disagreement with someone, beware of compromising too easily today and giving away the world—you'll need some of it tomorrow.

VENUS CONJUNCT MARS

Your sexuality is aroused, but even if you lack a sexual partner, you'll enjoy being with other people. A new love relationship may begin, but this transit by itself is not enough to make it last. It will be a good one while it does, though.

VENUS SEXTILE MARS

This is a good time to party or to be with others to have fun in one way or another. You find it easy to just be yourself, and your vitality is attractive to one and all, including members of the opposite sex.

VENUS SQUARE MARS

Your sexual energies are aroused; though without mutual consideration and possibly compromise, there can be discord in a love relationship. A relationship that begins under this transit may be short because of its basis in physical attraction only.

VENUS TRINE MARS

You're able to relate in a mature manner today, retaining your individuality in a relationship without being either overbearing or submissive.

VENUS CONJUNCT JUPITER

This is a banner day for any kind of relationship. You'll enjoy being with people and they'll enjoy being with you. You may meet a new friend or lover.

VENUS SEXTILE JUPITER

You're feeling kind, lighthearted, and sociable. This is a good time to enjoy being with friends. If a new relationship begins under this transit, it will elicit your best and highest character.

VENUS SQUARE JUPITER

This is a good time for socializing or doing anything you like to do. Others will relish your company, too, unless you start acting as if you can do no wrong.

VENUS TRINE JUPITER

This is a prime time for socializing, and you may meet someone who will be helpful to you in the future.

VENUS OPPOSITION JUPITER

A very pleasant day for relationships. Try to look for the deeper, inner qualities of others, though, and do not let the superficial unduly impress you.

VENUS SEXTILE SATURN

Saturn brings duty to your attention, and you'll be aware of the duties required in a healthy relationship. Fulfilling them will bring you pleasure. This would be a good time to discuss each other's views and expectations. You may feel drawn to older persons and wish to seek their advice.

VENUS SQUARE SATURN

You're apt to be a little reserved and calculating in your relationships today. You're assessing them to better understand yourself and your specific give and take within them. You may feel withdrawn and depressed. Be aware, though, that under this transit things usually appear worse than they actually are.

VENUS TRINE SATURN

Realism overcomes romanticism under this transit, and you can dispassionately thrash out difficulties if necessary. A relationship initiated now will probably be practical, sober, and stable. There may be substantial differences between the partners, but this won't hinder the alliance at all.

VENUS OPPOSITION SATURN

Today you may not feel like responding to others as usual. If so, don't try to fake it; just wait for this transit to pass—it will do so shortly. We all have days when we're not at our brightest.

VENUS SEXTILE URANUS

In your search for the new and exciting, you may very well meet new friends or a new lover. Unfortunately, these relationships, though probably stimulating, aren't likely to endure. If one does, though, it may radically change your life. There will have to be unusual freedom granted in the relationship, and this in itself may be a new experience for you.

VENUS TRINE URANUS

You'll run into people today unlike those you usually associate with. A relationship that begins now will probably be exciting and stimulating, but brief. (Alas.)

VENUS OPPOSITION URANUS

There may be unexpected events in relationships now, and whether this is unsettling to you probably depends on your inherent flexibility. (Uranus just loves to stamp out rigidity and routine.) If a relationship begins today, it's apt to be unusual but short-lived—unless you're the type that thrives on this sort of relationship as a rule.

VENUS CONJUNCT NEPTUNE

This transit brings out your ability for unconditional loving, and you're willing to give your all for a friend or loved one. You may tend to idealize, though, so it's not a good time to make permanent commitments.

VENUS SEXTILE NEPTUNE

If you can find your way out of your lovely daydreams long enough today, you'll be able to feel at one with those you love. You'll tune in to their needs and fulfill them without losing yourself or your own happiness in the process.

VENUS SQUARE NEPTUNE

You'll tend to see everyone through a mist of romantic idealism today and may be disappointed when they can't live up to it. This is usually not harmful in moderation; however, it would help if you at least tried to stay grounded in reality. Relationships that begin today may be based totally on romantic fantasy. Commitments to them should not be made hastily.

VENUS OPPOSITION NEPTUNE

Be careful. You may over-idealize someone and then be disappointed when they turn out to be only human. Also avoid the ego trap of playing the martyr. A new romantic relationship that begins now may turn out to be wonderful, but keep your eyes open and don't commit right away. There is the possibility that you'll be deceived.

VENUS SQUARE PLUTO

Relationships of any kind are apt to be emotionally intense at this time, though not necessarily unpleasant. Allow growth and change to happen.

VENUS CONJUNCT MIDHEAVEN

This is a great day for socializing in any way. All your relationships will go well. Get out and have some fun with your friends. You may even fall in love.

VENUS SEXTILE MIDHEAVEN

You get along well with one and all today—you're unwilling to disturb the peace for any reason and are more forgiving of others. Plus, you really want to help others if you can. This is a day to be with people.

VENUS TRINE MIDHEAVEN

You want to express your deep feelings of love to those you care about, and this is a good time to do so. It's also good for working out any problems you may be having with someone.

VENUS OPPOSITION MIDHEAVEN

This is an excellent time to entertain in your home, as you'll be able to make your friends feel welcome and loved. You may even meet someone new to return that love.

VENUS CONJUNCT ASCENDANT

All relationships are favored today. You'll feel good, sociable, and affectionate, and this will be reflected in those around you. Make plans for entertaining your friends. Perhaps you'll meet someone new to love. It's also a good time for resolving any problems in a relationship.

VENUS SEXTILE ASCENDANT

You're in a lighthearted mood, feeling just plain good, and want to spread it around. You'll enjoy being with people and they with you. You won't even feel as shy as usual and will make good impressions. You may meet someone who will become your lover.

VENUS SQUARE ASCENDANT

All goes well in relationships today. You'll enjoy being with your friends and having fun with them, and you may meet someone who'll become important to you.

VENUS TRINE ASCENDANT

This is a good time for socializing. You'll have a very good time but may tend to overindulge if you don't watch yourself. Be with friends and loved ones as much as you can.

VENUS OPPOSITION ASCENDANT

Relationships, especially of the twosome variety, are successful today. If there are existing difficulties, this is a good time to resolve them. Take a moment to be aware of how much you mean to each other. You'll favorably impress anyone you meet, and all else being equal, you may attract a new love.

MARS IN FIRST HOUSE

It would probably be best for you to be alone as much as possible today. Though you're not in a belligerent mood, your ego energies are so high you're not particularly willing to compromise enough even to be moderately civil.

MARS IN THIRD HOUSE

You're apt to be in a contentious mood, and there may be conflicts. If you can productively harness this energy and avoid conflict, however, you can accomplish a great deal with others.

MARS IN FOURTH HOUSE

There may be family disputes or quarrels—particularly with parents if you're living with them—if you don't consciously try to ameliorate the tensions. Pay attention. Subconscious drives or motives may be at the heart of any problems that arise.

MARS IN FIFTH HOUSE

Sexual energies are strongly aroused in love relationships now. In addition, there may be difficulties with your children, largely stemming from an overabundance of energy—yours and theirs. Keep the both of you physically active to best use this transit. Sports or vigorous games would be good.

MARS IN SEVENTH HOUSE

There is a need for cooperation between close partners, but due to ego energies, the tendency is toward conflict now. This can be avoided, and much can be accomplished, by making a concerted effort to employ the true spirit of compromise and cooperation. Should there be real problems, though, go for it—you may just clear them up now.

MARS IN TENTH HOUSE

Unless you can convince others that your interests are mutual and remember their needs, too, they are likely to feel threatened and oppose you at this time.

MARS IN ELEVENTH HOUSE

This is not the time to be a lone wolf but to work with others. This doesn't mean that you have to take a back seat, but that your energy would best be used and your ends best served by working through or with groups at this time. Otherwise, ego conflicts are likely.

MARS CONJUNCT SUN

Your high ego energies may land you in conflict situations today if you're not careful, especially with those in authority. You don't have to be a pansy, but don't forget that others have egos, too. Physical activity will help dissipate some of your excessive energy today.

MARS SEXTILE SUN

Your self-confidence, as well as your physical energy, is up today. You'll be able to work well with groups without creating ego conflict.

MARS SQUARE SUN

You may find yourself in ego-driven personality conflicts today if you're not careful. Yes, defend your positions, but do so with a spirit of willingness to compromise for the best results. Otherwise, in about six months even more difficult relationship problems may arise.

MARS OPPOSITION SUN

This can be an "either-or" transit. If you've been considerate of others and their ideas and have included them in your projects, all may go pretty well now. If not, opposition and conflict may occur. You may find yourself being more irritable with others than usual. In any event, making an effort to get along smoothly now is your best route.

MARS CONJUNCT MOON

You're likely to feel angry with others today, especially family and close friends, without realizing why. It may very well have to do with anger you've suppressed in the past which is being triggered by some "trivial" incident or comment now. You'll also be disinclined to back down on anything (which *can* be helpful at times) and will take everything as a direct ego challenge (which is seldom beneficial).

MARS SEXTILE MOON

Your emotions are intensified now, and you want to be with people who appeal to or arouse these emotioms. Sexual relationships will also be intensified, and you may be looking for just such an encounter.

MARS SQUARE MOON

You're feeling irritable, moody, irrational, and downright hard to get along with. You may want to revert to childish behavior, but you can control and prevent such irrational, unproductive actions. Hidden tensions with family members may surface. Be aware, however, that these tensions or conflicts may not be what they seem; you may have to dig for the real root of the problem.

MARS TRINE MOON

Your emotions are strong and at the forefront of your life now.

You want to be with people you can relate to on this level. All of your encounters now will be emotionally intense and can be very satisfying.

MARS OPPOSITION MOON

This is a time when you can come to greater self-understanding through your close relationships. This may or may not be pleasant—there may be conflict, but emotional experiences can be enlightening if you can remain self-aware and observant of what is going on.

MARS CONJUNCT MERCURY

You're likely to be cranky today and will tend to take everything that's said personally. This, naturally, could lead to conflicts. If, however, you can turn those energies to something that keeps your mind occupied and out of disputes, you'll be able to accomplish a great deal or make a good impression on anyone you need to.

MARS SEXTILE MERCURY

Your vigor, enthusiasm, and positive attitude now make it easy for you to communicate or work with people, and you can make a good impression on them.

MARS SQUARE MERCURY

You'll tend to be touchy and irritable today and will want to take everything as a threat to your ego, whether it is or not. If a matter is truly important, this is a good day for a dispute because you'll be able to stand up for yourself well. Otherwise, you're creating antagonism for nothing. Stop and look at yourself. You may be inciting others with your attitude, if not your words.

MARS OPPOSITION MERCURY

Disputes are likely to occur today because you or someone else is so darn touchy. Don't try to get altercations totally resolved now, though; you'll both be too stubborn to give even a little.

MARS SEXTILE VENUS

Sexual energy is aroused now, and if not in a current relationship, you'll probably be looking for one. This is a good time to get out and have some fun with your friends. You'll have a good time. Don't stay in and talk to the cat under this transit if you can help it.

MARS OPPOSITION MARS

You're very likely to encounter opposition from others now, and it may be partly or even largely your own fault. Your ego level is high, and you may be asserting yourself in a manner that riles others. Deal with any problems openly as they occur.

MARS OPPOSITION JUPITER

You'll have to remain aware of yourself and what you're doing, or you're liable to come across to others as bossy and high-handed. Of course, no one likes this, and problems may occur now or later.

MARS CONJUNCT SATURN

You may run into all kinds of frustrating irritations today, and will be doubly frustrated because you'll have little chance to vent any resulting anger. If this should occur, hard work requiring concentration will be a help, if it doesn't involve sharp tools. Be as patient as you can; this, too, shall pass.

MARS CONJUNCT URANUS

You want to be free of all restraints, and you feel downright rebellious. This can lead to difficulties with others, especially authority figures. You want to assert yourself and will probably do so, come hail or high water, so do it by starting new projects instead of fights.

MARS SEXTILE URANUS

You're restless and looking for newness and excitement. You may make new friends or seek out current ones who are stimulating and unpredictable.

MARS SQUARE URANUS

Feelings of restlessness and rebellion may propel you to impulsively lash out at others, especially anyone you feel is trying to restrict you in some way. Unfortunately, they are usually the people closest to you, whom you value the most.

MARS OPPOSITION URANUS

You're likely to be irritable and impatient with anything or anyone you feel is limiting your progress, and you may suddenly lash out. Or someone may explode at you. Alternatively, you may be making necessary changes for your own growth that others will resist. How you react to them will have repercussions about six months from now. You're trying to liberate yourself in some way; don't give up.

MARS SEXTILE NEPTUNE

You're well tuned in to the needs of others, and you want to help them if you can. You may find yourself working with groups toward this end.

MARS OPPOSITION NEPTUNE

Others may be depressing to you today, and someone may try to deceive you. Make an effort to see things and people as they really are, not as you'd prefer. Also try to make all communications extremely clear and precise. Don't attempt deception yourself. The best way to use this transit is to work in a truly selfless way for others.

MARS CONJUNCT PLUTO

There can be strong ego clashes, even ruthless confrontations, under this transit. You both want power. This energy can be used constructively, however, if you make an effort and if you're aware of what's going on. Make it abundantly clear to others that your objectives are not antagonistic to theirs.

MARS OPPOSITION PLUTO

Hassles and struggles for power are a distinct possibility. Avoid deviousness (it won't work now), and if others try it on you, seek help. Don't make others angry at you; they could turn violent. Stay away from dangerous areas and situations.

MARS SEXTILE MIDHEAVEN

Others will not see you as a threat today; you come across as self-confident and assured. You can obtain all sorts of assistance from others more easily than usual.

MARS SQUARE MIDHEAVEN

You're feeling self-assertive today, which, of course, could be either helpful or detrimental. Used positively, this energy can help you get a lot done; use it negatively and conflicts are likely. This would be a good time either to work or be alone, if you can.

MARS OPPOSITION MIDHEAVEN

Anger, tensions, conflicts are apt to erupt at home with parents, family, or spouse today. Something may release repressed problems, and each person may respond automatically, unconsciously bringing up old hurts and frustrations. Go ahead, clear the air, but fight fair and try to get at what the real problems are—the heart of the trouble. Kneejerking leads only to sore noses.

MARS CONJUNCT ASCENDANT

Conflicts are likely, especially if you follow your impulses to try to dominate others. If you consider their feelings, things will go much more smoothly. If you do get angry with someone, go ahead and have it out now, but get at the real reason for it or nothing will be accomplished.

MARS SEXTILE ASCENDANT

This is a good time for expressing yourself to others, as you'll be able to do it without causing a ruckus. If you can have a great deal of say-so, working with a group or team will go smoothly today—if, that is, the others can keep up with your tremendous energy.

MARS SQUARE ASCENDANT

The course of true love, or any other relationship, is not likely to run smoothly now. Nobody wants to compromise. Go ahead and have it out to clear the air, but don't count on getting things resolved under this transit. Teamwork is not your long suit today, so work alone if you can.

MARS OPPOSITION ASCENDANT

Conflicts, disputes, ego clashes, and confrontations are a distinct possibility today. Even normally smooth relationships may develop a few glitches. You may have to battle, but don't rule out some compromise, especially in close partnerships. If you can channel this energy into goals you both agree are of mutual benefit, you can do amazing things.

JUPITER IN THIRD HOUSE

You'll get along with your relatives superbly now, and it may be they'll be a boon to you in some way.

JUPITER IN FOURTH HOUSE

Beneficial support may come from your family now. This is a good time to be with them and to clear up any existing problems.

JUPITER IN FIFTH HOUSE

Your relationships with almost everyone will improve and be most rewarding at this time. Relationships with children or with lovers will be very good.

JUPITER IN SEVENTH HOUSE

All sorts of relationships are favored under this transit, especially close partnerships and friendships, either business or personal. You'll learn more about yourself and the world through relationships now, and may begin one totally unlike any others you've had, perhaps with someone from another country. This is also a good time to seek advice or counseling of any kind.

JUPITER IN NINTH HOUSE

You're very apt to encounter persons from backgrounds unlike your own (possibly from other countries), through their travels or your own. If you keep an open mind, this can be a broadening and maturing process for you.

JUPITER IN ELEVENTH HOUSE

Now is the time to work with and for others; the benefits will be mutual. You may form new friendships that will be valuable to you in the future.

JUPITER SEXTILE SUN

Everything runs smoothly now. You like being with your friends, and everyone will have a good time. You can resolve any differences to the benefit of all concerned.

JUPITER OPPOSITION SUN

If you allow yourself to be overbearing and to step on others on your way up now, your successes will prove hollow. Find someone to grow with spiritually, and make it a mutual journey; you'll each find your direction.

JUPITER SEXTILE MOON

You feel friendly toward everyone today, even yourself. It's likely that you and a friend will be of mutual benefit to each other today. This is a good day for dealing with groups or the public in general.

JUPITER SQUARE MOON

You want to help and protect others. And, if you don't come on as "holier-than-thou," you can help a great deal. In close relationships, you're torn between commitment and freedom. Unconscious elements from your past may be complicating matters. Observing the situation as objectively as you can will help.

JUPITER OPPOSITION MOON

You'll either feel very warm and generous with others or turn these feelings onto yourself and be very self-indulgent and demanding of others. Your relationships, especially with women, will consequently be either good or bad. Here's a chance for self-observation and, if it's necessary, for change.

JUPITER SEXTILE MERCURY

If there are any differences or outstanding disputes between you and someone, now is a good time to settle them. Your sincere and tactful manner will carry the day, and all parties will be happy with the results. There is likely to be much communication today, and some of it may be good news from a friend.

JUPITER CONJUNCT VENUS

Now is a good time to resolve difficulties in any relationship. Also, you're feeling sociable and want to go out and have a good time. Relationships generally run smoothly now, and a new love relationship may begin. If so, it will probably be a good one.

JUPITER SEXTILE VENUS

Relationships of all kinds are favored now, because of the warm, friendly vibes you're emitting. Your sincere and honest attitude will attract others who are the same. A new love may enter the scene. You'll probably do some flirting at any rate.

JUPITER SQUARE VENUS

Sometimes this transit signifies the beginning of a meaningful relationship, which is not likely to be placid. You'll learn and grow from it, though that may not be clear to you till later. The problem is Venus wants to be possessive and nurturing, and Jupiter wants to be free. It *can* work, but you'll have to go slowly and with caution.

JUPITER TRINE VENUS

You're in a lighthearted mood and will want to be with friends to have a good time. A love interest that begins now is likely to be very pleasant, though probably not enduring.

JUPITER OPPOSITION VENUS

This can go one of two ways. Either everything will be pleasant and harmonious, with you wanting to give and receive love, or there will be tension in a relationship about freedom and possessiveness. In the latter case, bring everything out into the open and try to take care of the problem now. Also, it's possible that an important new relationship will begin for you.

JUPITER TRINE MARS

If you're having problems with anyone, this transit affords an opportunity to resolve the difficulty. Your personal integrity will carry the day.

JUPITER OPPOSITION MARS

A clash with someone you feel has been restricting you may occur, and you may want to end the relationship. Reflect on this carefully, and don't act impulsively under this transit.

JUPITER OPPOSITION JUPITER

Relationships with authorities may be a problem now. Unless you do intend to be a threat to them or their position, better assure them that you're not. Be prepared to compromise; they'll be equipped with big guns.

JUPITER TRINE SATURN

You may want to play mama or papa to the world today, which is OK as long as you don't go too far. People have to learn to handle their own problems, their own karma.

JUPITER SQUARE URANUS

You may be so impatient with any restrictions in your life, real or imagined, that you become disruptive to a relationship. There may be many changes in your life now, but try to keep your head and determine which ones would be truly beneficial to you. Wait awhile and things may suddenly become clear to you.

JUPITER OPPOSITION URANUS

You will struggle for freedom under this transit, especially within close relationships. Breakups sometimes occur. It may be the other person who seeks more freedom. If so, give it. Not to do so would certainly result in losing him or her, and besides, you want freedom, too.

JUPITER OPPOSITION NEPTUNE

Relationships sometimes begin under this transit in which either of you idealizes the other one as almost godlike in stature. This is obviously undesirable and may include outright deception. Make an effort to see and to accept people as they really are, not as some archetypal perfect being.

JUPITER CONJUNCT ASCENDANT

Your relationships will be very pleasant, and you're likely to be meeting more new people than usual. The positive vibes you feel and project will be returned by those you meet. Take care not to "put on airs," though.

JUPITER SEXTILE ASCENDANT

All kinds of relationships, new or old, close or not, will bring you benefits today. And, your air of kindness and generosity with one and all elicits a like response from them.

JUPITER SQUARE ASCENDANT

If you can refrain from arrogance and try not to overlook the little details that promote good relationships, this may turn out to be a time when you can grow and benefit through relationships.

JUPITER TRINE ASCENDANT

Your relationships at this time will be a source of personal growth, and someone new may come along who will be of particular help to you. You are ready for spiritual growth, at whatever level.

JUPITER OPPOSITION ASCENDANT

Relationships will be mutually beneficial at this time. Someone who will be of some sort of assistance to you may enter your life. In some cases, a new love relationship appears, but not necessarily. A marriage will either run smoothly now or, if there are problem areas that just won't mend, break up entirely.

SATURN IN THIRD HOUSE

There are many changes going on within you which, of course, affect your outer world. Basically, your ways of relating and communicating with others are changing, and there may be some problems until your friends and relatives have time to adjust to the new you. Don't be discouraged and don't try to live up to outmoded ideals.

SATURN IN FOURTH HOUSE

At this time, your personal and domestic environment must be put on firm footing. This could mean anything from making home repairs to making sure your relationships and your inner world are in order. Problems must be brought out and handled now, or they'll be a source of difficulty later. You're creating a foundation on which to build your future.

SATURN IN FIFTH HOUSE

Relationships may be a little strained at this time, especially if they do not allow the free expression of the new self you've been restructuring these last few years. Children may become more of a problem. Love affairs may be troublesome. There may be emotional encounters with others. These encounters should not be avoided, however, as they can prove to be a beneficial learning experience for you. Hey, nobody ever said growth had to be easy.

SATURN IN SEVENTH HOUSE

Your relationships are likely to become more demanding, and you'll have to give them a great deal of your attention. Some may even end. Persons with a relationship on good footing will have to face and resolve difficulties that may have been more or less ignored till now.

SATURN CONJUNCT SUN

If a relationship ends now, bear in mind that it had probably served its purpose or was not good for your growth and development now. You may feel lonely for a while, but take comfort knowing it will pass.

SATURN OPPOSITION SUN

This is a time of endings, and this may include some relationships. Be patient. A time of beginnings will come soon.

SATURN CONJUNCT MOON

You may find relationships hard to handle and may want to withdraw from people, particularly women. This is a time for deep introspection, but not for making important decisions regarding relationships. Wait until this period has passed and your vision and perspective have cleared. Right now you're probably being too hard on yourself.

SATURN SEXTILE MOON

You have more emotional control and objectivity now and can therefore handle difficult relationships more readily. Now is a good time to make any necessary changes. Your family and your parents may become meaningful to you now, and these relationships can be helpful and worthwhile at this time.

SATURN SQUARE MOON

There may be problems in relationships now. Possibly your work or other responsibilities (Saturn) have gained too much dominance over your personal life (Moon), or *vice versa*. A period of realignment is called for, and when the two segments of your life are back in harmony, all will be right with your world again.

SATURN TRINE MOON

Relationships run smoothly now, because you've achieved a good working balance between your inner and outer worlds. This is a good time to make plans for the future and to seek the advice of older people, especially women.

SATURN OPPOSITION MOON

You may feel lonely or cut off from others. Relationships may end or undergo great stress. The problem is you've let your personal and professional spheres get out of balance, paying more attention to one (probably the professional) to the detriment of the other. This just won't work—they must be in balance for the sake of your growth and emotional health. You'll have to make some changes, and this probably won't be easy, but you'll emerge from the fray a happier and more complete person.

SATURN CONJUNCT MERCURY

You are entering a new cycle in which your attitude is more

serious and your focus narrower. You may become obsessed with perfection—in yourself and in others. This, of course, could lead to problems, and some relationships may not be able to stand the strain.

SATURN SQUARE MERCURY

Make an effort to work out all conflicts with others. You may have to defend and explain what you feel and think, but this will help get it straight in your own mind and show up any areas that have become too rigid and need changing.

SATURN OPPOSITION MERCURY

You may find yourself ending relationships because of differing opinions and communication breakdowns. If you can be flexible and open-minded—willing to change your thinking, if necessary, in order to improve your ideas or opinions—this may be avoided.

SATURN CONJUNCT VENUS

At this time, you'll retreat somewhat to assess yourself and which relationships are truly important to you, whether you realize it or phrase it in those terms or not. Some may fall away and some will survive, strengthened. A new relationship that seems "meant to be" may begin now.

SATURN SEXTILE VENUS

You'll assume a very practical approach to relationships now, eschewing idealistic romanticism for the time being. Business relationships or partnerships are especially favored under this transit.

SATURN SQUARE VENUS

Relationships will be difficult now; some may even break up. Relating seems to take more effort than you care to put into it. There is a conflict between your need for freedom and the rewards and obligations of a relationship.

SATURN TRINE VENUS

Pursuing personal growth and a better understanding of yourself through your relationships is a worthwhile endeavor now. Evaluate the role you play in the give and take of any relationship.

SATURN OPPOSITION VENUS

Personal relationships are being tested, and things could get a little problematical for a while. Only those relationships that are truly valuable for your life will survive, strengthened. Don't be willing to give one up too quickly, though; not until you know, deep down, that you've given it your all and it's useless. Otherwise, you may simply jump into another one just like it.

SATURN SEXTILE MARS

You are able to sublimate your ego and discipline your energy so that you can work well with others on long-term projects now.

SATURN SQUARE MARS

Conflicts may very well occur at this time. You may tend to suppress your anger against those who're really aggravating you, only to explode at the least little blunder by someone else. Learning to handle anger properly would greatly improve your life and your relationships.

SATURN CONJUNCT JUPITER

One effect of this transit could be to make you want to seek solitude, to withdraw from others, to work alone.

SATURN SQUARE JUPITER

You're antsy and impatient with restriction, but don't make any hasty decisions regarding relationships under this transit. Let it pass first, then reconsider when you're calmer.

SATURN OPPOSITION JUPITER

Relationships you feel have been restricting your freedom too much may be severed at this time. Though painful, this may ultimately be to your good.

SATURN CONJUNCT SATURN

You may feel the effects of this very important time in your life as much as a year before the transit is exact. If you are in an inappropriate relationship, it will end or must be substantially changed. You'll be better off if you voluntarily go along with the changes that will be occurring. Your life is preparing for a new direction.

SATURN SQUARE SATURN

You may be going through a period of reevaluation of your life and goals and identity. Some relationships may end. Don't relentlessly agonize over them if they do. Pick up and go on with your life.

SATURN OPPOSITION SATURN

If during the last square of Saturn to your natal Saturn you did not eliminate inappropriate relationships or take the opportunity to improve those which needed it, they will very probably not withstand the turmoil of this transit. Good, mature relationships, however, will be extremely satisfying.

SATURN CONJUNCT URANUS

You are undergoing changes—seeking excitement, freedom, new horizons. This may mean that some relationships will fall by the wayside. You may abandon a relationship suddenly, without warning— or you may need to radically restructure it.

SATURN SEXTILE URANUS

After undergoing some upheaval about seven years ago, your relationships have probably now stabilized and are working well.

SATURN SQUARE URANUS

You now have the opportunity to make creative changes in your life and to eliminate anything that is not appropriate for your growth and development. Relationships not open to change and improvement will end. Willingly going along with Uranian changes can make them exciting, not disruptive.

SATURN OPPOSITION URANUS

"Don't fence me in" is your battle cry at the moment. Any relationship that you feel does restrict your freedom or which resists any change or readjustment in its structuring will probably break up.

SATURN TRINE PLUTO

Others will respect your inner strength and ability to work hard and effectively and will want to work with you.

SATURN SQUARE MIDHEAVEN

If you've favored either your professional or your personal life over the other in the past, you're going to have to make some changes. Realize that you need the emotional support of relationships, but neither should they deter you from your life's work. You need to, and will be able to, make the necessary adjustments at this time. It will be incredibly more difficult to do later.

SATURN CONJUNCT ASCENDANT

This is likely to be a time when good relationships are "polished up" and bad ones eliminated. You'll be busy, but don't neglect relationships. This is also a good time to talk with, and possibly get advice from, older persons.

SATURN SEXTILE ASCENDANT

The standards and routines you establish in relationships now will define them for a number of years, so it behooves you to be aware of what you're doing and not to act or react mindlessly. Consulting respected, older persons will be helpful in learning more about yourself and how you relate. Don't necessarily take anyone's word as law, however.

SATURN SQUARE ASCENDANT

Relationships that are inappropriate for you and your personal goals will end now. You may feel a keen sense of loss, but this will soon be replaced with a feeling of relief and freedom. You must consciously evaluate your relationships or be forced to do so by others or circumstances.

SATURN TRINE ASCENDANT

You're stabilized in your relationships, and are in no mood for changes or sudden surprises. You'll be attracted to more mature people, and, in fact, may come across as being older than you actually are yourself. Someone who may turn out to be very important in your life may enter it at this point, but you might not appreciate this until later.

SATURN OPPOSITION ASCENDANT

Relationships, especially close partnerships, are likely to be severely tested at this time. Handle problems immediately. Some relationships may, in fact, end. Or, some people may oppose you because they feel threatened. Try to understand the reasons, whatever they are, and get rid of them. (The reasons, not the people!)

URANUS IN FIRST HOUSE

There may be some difficulties in relationships because you are suddenly seeking more freedom to express yourself as you really are, and if a relationship cannot handle that, it may end. Others will adjust after a while.

URANUS IN FOURTH HOUSE

There are apt to be disruptions in your home life at this time. Basically you yourself are changing at a deep psychological level, and if there are interpersonal problems you've been ignoring, they'll come to a head now. Some relationships may end. This will be upsetting at the time, but in the long run, you'll be freer to be yourself than before. Try to be flexible to facilitate the process.

URANUS IN FIFTH HOUSE

If you have children, they will be demanding of your attention in one way or another. Exciting, dramatic things may happen with, through, or to them. Unexpected pregnancies sometimes occur at this time. Unusual and exciting, but not long-lasting, romances may occur, too.

URANUS IN SEVENTH HOUSE

There may be open conflicts and confrontations with just about anyone you know. Problems that may have been stewing for years will come to a boil. Uranus does not allow situations or routines that are not for our ultimate good to continue. Correct the problems consciously, and this transit need not be so troublesome.

URANUS IN ELEVENTH HOUSE

You'll be meeting new friends and perhaps saying goodbye to some of your old ones. Friends may involve you in new and different experiences. The same applies to groups you belong to or may join. As always with Uranus, be flexible and open-minded.

URANUS IN TWELFTH HOUSE

Difficulties with "secret enemies"—actually only people who subconsciously react to your subconscious signals—are likely. The difficulties will probably concern secret or hidden aspects of yourself. Becoming aware of the unconscious memories or behavior patterns that may be emerging is your best course now. Psychotherapy, meditation, or other techniques of self-knowledge will be helpful in accomplishing this.

URANUS SEXTILE SUN

Any relationship that begins now will be an embodiment of your need for greater self-expression and control over your life. Old relationships will very likely adjust in order to come more in line with this need.

URANUS TRINE SUN

New relationships that begin now will be exciting and will allow you to be yourself. Established relationships will have to change to allow this, too, if they haven't already.

URANUS OPPOSITION SUN

Relationships may end suddenly under this transit—possibly, but not necessarily, due to a death. If they do, it's because their purpose has been accomplished or they were inhibiting your ability to truly express yourself.

URANUS CONJUNCT MOON

Sudden and surprising changes in your family or home life may occur, possibly concerning your mother or another female relative.

URANUS SEXTILE MOON

Your emotions are aroused and you experience yourself and the world through your feelings. You're subjective, yes, but it's a wonderful experience. You give and require more emotional support and expression from all around you. If they can't give it, you'll find someone who can.

URANUS SQUARE MOON

Seemingly sudden problems with parents or other close relationships may erupt now, expressing tensions that may have been buried for years. Some sort of split-up may even occur. Working out these problems, however, would be better than chucking a relationship for a new one now.

URANUS TRINE MOON

Really pay attention to your friendships and other relationships now. You may have been taking them for granted. Changing your attitudes now will be relatively easy and will allow you new emotional insights and rewards. Something may happen that gives you new understanding of a past incident.

URANUS OPPOSITION MOON

You're undergoing emotional changes and growth, either by choice or through the force of sudden events. This growth may affect any or all relationships you have, especially with women, and a relationship must either change to reflect and allow for your growth or end. When the changes are made, you'll feel freer and more your Self than ever before.

URANUS CONJUNCT VENUS

You suddenly cannot stand the boredom and routine of settled-in relationships, and you'll pursue new freedom and excitement at almost any cost. Either you'll look outside current relationships or they'll change and develop into something new. It's best to let this transit pass before making any definite and binding decisions concerning any relationship.

URANUS SEXTILE VENUS

New and different people will enter your life now, and your relationships with them will be totally unlike any of your previous ones. For one thing, you'll give each other unusual freedom, and that alone may be a new experience for you. If you preserve their freedom and excitement, these relationships can be long lasting.

URANUS SQUARE VENUS

Relationships are not likely to be too stable or predictable at this time. Basically, the problem is that you are seeking more freedom and excitement, an escape from dull routine. You'll look for people totally different from those you usually associate with. And, as long as the excitement lasts, so will the relationship. Existing relationships will have to change and grow to endure.

URANUS TRINE VENUS

Freedom and exhilaration are the key words right now. If an existing relationship doesn't have it, now is a good time to transform it so it does. A new love relationship may begin if you're not in one already. It will be unusual in some way compared to previous ones, and it may very well last, preserving its interest and freedom right along. Friendships, too, will prove exciting and different now, even the ones you already have.

URANUS SQUARE MARS

Your insecurities may be showing, and you may feel compelled to prove yourself in some way. You may act rashly and find yourself in disputes and confrontations. It's OK to assert yourself, but it will help to think before you act.

URANUS OPPOSITION MARS

You are needing to be more self-assertive, but don't let your "damn the torpedoes" mood lead you into rash actions. You do need to make changes in how you relate to others, but, without suppressing these energies totally, do try to manage a little caution and rationality. Otherwise, expect possibly explosive confrontations.

URANUS OPPOSITION JUPITER

You'll want to break free of any less-than-ideal situations you've been putting up with. Or, someone may want to break free of you. Though possibly unpleasant at the time, you'll probably be glad later it's finished.

URANUS CONJUNCT SATURN

If any relationship has been restricting your ultimate growth, whether you're consciously aware of that fact or not, it will be subject to sudden, perhaps explosive, change at this time. This may include breaking up. Do not resist or suppress this energy. You'll be better for the change in the long run.

URANUS SEXTILE SATURN

Here, Uranus gives you a chance to modify the structures of Saturn so that they don't eventually become too rigid and confining. You can do this within all relationships with relative ease now.

URANUS SQUARE SATURN

Relationships that limit you in some way will be a source of unbearable tensions. You'll want to be free no matter what the consequences. Find someone you can talk with to help alleviate the stress until you're in a better space to decide on the appropriate course of action.

URANUS OPPOSITION SATURN

Uranus may throw you a curve ball to break through your perhaps quietly smug, arrogant attitude that you, the great guru, now have all the answers. Uranus says, "Listen, kid, you're not through growing yet." Unexpected events or circumstances will force you to reevaluate your thinking. In relationships, tensions hidden for a long time may choose to manifest now. Handle them as positively as you can—confront the problems, be flexible, and let yourself grow.

URANUS TRINE NEPTUNE

This is a harmonious time for most relationships. Your compassion and understanding for all will increase or surface, and you'll want to help those less fortunate than you.

URANUS CONJUNCT PLUTO

Relationships may become deeper and more important to you now, and you may meet people who are unlike any you usually associate with. These new relationships may not be long lasting, though. A friend may help you grow in some way.

URANUS OPPOSITION PLUTO

Some relationships may end under this transit, possibly through death or other separation. It's all part of sweeping out the old order to make way for the new in your life. You'll have to be flexible to minimize any turmoil.

URANUS CONJUNCT MIDHEAVEN

Sudden changes regarding your parents may alter your life in some way. This need not be bad, and could very well be positive.

URANUS SEXTILE MIDHEAVEN

You'll be seeking more freedom in your relationships in order to pursue your objectives unhindered. And you may make changes in those objectives.

URANUS SQUARE MIDHEAVEN

There may be sudden, unsettling changes involving your parents. Or there may be problems with friends or relatives, probably because you're wanting to break free from any restrictions in order to be truly yourself. You may be expressing this urge as rebellion against any authority or authoritative voice you hear.

URANUS OPPOSITION MIDHEAVEN

There may be sudden family disruptions, such as illness or accident, particularly regarding your parents. There may be disruptions within your family for other reasons, too. All this is happening, no doubt, largely because there are changes going on with yourself. Try to be aware of yourself, open to inner insights, considerate of others, and the disturbances may be avoided or kept to a minimum.

URANUS CONJUNCT ASCENDANT

Freedom to be oneself is the issue with this transit, and relationships must change to allow it. Also, you may meet people who are totally different from your usual friends.

URANUS SEXTILE ASCENDANT

You're undergoing inner changes, and your old associations may suddenly seem outdated or too conservative. New and unusual people may enter your life. All this may bother you if *you* have become too rigid and conservative, but it's all necessary for your growth, so go along with what's happening. New partnerships, friendships, even marriage opportunities may come to you now. At the very least, you'll find this a stimulating time.

URANUS SQUARE ASCENDANT

New freedom of personal expression is what you seek now, and this may take the form of overthrowing old, outworn aspects of your life. This will certainly affect relationships. Old ones may end or change and new ones begin. Don't make binding committals for quite some time, though.

URANUS OPPOSITION ASCENDANT

Relationships, even good ones, are apt to be disrupted at this time. Basically, one of you wants a greater say and perhaps more freedom within the relationship, resisting efforts of the other to totally control it. If either person is too rigid to accept change, the relationship will probably break up. This applies to business partnerships as well.

NEPTUNE IN FOURTH HOUSE

Your home life and family relationships are very likely to experience some sort of change or transformation. Dealing with family members, especially parents, may be difficult. Or, if there are afflictions to the fourth house, a parent may be hospitalized or require your care. This can be a confusing time, reflecting deep inner changes going on within you.

NEPTUNE IN FIFTH HOUSE

If you have children, they may be something of a problem now. For one thing, you may be over-idealizing them. Open your eyes and see them as they really are. The same applies to everyone you know; beware of delusion and illusion. Be careful of unwanted pregnancies.

NEPTUNE IN SEVENTH HOUSE

There can be difficulties in relationships due to faulty communication, misunderstanding, or deception. Consequently, now is not a good time for consulting a professional in any field. In any case, try to make all communications as clear and precise as you can. Spell everything out. This is not a good time for forming partnerships.

NEPTUNE IN ELEVENTH HOUSE

You may meet new friends who are psychic or artistic in some way, or you may join a group interested in psychic matters. Your friends will share your ideals and help you work toward them— unless, of course, you're all living out some mutual daydream. Neptune is famous for making illusion seem reality. Try to see people as they are, not as you'd like them to be. Also, you'll want to help people in some way, but make sure they really need such help.

NEPTUNE CONJUNCT SUN

If you are able to handle the focus of higher consciousness that Neptune can bring and are willing to leave your ego behind, you'll experience this time as enhanced sensitivity both to others and their needs and to the metaphysical aspects of the universe.

NEPTUNE SEXTILE SUN

You'll be especially sensitive and selfless with one and all. You'll begin to appreciate the real meaning and importance of human relationships.

NEPTUNE SQUARE SUN

You may be confused and disoriented. Your grasp of reality is not quite up to par. Consequently this is not a good time to sever or commit to a relationship, nor to withdraw from society as a whole. You need grounding. Hang in there, and wait for this transit to pass.

NEPTUNE TRINE SUN

You're willing to selflessly help others and seek nothing in return but the actualization of your ideals.

NEPTUNE OPPOSITION SUN

There is danger of self-delusion and delusion by others. Be very specific with your communications and make sure others are, too. Misunderstandings or deceptions are quite possible. Do not accept anything or anyone uncritically.

NEPTUNE SQUARE MOON

There may be difficulties in relationships due to misunderstandings. Be very precise and specific in your communications and try not to take your moods and emotions too earnestly at the moment. You're very sensitive to the feelings of others, and they may influence you more than they should. Avoid being around anyone giving out negative vibrations.

NEPTUNE OPPOSITION MOON

What you're seeing or feeling at this time just "ain't necessarily so." You're not interpreting people and events as they really are. Don't make any emotional commitments under this transit. Handle all problems on the home front as soon as they arise.

NEPTUNE TRINE MERCURY

Your heightened intuition and sensitivity under this transit make understanding and communicating with others effective and rewarding.

NEPTUNE CONJUNCT VENUS

You'll be intuitive and sensitive about others' feelings but may still be in a fog when it comes to bestowing your affections. You may over-idealize, you may play the selfless martyr or attract someone else who plays that role—all of which may be fine and fun until the transit passes. It would be unwise to make any permanent arrangements until this transit is over.

NEPTUNE SEXTILE VENUS

You'll be intuitively sensitive to others, willing and able to be self-less in your devotion to them, but may be romanticizing or idealizing them all out of proportion to their true worth or merit. You will not greatly suffer from this, though, even if things turn out not to be what they now seem when this transit is over. And if they are what they seem—so much the better.

NEPTUNE SQUARE VENUS

Your ability to wade through illusion and idealization with regard to personal relationships will be tested. You must learn to see and to accept people as they really are, including yourself.

NEPTUNE TRINE VENUS

Your sensitivity to, and appreciation of, others is enhanced. You'll have a pleasant and enjoyable, perhaps dreamy, time with others. You'll be very romantic, and such a relationship may begin.

NEPTUNE OPPOSITION VENUS

Difficulties may arise in almost any relationship, possibly due to over-idealization, misunderstandings, poor communication, or even deception. Don't try anything sneaky yourself, and work at clearing up all problems as they occur.

NEPTUNE SEXTILE JUPITER

Benefits to and from friends and relatives are a possibility now. At any rate, there aren't apt to be conflicts, and you'll enjoy being with them and will want to help them in some way if you can.

NEPTUNE OPPOSITION SATURN

Someone may enter your life now who challenges your views and makes you justify them. This is helpful both in forcing you to put your opinions and beliefs into words and for showing you how well you've actually thought things through.

NEPTUNE OPPOSITION MIDHEAVEN

It's time to start a new cycle. Let the old go if it wants to. This is a very good time to stop and take stock of your life and relationships and the direction you want them to go.

NEPTUNE CONJUNCT ASCENDANT

This is another transit that may prove the adage, "love is blind," though any relationship can be involved. Your idealism is so aroused you may not see, or refuse to see, the faults or ploys of others. This is not a good time to make permanent relational arrangements or to sign any contracts. Don't become so starry-eyed you can't stand up for yourself, either.

NEPTUNE SEXTILE ASCENDANT

Your intuitive awareness of others will increase and, consequently, so will your compassion. Your ego is banked a bit, and you're able to be more selfless, less selfish. Old acquaintances will suddenly mean more to you, but you may over-idealize new ones, which, of course, is nonproductive all around.

NEPTUNE SQUARE ASCENDANT

Confusion under this transit is probable. You're not seeing yourself and others realistically. Try to analyze whatever is happening in terms of what you can learn from it—even if a relationship ends. Be very careful about signing anything.

NEPTUNE TRINE ASCENDANT

You'll have much more compassion for others, but you may tend to over-idealize them, too, thinking they are wonderful and you are a nobody. This may be especially true in a love or spiritual-guide relationship. Hang in there; make no permanent commitments, and reappraise what you've learned after this transit of about one year is over.

NEPTUNE OPPOSITION ASCENDANT

This is not a good time to consult anyone, including professionals, for advice. There is a possibility of deception in almost any relationship at this time, and communications are poor. Rectify this as best you can by being totally explicit in any communication and getting any deception out into the open immediately.

PLUTO IN FOURTH HOUSE

Your family relationships, especially with parents, are apt to change a great deal due to one cause or another—divorce, death, separations, or just a change in the dynamics of the relationship. The changes won't necessarily be negative and can just as easily be positive.

PLUTO IN FIFTH HOUSE

Your relationship with your children is very important now. There may be a power struggle with them. But whatever you do will affect them profoundly, which, of course, could be all to the good. If planets in this house are severely afflicted, be especially careful of your children's health and safety. Love affairs or existing love relationships will be intense.

PLUTO IN SEVENTH HOUSE

Relationships will undergo definite and significant changes during these years. If they don't or won't change, they'll end. You, too, will of course be changing in the process. Opponents may be a problem, and they may even resort to underhanded techniques. Don't try it yourself, though; it won't work. Wherever there are problems, look within for the answers. Remember, we subconsciously attract everyone we know and must deal with. This is not a particularly good time to begin any type of partnership.

PLUTO IN ELEVENTH HOUSE

No longer content with shallow relationships, you'll change the type of friends you wish to associate with. You may even meet someone who profoundly changes your life. Be careful, though, not to associate with unsavory types or to give your allegiance to spiritual charlatans.

PLUTO CONJUNCT SUN

This is not a time to try to dominate others. Whatever you do must be done for the good of all, not just yourself.

PLUTO SEXTILE SUN

If you feel the need to make some changes in any relationship, now is a time when you can do so creatively and with little trouble.

PLUTO OPPOSITION SUN

This may be a pretty rocky period in relationships. Absolutely do not for any reason try to dominate someone, and if they should try to run roughshod over you, resist.

PLUTO CONJUNCT MOON

There may be intense encounters with friends and family, especially women, possibly your mother. Separations may occur, sometimes through death. Remember, when the old falls away, the way is being prepared for the new. You are entering a new cycle of life.

PLUTO SEXTILE MOON

You'll have greater emotional rapport and understanding with your family now. You feel supported, that your foundation is firm. If you think there is a need to make any changes in a relationship, now is a good time to do it.

PLUTO SQUARE MOON

Buried feelings or drives are emerging now, forcing you to confront them. There may be deep, possibly subconsciously motivated, emotional conflicts with family members, probably women. There may be psychological power plays or guilt trips. Try to avoid such mind games. But pay attention to what's going on within you, and you'll learn a great deal about yourself.

PLUTO TRINE MOON

Your emotional understanding of yourself and others is heightened. This reflects positively in all relationships. This is an excellent time to make any changes or improvements in your relationships. A new relationship may begin which will have a profound effect on your life.

PLUTO OPPOSITION MOON

There may be emotional turmoil and conflict in relationships. Either party may stoop to emotional manipulation. Try to avoid this. The best course is for each to be completely frank with each other. Otherwise, the relationship may end. And probably should.

PLUTO SEXTILE VENUS

Your relationships will serve as a basis for insights into yourself and the meaning others have for you. You'll find your capacity for love deepened. New relationships may begin that will prove very meaningful and enlightening.

PLUTO OPPOSITION MARS

There may be ego conflicts and power plays with others, at work or otherwise. Your ego energies (and possibly theirs) are high. Do try to control them. Avoid stepping on others, questionable tactics, and underground elements.

PLUTO OPPOSITION SATURN

Relationships sometimes end under this transit. If so, let them go as being part of another cycle, another era of your life.

PLUTO SQUARE URANUS

Don't neglect the human, emotional needs of yourself and those around you, as you may be inclined to do so at this time.

PLUTO TRINE URANUS

Old relationships may fade away or even end suddenly. New friends who more accurately reflect the new you that is now evolving will enter your life.

PLUTO OPPOSITION URANUS

Outworn or outgrown relationships will fall away now, and you should let them, or else make revolutionary changes in their structure. In whatever case, change they must, and you must be flexible enough to allow, indeed to assist, their changing.

PLUTO CONJUNCT NEPTUNE

You are undergoing many changes, and some relationships may fall by the wayside as a reflection of the new you now emerging.

PLUTO CONJUNCT MIDHEAVEN

There may be important changes in your relationships, particularly within your family. Some relationships may end entirely. If so, let them go as part of a necessary evolutionary process.

PLUTO SQUARE MIDHEAVEN

Any tensions in your family life that you've been putting up with or trying to ignore are very likely to come into focus now, and you will be forced to face them. Now is the time to work together to improve and change the relationship so that it can grow.

PLUTO OPPOSITION MIDHEAVEN

There are apt to be great changes in your relationships now—

possibly, but not necessarily, including divorce, separations, or death. The past is clearing away to make way for the new. This could simply mean creative, positive changes within relationships. Don't resist; in fact, assist.

PLUTO CONJUNCT ASCENDANT

There may be power struggles or other difficulties in relationships now. You're experiencing a personal transformation in which aspects of yourself are emerging that you may have attempted to hide or ignore in the past. Whether you are aware of these surfacing aspects or not, others will begin to behave differently toward you, causing you to react. And change. Do not attempt to ignore this phase in your development.

PLUTO SEXTILE ASCENDANT

Your relationships will become more intense and meaningful to you, and you'll have an opportunity to change your life through them. Or, you may be an instrument for important change in another's life.

PLUTO SQUARE ASCENDANT

There are apt to be power struggles or other unpleasant encounters with others during this time. Some relationships may end. With difficult relational problems, look within yourself to discover what possible subconscious "strings" someone is pulling, and deal with those strings. Do not stoop to devious methods of any kind. Nor should you shrink from unpleasant encounters. It's best to just get them over.

PLUTO TRINE ASCENDANT

You are changing and growing, your self-understanding deepening, and this is likely to occur through, or be partly helped by, your relationships now. They, too, are evolving. You are not interested in the shallow; your relationships will be intense.

PLUTO OPPOSITION ASCENDANT

The need for change in relationships, especially close ones, will come to a head now. You must confront your difficulties, clear the air, and try to work them out, or the relationship is likely to end. Your life will be transformed somehow. Someone who opposes you vigorously may figure into this equation somehow—perhaps an enemy or someone who feels threatened by you; or perhaps a good friend who will help you immensely.

Chapter 18

Your Self, Its Status and Growth

Your Self—its status and growth—is your prime responsibility. Only you can live out your karma. And while you can love and help others, only they can live out their karma. Each must take the responsibility for his or her own Self. Each can grow only when ready, no matter what any of the rest of us may do. This is The Law, which is Love. If all of us were to truly live up to The Law, then, each would be taken care of and all would be taken care of.

But it's no rose garden, this task, and just knowing what's going on sometimes can be a relief. Knowing that "this, too, shall pass"—and when—or that it's just your ego kicking up now instead of the rest of the world going crazy can save you a lot of anxiety and help keep you on the right path. Keeping up with your transits concerning Self can make your prime responsibility easier, perhaps even more of a joy, to fulfill.

Transit Descriptions

SUN IN FIRST HOUSE

This is a time when you should take care of your own needs and energize yourself for the rest of the year. This transit lasts about a month, during which you'll experience a surge of greater self-confidence.

SUN IN SECOND HOUSE

You'll be concerned with things or philosophies you value, as well as with getting ahead and making money. This is a good time to think about and assess your values.

SUN IN THIRD HOUSE

You'll probably be restless and want to do something out of your usual routine. You'll also find the pace of your life and interactions with others picking up. Make an effort to communicate effectively, taking care to truly listen to others, too.

SUN IN FOURTH HOUSE

A subjective time, valuable for self-contemplation and evaluation, particularly in safe and familiar surroundings. This month each year can be very important and helpful for growth. Pay particular attention to unconscious drives or habits generated by early family training.

SUN IN FIFTH HOUSE

This is likely to be a lighthearted time when you'll want to be, and will feel free to be, yourself. It's a good time to enjoy yourself but also to try to know yourself better.

SUN IN SIXTH HOUSE

The emphasis is on whether you can sublimate your own ego demands enough to be of service to others in your work—and enjoy it. Don't worry; you don't have to be a sainted martyr. The satisfaction you'll gain from such service will more than compensate your delicate little ego, my friend.

SUN IN SEVENTH HOUSE

Self-observation of your actions, reactions, and motivations as you interact with others would be profitable at this time.

SUN IN EIGHTH HOUSE

You'll be more in touch with your feelings and more concerned with the deeper levels of yourself during this transit. And you should be. Self-contemplation is favored now, and if you can't get a time or place to do this, you'll feel out of sync with yourself. Psychological or philosophical changes may occur or begin at this time each year. The subject of survival after death may interest you more than usual.

SUN IN NINTH HOUSE

You're unusually mentally restless and active—an excellent time to begin a new study or to do something different. Your interest in metaphysical, spiritual, or occult matters is heightened now, and you may begin a study in one of these areas. The main thing is, you're trying to stretch yourself and grow.

SUN IN TENTH HOUSE

Be yourself, without show or pretense in any context now. "Faking" anything will only harm you in the long run. You may find yourself in the public eye to some degree, possibly connected with your job or career. Critically have a look at yourself and see if you're on the path you really want to be on.

SUN IN ELEVENTH HOUSE

Now you are reassessing yourself in relation to the groups you belong to and the friends you have. No one enters your life unless drawn by you. What facets of yourself are mirrored in them? Are they appropriate to your ideal of yourself?

SUN IN TWELFTH HOUSE

Your personal year is ending, and it's a good time to get in touch with your subconscious and evaluate with absolute honesty this reality and your methods of relating with others. Behavioral responses learned in childhood are unsuitable now, and observing yourself with objectivity can help you release them and grow in maturity.

SUN CONJUNCT SUN

This transit signifies your real birth time, whether it falls on your birth *date* or not. You'll feel reenergized and special. It's excellent for reassessing yourself and your goals and making new beginnings. Things begun today have a good chance of turning out well for you.

SUN SEXTILE SUN

This transit affords you two excellent opportunities a year to assess how you're doing and to make adjustments if necessary. At about two months before your birthday, you should take stock of your achievements since your last birthday. Analyze what has and hasn't panned out, and prepare to try again on your approaching birthday. The second chance at course correction occurs about two months after your birthday, during which time you should scrutinize how well you're progressing in the direction you've set for yourself. If you pass up these opportunities, you'll meet unexpected difficulties in about a month.

SUN SQUARE SUN

You'll be presented with some sort of difficulty when this transit rolls around about three months before and after your birthday. The challenge may come from within yourself or from someone else. Basically, it's another opportunity to prove to yourself and others that you're on the right trajectory. Three months before your birthday it may have to do with something you're attempting to create; three months after, it probably will concern your ability to stick with a project and finish it.

SUN TRINE SUN

This transit will greet you approximately four months before and four months after your birthday. Your energy level is high, and all is right with the world. Obstacles? What are *they*? You'll meet very few. It won't always be like this, though, and now is a good time to take stock and make sure that all is battened down to withstand any storms of success or defeat that may arise later on. If there are failures, forget them and get busy trying another direction.

SUN OPPOSITION SUN

Things begun some months ago are now coming to a head—some successfully, some not. Accept the losses and start over. Don't despair—you'll have learned something about yourself if you've been paying attention. Your successes will also teach you about yourself if you can see them as an integral part of your life and growth patterns.

SUN CONJUNCT MOON

Your emotions are going to be more to the fore today, so it's a good chance to try to understand them better. If you can honestly and fearlessly look at what emerges, there can be significant new beginnings on the psychological level.

SUN SEXTILE MOON

You are in a state of inner and outer harmony now, and this benefits all areas of your life, especially relationships.

SUN SQUARE MOON

You may feel as if you're the rope in a tug of war if you haven't been handling your emotional self and the pressures of the outside world well. Hiding or trying to ignore problems never works, as you're finding out now if you've tried to do so. This may erupt as irritability in yourself and possible conflicts with authority figures or your family.

SUN TRINE MOON

Today you are calm, serene, and tranquil. Your emotions and intellect are balanced. This is a good day to look inward for self-understanding and outward to help others understand themselves. If the Sun is moving toward the natal Moon, this is a good time to assess the period of turmoil and tension you've probably just been through for lessons learned and aspects of yourself revealed.

SUN OPPOSITION MOON

Unless you've kept in touch with your inner self and managed to keep a balance between your emotions and intellect, you're apt to feel like that rope in a tug of war again (Sun square Moon). Your professional and personal life may conflict, or your conscious desires may be at odds with your subconscious ones. Whatever. You're being shown the necessity of not favoring one aspect of yourself over another. If you have maintained a balance between your inner and outer selves, this can be a very pleasant and satisfying day.

SUN CONJUNCT MERCURY

You may tend to be too self-preoccupied today. Don't forget to listen to others, or you'll miss something important.

SUN SEXTILE MERCURY

A good day for getting in touch with yourself—for looking at your hopes, desires, and objectives and how your efforts to achieve them are succeeding.

SUN TRINE MERCURY

This is an excellent time for self-examination with an eye toward enhanced knowledge of yourself and your purpose. You can see the broad overview now.

SUN OPPOSITION MERCURY

Remain objective and listen carefully to others and your inner self.

SUN CONJUNCT VENUS

You'll feel more at peace today if you can surround yourself with beauty and be with others.

SUN SEXTILE VENUS

This is a good time to examine your role in relationships to see if you're giving as much as you receive. You'll be happier and more satisfied if that is the case.

SUN CONJUNCT MARS

How you react to situations today can be a clue as to how you really feel about yourself and your inner foundation, your inner security—or lack of it. If your reactions are generally negative, it's probably time for reevaluation and change. Physical activity will help your mood somewhat today.

SUN SQUARE MARS

This is a potentially explosive combination, and you should make a concerted effort to be very aware of what you're doing today and for what reasons. You'll likely be challenged in some manner, and if you react subconsciously, without thinking, you're apt to blow it. This is not to say you should suppress any feelings of aggression you may legitimately have—this could lead to accident or illness—but be in conscious control of them. Physical activity will help.

SUN TRINE MARS

This day can best be spent in creative visualization of the various projects you're working on—how you're handling them and how you will handle them, even under possible challenge, as they reach culmination. And if you can do this while being physically active (perhaps on the project under consideration itself), so much the better. The purpose is not so much to better the projects, but to know yourself better in relation to them.

SUN CONJUNCT JUPITER

You want to have all kinds of experiences and broaden your life, which you tackle with energy and enthusiasm now. Depending on your subconscious attitude toward personal growth, you may react with generosity or arrogance toward others.

SUN SEXTILE JUPITER

This is one of those pleasant, happy days when everything seems to go right for you—not because of "luck," but because of your positive attitude. This is a good time to survey your life and objectives, working out plans for the future, because today you can see the whole picture.

SUN TRINE JUPITER

Unless there is some very powerful aspect against it, this will be one of the most positive days you've experienced in a long time. This is a good day to review your life and make any necessary changes. It will be easy for you to do today, and visualizing everything working out as you wish will be immensely effective.

SUN OPPOSITION JUPITER

This transit will raise you up the optimism scale by several degrees and increase your self-confidence. If you can manage not to go so far as arrogant self-righteousness, everything should work out well. Overextension in any area is best avoided, too.

SUN CONJUNCT SATURN

You may feel depressed and lonely, but if you'll just get up and do what you have to do anyway, you'll feel better and maybe even end up with a degree of happy satisfaction.

SUN SQUARE SATURN

You feel on the horns of a dilemma today: How much of yourself do you owe to others? *Ask.* You may be making specious assumptions about what you "have" to do. Your own choices or erroneous ideas may be restricting you. Problems today will show where to concentrate your energies to develop more self-confidence.

SUN TRINE SATURN

Now is a good time to look at your life, your plans, your family, your job, your environment, or whatever to see what's working and what isn't. You're apt to learn a good deal about yourself by so doing.

SUN OPPOSITION SATURN

As with the square, you're in conflict between your own needs and the needs and demands of others. Communicate this frankly and be willing to compromise if necessary. Don't be resigned and inactive, don't be resentful, don't let depression or loneliness drag you under. Make the effort to communicate.

SUN CONJUNCT URANUS

Get out of your rut! Do something different and exciting, or Uranus will do it for you in a manner that may not be totally pleasing to you.

SUN SEXTILE URANUS

Today is apt to be pleasantly interesting, possibly even exciting, with everyday events or relationships sparking off new insights. You're not in the mood for self-discipline today, but letting it go once in a while can also be important. Sometimes, as the ancient Persian poet Sadi wrote, we must "buy hyacinths to feed the soul."

SUN SQUARE URANUS

There are two primary bits of advice that will apply today: 1) expect the unexpected, and 2) voluntarily do something out of your ordinary routine. If you feel irritable and impatient with restrictions, look for the real root of the problem and do something about it.

SUN TRINE URANUS

You're lively and excited, and if you don't spend this day in new endeavors and making discoveries, you're wasting a lot of valuable

Uranian energy. You won't try to deceive yourself today, so it's a good time to learn all you can about yourself in new ways, though this is not the best of all possible times to sit quietly and meditate. Get out and experience!

SUN OPPOSITION URANUS

Facets of yourself that you may not have dealt with or even been aware of heretofore may be brought to your attention today through surprising, upsetting, or unexpected turns in a personal or business relationship. Take note now; deal with their practical aspects later.

SUN CONJUNCT NEPTUNE

You may be so in tune with others you forget yourself, or you may wish to totally withdraw from reality. If you react in the latter fashion, don't try to escape through drugs or alcohol at this time. Daydream or meditate instead. You're also more aware of, and may find yourself more than usually interested in, the spiritual or occult.

SUN SEXTILE NEPTUNE

You're more spiritually aware today and would greatly benefit from going off by yourself to meditate. You're able to achieve greater self-understanding than usual. You're also more aware of and sensitive to others.

SUN TRINE NEPTUNE

Your idealism is triggered, and you may be tempted to see yourself and others through rose-colored glasses. This is not inherently bad, as long as you can retain some semblance of contact with reality. You wish to understand more on a spiritual level and may delve into such matters. Your spiritual sensitivity is heightened, and you may experience ESP or something mystical. A good day for solitary contemplation.

SUN OPPOSITION NEPTUNE

You're not feeling very confident or assertive today and may even be enmeshed in confusion. This would be a good day to simply contemplate yourself and your life and what you've learned, without trying to understand it all. Avoid confrontations or commitments under this transit.

SUN CONJUNCT PLUTO

Whatever happens today will occur or affect you on a deeper level than usual. This transit calls for you to get really involved in all your experiences. Try to observe from an inner level of knowledge.

SUN SEXTILE PLUTO

Transformation is a word often associated with Pluto, and now would be a good time to embark on a journey of personal transformation. You might want to look into occult subjects—psychology, yoga, meditation, or whatever appeals to you in this area to aid you in your quest.

SUN SQUARE PLUTO

This is a good time for changes, including those of the inner self. Be prepared to let go of the old and embrace the new, for you will be challenged to do so.

SUN TRINE PLUTO

You're apt to encounter intense experiences today that will help teach you more about yourself and the world. The inner you knows if any changes need to be made, either in your inner or outer life. Listen. Then make them. They will come easily now.

SUN OPPOSITION PLUTO

Air-clearing encounters with others may give you insight into areas of yourself perhaps hidden or submerged till now. Pay attention and set about making corrections. You can make vital changes in your life now but must seek to benefit all involved, not just yourself.

SUN OPPOSITION MIDHEAVEN

Today is best spent introspectively and in the company of close friends and family. You're recharging yourself and must pay attention to your inner needs.

SUN CONJUNCT ASCENDANT

You're infused with new energy, vigor, and joy for living. This is a new beginning, a personal new year—take advantage of it.

SUN SEXTILE ASCENDANT

Today you need to be "stroked," to be acknowledged by your

family and friends. Don't be afraid to let people know you need them, too.

SUN TRINE ASCENDANT

You're feeling good and sociable. Go out with your friends and have a good time. Save hard work for later, if you can—unless you really get your kicks from your work.

SUN OPPOSITION ASCENDANT

Be aware of your reactions to others and of theirs to you, and you can learn a lot about yourself today.

MOON IN FIRST HOUSE

You'll be in tune with your feelings and able to give emotional support to others. Or, you may crave it yourself. You won't be able to muster much objectivity now.

MOON IN SECOND HOUSE

You'll enjoy being surrounded by old, familiar objects. Your possessions have sentimental value, and you feel very attached to them. This is obviously not a good time to clean out the attic or garage, unless you can recognize it's the emotion, not the object itself, that you value.

MOON IN FOURTH HOUSE

Now is an excellent time to meditate on your own inner workings and behavior patterns. Look within and see if, in certain situations, you may not be automatically acting from childhood training or past habits that are no longer necessary or appropriate.

MOON IN FIFTH HOUSE

Your emotional self is intensified now, and you shouldn't try to hide your feelings, except to avoid being overpossessive or over-protective in a relationship. Your nurturing nature may be triggered, which is fine and can be beautiful if not allowed to get out of hand. A woman may be very meaningful in your life now, showing you, or bringing out, aspects of yourself you may not have realized were there before.

MOON IN SIXTH HOUSE

Do not repress, suppress, or disguise your feelings. Show them.

Don't put on your martyr mask, either.

MOON IN SEVENTH HOUSE

All your relationships, but especially those with women, are apt to be more emotional than usual. Pay attention to what you're doing, saying, and feeling, and you'll be able to learn things about yourself you're not usually aware of. Try to observe what's happening.

MOON IN EIGHTH HOUSE

You're likely to be more emotional than usual and may even feel not quite yourself during some of these transits. (It occurs once a month.) You may have more psychic experiences during this time. You may feel possessive about joint property or belongings. Consider: Is this a productive attitude?

MOON IN NINTH HOUSE

You want to get out of your normal, everyday routine and yet don't want to leave the security of the familiar around you. How about beginning a new study or cerebral adventure at home—like reading a book, meditating, or daydreaming yourself elsewhere?

MOON IN TWELFTH HOUSE

Subconscious moods or attitudes may be affecting your life and relationships. You may feel like retreating, which is not what you should do—at least not totally. It would be helpful to discuss your deep, possibly buried, feelings with a trusted friend and also to meditate alone on any feelings or attitudes you'd rather keep hidden. Facing them will probably show you they're not as terrible as you thought.

MOON CONJUNCT SUN

Unless under another, longer, depressing transit, you'll feel harmoniously integrated in body, mind, and soul today.

MOON SEXTILE SUN

A time of harmony—a brief respite from the daily crush of events. A good time to appraise yourself and your situation, but also to be with others.

MOON TRINE SUN

Barring strong counter-indications, you'll feel good, harmonious, and in sync with the world during this time.

MOON OPPOSITION SUN

You may be conscious of a dichotomy between your emotional and your mental natures, or, to put it differently, between your left and right brain selves. Make an effort to harmonize these conflicting portions, and your life will go more smoothly.

MOON CONJUNCT MOON

You probably feel the need to be alone for a while. You'll be very emotionally aware and intense under this transit, and women may be very important in your life now. You'll want to be in familiar surroundings.

MOON SEXTILE MOON

You need intimate, in-depth encounters with others today, and will probably be in tune with women more than men. You seek to be with close friends and relatives, if anyone.

MOON SQUARE MOON

Your emotions seem to be at odds today and this, of course, reflects in your outer life. Women, especially, may be a source of conflict, but you can learn about your emotional self through these encounters.

MOON TRINE MOON

You feel emotionally calm and integrated. This will manifest in a generally harmonious outer life, and you'll want to be surrounded by close friends and family. This is a time for inner recharging, not for slaying dragons in the wide, wide world.

MOON OPPOSITION MOON

There may be emotional conflicts today, which, if you can rise above them and observe how others are affected, can lead to personal growth and understanding. This probably won't be easy, but you should try.

MOON CONJUNCT MERCURY

Your moods will have the upper hand for the brief span of this transit, and you can express your feelings more easily than usual. This is not a good time to make decisions, but you can find out what your feelings really *are* about something and use that knowledge later.

MOON TRINE MERCURY

You're very much tuned in to your emotions and can express them easily. Your logical faculties are not eclipsed, which gives you an unusual and helpful balance. This is a good time to tell someone how much you love them and to make insightful, reasoned decisions in almost any area.

MOON OPPOSITION MERCURY

You may be able to gain great insight into your true, inner self, either alone or with the help of another. Recognize that you're not apt to be too rational today, and you can learn much about your emotional self.

MOON CONJUNCT VENUS

Your mood is cheerful and you'll want to socialize. Go ahead. It's a great time for it.

MOON SEXTILE VENUS

You feel pleasant and cheerful and happy and in rapport with one and all. Fight the passive self-indulgence you may also be feeling, and get out there and have some fun.

MOON SQUARE VENUS

You feel very pleasant and sociable now. Enjoy.

MOON TRINE VENUS

You feel lazy, pleasant, and self-indulgent now, and you'll get along well with others. The more altruistic side of your nurturing instincts may be evident today; you won't try to be overprotective.

MOON OPPOSITION VENUS

Aside from your tendency to overeat, overdrink, or overspend, this is apt to be a very congenial time. You want to be with others, and if you are observant, you can learn and grow through your interactions, even negative ones.

MOON CONJUNCT MARS

You're likely to feel irritable and want only to have your own way.

Your best bet is to cool off, get control of yourself, and be willing to compromise.

MOON SQUARE MARS

You may feel irritable and rash or singled out to be picked upon by others, depending on your temperament. The trick is to direct your emotions reasonably and properly. Be careful of turning them in on yourself, perhaps in the form of an accident.

MOON TRINE MARS

You feel confident and courageous today, able to communicate well and reasonably.

MOON OPPOSITION MARS

This may be an irritable and emotional time. Try to stay cool and in control; the storm will pass rather quickly.

MOON CONJUNCT JUPITER

You have good feelings toward everyone, and they'll be reciprocated. Contact with women will probably be mutually beneficial. You may begin a search on an intuitive level for metaphysical insights during this brief transit.

MOON SEXTILE JUPITER

Your genuine warmth and affection for others will show during this transit and will be reciprocated. You'll especially enjoy being with old friends. Contact with women may be especially beneficial.

MOON SQUARE JUPITER

Your intellectual interest in religion or other topics above the mundane is likely to perk up during this transit. You'll be feeling good about yourself, and if you can sidestep the pitfall of acting holier-than-thou, this will probably be a very pleasant time.

MOON TRINE JUPITER

You feel good about yourself and others now, and you genuinely want to help them on a practical level. You realize that doing so helps you, too.

MOON OPPOSITION JUPITER

You may go through a period of uneasiness now, during which

you'll seek more personal freedom. You'll wonder if you're heading in the right direction and may even question whether your basic assumptions are valid. Now is a good time for this type of soul-searching.

MOON CONJUNCT SATURN

You're very likely holding in or trying to evade your emotions. You feel lonely and deserted by all humankind. Pessimism is attempting to reign supreme. On top of all that, you may be trying to deal with some sort of guilt. Relating to women may be difficult. However, take heart—this is a relatively brief transit, and besides, things are probably not really as bad as they seem at the moment.

MOON SEXTILE SATURN

You're tranquil and thoughtful now, and would just as soon be with no-nonsense people or no one at all. Your emotional needs are well-balanced with the rest of you now.

MOON SQUARE SATURN

You're tending to see only the negative now—in yourself, in others, in life in general. Don't wallow in this or take everything so gravely. Your outlook is off at the moment. Things will brighten up very soon.

MOON TRINE SATURN

You're able to handle and to view yourself and your emotions dispassionately. This is a good time to be alone to think about yourself or to talk with a respected older person about problems. You won't feel lonely even when alone, however, but full of inner strength and peace.

MOON OPPOSITION SATURN

You're apt to be in a "down" mood now, giving in to depression more easily than usual—depression that is usually baseless. You may feel lonely and cut off from others, yet seem to repel them even if they do try to cheer you up. Fortunately, this transit is rather brief. Simply waiting for it to pass works best.

MOON CONJUNCT URANUS

For the few hours this transit is in effect, you'll feel impulsive, perhaps rash, and restless with your usual routine. OK, so break out of your mold for a while—just try not to be *too* wild and crazy, or you could be sorry very, very shortly.

MOON SEXTILE URANUS

This transit stimulates an inner excitement, an openness to new experiences and ideas. You may feel restless, but not uncomfortably so.

MOON SQUARE URANUS

You're in a stubborn, rebellious, independent mood and don't want anyone telling you what to do. Your need for excitement is extreme; your emotions may feel scrambled. This is not a time to make important decisions.

MOON TRINE URANUS

You want the new, the unusual; you feel you absolutely require excitement. And you'll probably get it.

MOON OPPOSITION URANUS

You're feeling downright contrary and will very likely mutiny against anyone who tries to restrict you. You may be uptight, excitable, and possibly in for an emotional, disrupting surprise. This brief period is no time to make any important decisions.

MOON CONJUNCT NEPTUNE

Your sensitivity to others is enhanced. Try to avoid those of a negative turn for now. This is a good time for daydreaming or discussing problems with a friend, though there is some danger of misinterpretation, even self-delusion.

MOON SEXTILE NEPTUNE

You're very attuned to others during this transit, which can be detrimental if you're around those of a negative or destructive nature. You may want to spend some time daydreaming, either alone or discussing them with a good friend. Meditation or other means of self-knowledge can be very beneficial at this time.

MOON SQUARE NEPTUNE

You'll feel dreamy, possibly detached. There may be psychic insights or occurrences, or just daydreams. Whatever transpires, be aware that your sense of reality is askew under this transit. Be prepared to reevaluate everything later, after this transit is over, and to put off making decisions until then, too.

MOON TRINE NEPTUNE

You're in a mood to just daydream and let your imagination run free. You're psychically sensitive and are interested in this aspect of your life. Avoid being around negative people; you'll pick up their mood too easily. This would be a good time to spend time alone and get in touch with your inner self.

MOON OPPOSITION NEPTUNE

Your subconscious fears and complexes are coming to the fore and coloring all you see. You may feel confused and wish to retreat from the world around you. What's happening is that you're responding to inner, not outer, stimuli. Try getting in touch with your higher self and tapping into some inner wisdom to help you understand and get through this period.

MOON CONJUNCT PLUTO

Strong feelings, dredged up from the briny deep within you, are bobbing to the surface and the shore now. This is a good time for self-analysis or professional therapy. Insights that may seem like a direct pronouncement from the oracle may come to you, but wait for this transit to pass before deciding to set sail for Troy.

MOON SEXTILE PLUTO

Emotions from the deep will be emerging, possibly triggering intense encounters. If you try to understand these subconscious drives, you probably can. You'll be motivated to probe into the hidden and mysterious.

MOON SQUARE PLUTO

If you've been trying to hide or ignore your emotions, they're likely to emerge now in the form of powerful, irrational urges or explosive emotional confrontations. The best way to handle this intense emotional energy is to stop ignoring your feelings and courageously and frankly face up to them. Do not recoil from honest self-appraisal.

MOON TRINE PLUTO

Your emotions and your sensitivity are both heightened, and by observing your response to others and to life in general, you can learn a great deal about yourself and your feelings. Your encounters are apt to be intense—and probably rewarding. Express your feelings, but don't forget you have a mind, too.

MOON OPPOSITION PLUTO

Your deep, subconscious emotions are coming to the surface, and intense emotional conflicts with others are a distinct possibility. Reassess whatever occurs after this transit is passed; you may gain precious insight into yourself and others. Obviously, this is no time to make important decisions.

MOON SEXTILE MIDHEAVEN

If you're comfortable with your emotions, this will be a period of emotionally enriched experience o. yourself and your life. If not, you'll probably stumble through this transit on automatic pilot, unawares.

MOON TRINE MIDHEAVEN

You feel at one, emotionally in tune to all and everything in your world—a good time to quietly cherish your life and your emotional response to it and to others.

MOON OPPOSITION MIDHEAVEN

Now is a good time to be alone and meditate, to make contact with your inner self—or to be with close friends and family. You'll feel refreshed and reenergized.

MOON CONJUNCT ASCENDANT

More emotionally alive than usual, you can relate to others very intensely, unless dealing with emotions bothers you. If so, you'll probably react out of habit, perhaps from subconscious motives, and things might get a little unpleasant for you.

MOON SQUARE ASCENDANT

Your emotions will be powerful but changeable, and they may manifest either as total sympathy for others or as abject self-centeredness. Being with and relating to others will help in any case, bringing you face-to-face with reality.

MOON TRINE ASCENDANT

You're emotionally in tune now. Observe yourself and your reactions as you relate to others now. Greater self-understanding can result.

MOON OPPOSITION ASCENDANT

You're more sensitive to the emotions of others as well as to your own now. This is a time when you need to be with loved ones to both give and receive affection and emotional support.

MERCURY IN FIRST HOUSE

Your intellectual objectivity has shifted into gear. This is a good time to delve into yourself and observe.

MERCURY IN SECOND HOUSE

Whatever is of value to you, whether it be spiritual or material, will concern you now. You'll be either actively involved in it or planning, thinking, or talking about it.

MERCURY IN FOURTH HOUSE

Your thoughts and attention will turn to your private life now. Should you find yourself dwelling on the past, try to relate it to your present situation.

MERCURY IN FIFTH HOUSE

You'll be in the mood for intellectual fun and games. It's also a good time for you to communicate; just don't forget to listen.

MERCURY IN EIGHTH HOUSE

This is a good time to think about the deeper aspects of yourself and possibly of others. Interest in the occult, the hidden, or the mysterious is stimulated for you. You may have some esoteric intellectual exchanges.

MERCURY IN ELEVENTH HOUSE

This is a good time to examine your ideals and goals in relation to groups you belong to, whether clubs or demographic classes. Are the ideals really your own? Discussing this with (preferably unbiased) friends may help.

MERCURY IN TWELFTH HOUSE

You may want to keep everything inside yourself now, but it would be better to speak out frankly and communicate. You'll be more attuned to the deeper reaches of yourself.

MERCURY CONJUNCT SUN

Your mind is eager and restless, and you're in touch with your own goals and purposes. A good time to communicate, if you remember to listen to others, too. Travel would be an ideal learning experience now.

MERCURY SEXTILE SUN

Your curiosity knows no bounds today. You'll find meaning even in the most mundane around you.

MERCURY SEXTILE MOON

This is a good time for introspection and self-communication, or if you can't get a handle on something by yourself, to discuss it with someone. You're very much in harmony with your own and others' feelings today.

MERCURY SQUARE MOON

Because unconscious impulses and past habits of thought and behavior may surface today, this is a good time to examine your thoughts and feelings to see if they're really yours. Examining your unconscious or "automatic" responses will help you discover whether you're bringing on your own problems and, if so, to stop blaming others.

MERCURY CONJUNCT VENUS

You'll be able to see more clearly the unifying threads of various events and experiences warping and woofing through your life. This will help you to a better understanding and appreciation of the entire fabric of your current trek through material reality.

MERCURY SEXTILE VENUS

Relax, rest, enjoy pleasant surroundings or aesthetic pursuits. You need this day for recharging. Really. Do it.

MERCURY SQUARE VENUS

Today you'll probably feel just plain good and may be tempted toward various forms of self-indulgence. Okay, but do try to exercise *some* restraint.

MERCURY TRINE VENUS

You'll feel good today and will want to share this feeling. It's a good time for socializing.

MERCURY OPPOSITION VENUS

You feel more like enjoying and possibly indulging yourself than working. You don't even want to talk about anything serious.

MERCURY CONJUNCT MARS

You may feel irritable today and want to argue just for the fun of it. Appropriately or not, you may also feel defensive about almost anything.

MERCURY SQUARE MARS

You may be irritable, and the least little thing may set you off. Or, you may be OK but have to deal with someone else who's cranky. In either case, self-examination would be beneficial: Is what ticks you off symptomatic of some deeper, suppressed anger or frustration?

MERCURY TRINE MARS

Your self-confidence and physical energy are high. You feel as if you could take on the world single-handedly. Well, go ahead, give it a shot!

MERCURY OPPOSITION MARS

As with the square to Mars, you'll likely feel irritable or draw combative people to you. Again, self-examination will be beneficial. Suppressed anger or frustration is likely to be the culprit. Find out what it is and you can make some real progress.

MERCURY CONJUNCT JUPITER

Today the advantage of the broad overview of life is yours—an excellent time for self-examination.

MERCURY SEXTILE JUPITER

Today you can grasp how the little bits and pieces of your everyday life fit into a universal motif. Your self-understanding is thereby enhanced, and all areas of your world will benefit.

MERCURY SQUARE JUPITER

In your optimism today, you make grand plans because now you can see the broad view. You may tend to act a bit "grand" as well, however. Avoid this and all will go well.

MERCURY TRINE JUPITER

You have grand scope and optimism now, and if you can exert some self-discipline, you should be able to handle even difficult problems.

MERCURY CONJUNCT SATURN

You're in a somber, nit-picking mood. Details overwhelm the big picture for you. Make a concerted effort to think positively in all areas, and don't be afraid to speak out.

MERCURY SEXTILE SATURN

This is not one of your more lighthearted transits, though it won't go so far as depression, unless you lean that way anyway. You'll be able to concentrate well on details and the practical aspects of living. A good time to make necessary changes in your life or attitudes.

MERCURY SQUARE SATURN

You may feel detached and unwilling to make an effort to communicate. You may even feel lonely. It would help if you realized you're seeing only the negative side of life right now—and that this will soon pass.

MERCURY OPPOSITION SATURN

You may feel moody, broody, and gloomy today, wondering about yourself and your slot in the overall scheme of things. Positive thinking and constructive action are your shuttle tickets out of this space at the moment.

MERCURY SEXTILE URANUS

Do something different and spontaneous. Loosen up; you'll make exciting new discoveries. Just let the world happen today, and go along with it.

MERCURY SEXTILE NEPTUNE

Imagination and intuition are stimulated now, and you may feel like daydreaming much of the time. You may become more interested in the spiritual aspects of reality, in which case, new insights will amaze you.

MERCURY SQUARE NEPTUNE

You feel a little "spaced" today, having trouble keeping in touch with the realities of this world. Be careful of over-idealizing, or uncritically accepting, anyone or anything—including spiritual or mystical revelations.

MERCURY OPPOSITION NEPTUNE

This transit may bring increased spiritual awareness. However, some "great truths" that come to you today may bear closer inspection in a day or two. You may be in one of Neptune's famous fogs. Don't make any permanent arrangements until you've had awhile to be sure of them.

MERCURY SEXTILE PLUTO

This transit leads you to dig deeper for true and accurate knowledge, and what you learn will bring about beneficial changes in your life.

MERCURY SQUARE PLUTO

You want to get to the heart and root of any subject now, and if you can turn this probing searchlight within, you can gain valuable insight and self-awareness.

MERCURY TRINE PLUTO

As always with Pluto, you're not satisfied with the superficial. Going within to explore your inner dimensions would be very advantageous now.

MERCURY OPPOSITION PLUTO

This a good time for getting in touch with your subconscious and for learning about your inner dimensions, because you're willing to delve beyond the superficial.

MERCURY CONJUNCT MIDHEAVEN

This is an especially suitable time to consider your future and to make sure your goals and plans will really gratify your needs.

MERCURY SEXTILE MIDHEAVEN

Now you can agreeably and fruitfully spend your time making plans and communicating with anyone, including yourself. This is a time when you can truly know your own mind and feelings.

MERCURY OPPOSITION MIDHEAVEN

At this time, if you try, you can disregard dogma, indoctrination, and the hopes and fears of others. You'll be able to get a handle on what you really want, need, and hope to achieve during this lifetime.

VENUS IN FIRST HOUSE

You're in an extremely pleasant mood, and you'll benefit from indulging yourself in rest and recreation, fun and games, or just plain visiting during this transit.

VENUS IN THIRD HOUSE

You'll be in a lighthearted and sociable mood. This is an excellent time to notice and appreciate all the love and affection in your life. Don't keep it a secret; share it.

VENUS IN FOURTH HOUSE

You'll feel more in harmony with your family and loved ones during this transit, mainly because you're more in touch with yourself.

VENUS IN FIFTH HOUSE

This is not the best of all possible times to grind away at your duties. You just won't be in the mood. Treat yourself to a good time with friends and family, or work on creative projects if you can.

VENUS IN NINTH HOUSE

You'll want to seek the new and different in art, people, events, or places, simply for the joy and the experience of it. You'll expand your vision of life and probably will enjoy every minute of it.

VENUS IN TWELFTH HOUSE

To reap the best rewards from this transit you must be sincerely selfless in helping others, which you may very well find yourself doing at this time. If you serve only to "be rewarded" psychologically or otherwise, satisfaction will elude you.

VENUS CONJUNCT MERCURY

You'll be in a lighthearted, sociable mood. Enjoy. Tell someone you love them and watch their face light up.

VENUS SEXTILE MERCURY

Your mood is lighthearted and sociable. Go out and enjoy yourself with friends and loved ones.

VENUS SQUARE MERCURY

This transit finds you in a lighthearted, sociable mood. Enjoy yourself with friends and, if possible, leave serious work or philosophy until later.

VENUS SEXTILE VENUS

You're in a good mood, and events will probably bear out your feeling that all's right with your particular world today.

VENUS SQUARE JUPITER

You're feeling good and sociable, and you'll enjoy being with others. They'll enjoy it too, if you can curb a possible tendency to think you can do no wrong. Your willpower is low, so be careful when it comes to self-indulgence during all this socializing.

VENUS TRINE JUPITER

You feel happy, satisfied, and perhaps a little lazy. You'd very much enjoy social events during this transit.

VENUS OPPOSITION JUPITER

This is basically a pleasant day if you can scrounge up enough self-discipline to avoid overdoing anything to the point of imminent regret.

VENUS SQUARE SATURN

This is a good day to be alone and introspective, especially about relationships. You may learn a great deal about yourself in the bargain, but don't take steps to change anything until this transit is over. It tends to make things look gloomier than they are.

VENUS OPPOSITION SATURN

You're apt to feel depressed, possibly out-of-sync with the world, and events may compel you to recognize facets of yourself you generally try to ignore. Observe your reactions, and you may learn a great deal about yourself. But don't take this current case of the blues too seriously, however; this transit will soon pass.

VENUS TRINE URANUS

You're looking for the new and unusual, and you'll probably find it—either by doing something or going somewhere you usually wouldn't, or by meeting new types of people. Observe your reactions; you have an opportunity for self-realization under new circumstances.

VENUS CONJUNCT NEPTUNE

Your sense of reality is somewhat weakened today, but your sense of beauty and appreciation of it is enhanced. Dream on, dream on, and save practical planning for later.

VENUS SEXTILE NEPTUNE

You may find yourself drifting in daydreams today, unable to marshal enough ambition to do much of anything. If so, enjoy yourself; we all need recharging in never-never land once in a while.

VENUS OPPOSITION MIDHEAVEN

You feel pleasantly lazy today and are happy to stay home and leave windmill-tilting to others. You're in an affectionate and sociable mood and want to be with familiar people in familiar surroundings.

VENUS SEXTILE ASCENDANT

You're in a happy mood and will enjoy being with all types of people. You just plain feel great and want to let your "light" shine upon the just and the unjust.

MARS IN SECOND HOUSE

You'll be concerned with your values, beliefs, and possessions and may tend to excessively identify with them. Realize that you are no more what you believe or possess than you are what you do for a living, and remember it should you find yourself in disputes over any of this.

MARS IN THIRD HOUSE

You may be rather contentious today and feel that you have to defend your beliefs as though your honor was at stake. Obviously, this is not generally necessary; you are not your beliefs. However, if you do need to convince someone of something, you'll have the confidence and pizazz to do so—if you're careful not to come off sounding like an arrogant know-it-all.

MARS IN FOURTH HOUSE

Pay attention. Subconscious drives or motives, even memories, dredged up from the deep may surface and influence your actions during this time. By being aware of this and of what you're doing, you can exercise more control and learn a great deal about yourself.

MARS IN FIFTH HOUSE

You'll have a lot of energy, but not much self-discipline during this transit. Mostly, you'd just like to enjoy yourself. Well, go ahead if you can. Everyone deserves a break now and then. Do something physically active and demanding, but not dangerous.

MARS IN SIXTH HOUSE

You have much energy and the desire and discipline to get a lot of work done. Keep physically active and don't suppress frustrations.

MARS IN EIGHTH HOUSE

This transit is likely to trigger some sort of change or metamorphosis in almost any area of your life. When it's over, you or your circumstances will be altered somehow, either subtly or dramatically.

MARS IN NINTH HOUSE

Realize you are not your beliefs, and quit taking everything so personally. Nor should you try to cram your ideas into anyone else. It's better to spend your time broadening your own horizons. Seek your own enlightenment and let others alone to seek theirs.

MARS IN ELEVENTH HOUSE

Pursue your aims and ambitions now, but you and they will be better served if the achievement of your goals involves working harmoniously with others. Cooperation with others is the hallmark of the eleventh house.

MARS IN TWELFTH HOUSE

Look within, not without, for the source of your irritability and frustrations at this time. Emerging subconscious drives are probably at work. Relentlessly observe yourself and your actions. Work alone as much as you can during this transit, or help others through some sort of charity work.

MARS TRINE SUN

Your self-confidence is high, as is your energy, and you feel you can tackle anything. This is a good time to make decisions, take action, talk with or confront those in authority.

MARS SEXTILE MOON

Your emotions are powerful at the moment, even passionate. You're more subjective than usual now, so it's best to hold off on anything requiring rigorous objectivity.

MARS SQUARE MOON

You're apt to feel moody, irrational, irritable, impulsive, compulsive, and downright hard to get along with. You may find yourself acting, or wanting to act, childishly. Remain aware of what you're doing, however, and you can control it. Observe yourself and you can learn and grow.

MARS TRINE MOON

Your life will take on a deeply emotional quality now, but it isn't out of control. You can handle it and can appreciate the added dimension to your experiences.

MARS OPPOSITION MOON

You have a chance now to increase your self-knowledge through your relationships, especially close ones. It may not be completely pleasant, however. Unless you can remain acutely self-aware and observant, you'll either act out subconscious emotional drives or project them onto another who'll act them out toward you.

MARS SEXTILE MARS

Your energy and self-confidence are high now, and you create a favorable impression with everyone. This is a good time to get out and work hard with others or to play some vigorous team sport. You will all benefit.

MARS SQUARE MARS

You're likely to feel irritable, angry, rash, and impulsive today unless you can channel your very high energy appropriately, preferably into hard physical activity.

MARS TRINE MARS

You're full of self-confidence and energy, able to assert yourself appropriately. You'll miss valuable self-information and opportunity for growth if you waste this transit in idleness.

MARS SQUARE JUPITER

You have incredible energy and confidence now, but this can sometimes lead to overconfidence and impulsiveness. Try not to overdo in any area, especially in seeking self-glorification.

MARS TRINE JUPITER

This is a good time to pursue personal growth and to get involved in anything that can help you toward that goal.

MARS OPPOSITION JUPITER

If you can become and remain aware of what you're doing and avoid overextension of any sort, this should be a favorable transit for you, even "lucky."

MARS SEXTILE SATURN

You're capable of great self-discipline now. It's therefore a good time to pursue personal growth and self-understanding, or any other task with long-term rewards.

MARS SQUARE SATURN

There are going to be frustrations. Part of you says go ahead and another part says, "No, no. You're not good enough." Be aware of this and proceed with all deliberate speed. After a while you'll understand that most of your fears are irrational.

MARS TRINE SATURN

You're able to closely and carefully observe yourself now, and by so doing, may learn a great deal.

MARS CONJUNCT URANUS

You're feeling rash and impulsive and full of seemingly uncontrolled bursts of energy. You'll not tolerate any inhibition of your freedom whatsoever. Conflicts may arise. Surprising events may happen. Asserting yourself in appropriate fashions will help you cope with this transit.

MARS SEXTILE URANUS

You're restless and want excitement. The normal routine will bore you bananas. You'll seek new experiences and be open to new thoughts and insights.

MARS SQUARE URANUS

You may feel like revolting against almost anything under this transit, and indeed it is a time when change is necessary. If you resist making changes at this point, serious disruptions may occur. Change will be easier and less upsetting if done willingly now.

MARS TRINE URANUS

This can be an exciting time of personal growth and self-discovery. You'll feel wonderful, and because you're open to new experiences, you'll be able to find the inner strength necessary to step out of old routines and restrictions.

MARS OPPOSITION URANUS

Either you'll find yourself totally irritated with restricting persons or circumstances and will have an air-clearing row or, if you've been working to free yourself right along, you'll get a small, sweet taste of success. Others will resist the changes you're making, however, and give you a hard time. Don't give up, though. Creative change is necessary for personal growth.

MARS CONJUNCT NEPTUNE

You may feel irritable, down, or just "different" for no apparent reason. Delusions and illusions are rampant, and you won't really know what's what until this transit is over. But whatever you do must be done without a shred of ulterior motive.

MARS SEXTILE NEPTUNE

Your ego energies are somewhat dampened by Neptune right now. This is therefore a good time to meditate and engage in self-evaluation.

MARS SQUARE NEPTUNE

This transit tests your resolve roughly every six months, causing you and possibly others to challenge whether you're on the right track. Be aware that doubt, insecurity, and discouragement are inherent with this transit. Also, at all costs, don't give in to the temptation to do something underhanded.

MARS TRINE NEPTUNE

Your ego demands are relatively low now; this would be a good time to meditate on your life and yourself. On another level, selfless-ness is emphasized under this transit, and exercising it by doing some sort of charitable work is recommended.

MARS OPPOSITION NEPTUNE

You're feeling down, insecure, and possibly discouraged. Self-less work for others is advised. You'll not get ego-gratification under this transit, and if you go after it, things are apt to backfire. You'll get the same result if you stoop to deviousness. Whatever happens, keep your eyes open, face facts honestly, and get on with your life. Things *will* get better.

MARS CONJUNCT PLUTO

Your ego energies are strong now, and what you're really interested in is power. Trouble is, others may be, too, and intense ego conflicts could ensue. By being aware of all this, however, you can make an effort to control your own energies and use them creatively.

MARS SEXTILE PLUTO

Meditation and self-examination now will help clarify your ob-jectives in life and lead to better self-knowledge.

MARS SQUARE PLUTO

Try to retain your calm and your ideals and don't step on others for personal gain or resort to devious action, and this powerful energy can be channeled into creative change and accomplishment in your life.

MARS TRINE PLUTO

This can be a time of greater insight and self-understanding. Be open and it will come.

MARS OPPOSITION PLUTO

This is an excellent opportunity to use your considerable energies to effect transformation in your life, even if you meet opposition. Avoid any attempts at underhandedness, and seek help from others if your opposition should behave that way.

MARS CONJUNCT MIDHEAVEN

You're self-confident and assertive now, and if you can avoid operating totally out of egotism, all should go well.

MARS SEXTILE MIDHEAVEN

This is a time when your self-confidence is enhanced. Notice what it feels like and the results you get in the outer world, and try to regain that feeling at times when it's lacking.

MARS SQUARE MIDHEAVEN

You're able to assert yourself with considerable vigor, which, of course, could be either helpful or detrimental, depending upon your usual level of aggression. Either way, knowing this inner power is there and available during this time can help you moderate it or use it to the hilt in order to achieve your goals. Pay attention and you'll learn another lesson in the art of being you.

MARS TRINE MIDHEAVEN

You have a boost in self-confidence now, and this attitude, plus your high energy at the moment, enables you to accomplish much. You may achieve greater self-understanding through self-observation.

MARS TRINE ASCENDANT

You're self-confident, decisive, and dynamic and want to branch out in new pathways. Ask within for direction and you may end up surprising yourself with what you can do.

JUPITER IN FIRST HOUSE

A new 12-year cycle of spiritual growth and maturation begins with this transit. Seek to know yourself better now, and try to learn from everything that happens. You'll experience greater self-confidence and will therefore attract advantageous relationships and situations. This may very well be a fortunate and rewarding year.

JUPITER IN SECOND HOUSE

This is a time when you're likely to have the opportunity to learn more about yourself through the management of resources, whether they be material or not. Whatever you prize or desire may just come to you in spades. Just be sure it really is what you want. Be careful. Resources or possessions can sometimes manage you. Frankly assess your goals.

JUPITER IN FOURTH HOUSE

This is a good time to turn within for self-knowledge and evaluation while in the security and tranquility of your home and family. Facing truths, even unpleasant ones, about yourself will be relatively easy now and will help to straighten the path before you.

JUPITER IN FIFTH HOUSE

Self-confidence and assurance are yours now as never before. You're you, proud of it, and not afraid to show it. This is likely to be a time of growth for you as well.

JUPITER IN SIXTH HOUSE

Here, you are encouraged to develop a healthy attitude toward your duties and obligations. Realize that performing these tasks can be a meditation and a source of growth and satisfaction, and you'll be more than amply rewarded.

JUPITER IN SEVENTH HOUSE

With Jupiter in this house, you'll have the opportunity to learn more about yourself through your encounters with others, especially in any kind of close partnership. Pay attention; life is a school full of fascinating subjects—one of which is you.

JUPITER IN EIGHTH HOUSE

You may experience a powerful spiritual rebirth, whether it be along traditional religious lines or not, and delving into metaphysical subjects now could help you better understand yourself and the universe. At any rate, when this transit is over, you will have more insight into yourself in some manner.

JUPITER IN NINTH HOUSE

Your horizons are expanding as you're exposed to more and more experiences and ideas, and if you can maintain an open mind, you'll grow and mature in understanding of self and of life in general.

JUPITER IN TENTH HOUSE

Refrain from letting any success or recognition you may now receive go to your head and, on the whole, all should go well. Your confidence is boosted, and you'll probably feel wonderful.

JUPITER IN ELEVENTH HOUSE

Your efforts to further your ideals and ambitions should include or benefit others as well; unselfishness should be your motto. Work with and truly for others, and you'll be well rewarded.

JUPITER IN TWELFTH HOUSE

Your ego needs are somewhat dampened now, and you can quite beneficially engage in self-examination or soul-searching. You are very much interested in esoteric truth and growth. Someone who can guide you in this search may show up, or you may act in this capacity for someone.

JUPITER CONJUNCT SUN

This transit marks the beginning of a new 12-year cycle. You'll feel happy and upbeat and in the mood to expand your experience. This can be the beginning of one of your best years if you don't just sit around waiting for all that's good and wonderful to come to you on a silver platter. This is a good time to start anything new, especially continuing your education.

JUPITER SEXTILE SUN

You feel sure that all's right with the world and that things will turn out for the best. This positive attitude makes it a good time to reflect on your life and to plan for its future.

JUPITER SQUARE SUN

The question here is whether you can rein in Jupiter's exuberant expansionism and tendency to go overboard. If you can exercise self-discipline and not overdo in any area, this can be a period of increased personal insight. Especially beware of overconfidence and egotistical behavior.

JUPITER TRINE SUN

Seek out new experiences that can expand your understanding

and personal growth. Your self-confidence is high, and your sense of humor lends balance to the new perspective you can gain by looking around at the world and within yourself. You'll feel good and at peace.

JUPITER OPPOSITION SUN

This can be a period of intense personal growth if you allow it to be. If, that is, you realize that you do not have all the answers, that material success is not one of those answers, that you're going to have to seek within for the real answers. Now is the time to begin a journey of spiritual growth. This does not mean you have to join a monastery; just don't give all your attention to material success. Find someone to grow with and make it a mutual journey.

JUPITER CONJUNCT MOON

You're feeling secure within yourself and are able to give and receive on an emotional level. Women, especially, may be of benefit to you now.

JUPITER SEXTILE MOON

Jupiter's optimism and interest in the spiritual side of things permeate your being now. Insights will no doubt come to you, perhaps through your personal relationships, particularly with women.

JUPITER SQUARE MOON

You're more aware and in touch with your emotions than usual. In fact, if you're not careful, they can get out of hand. It's best to use your emotional impetus and sensitivity for helping others now. You may have to deal with areas of your past that you'd rather not face, but doing so will make you stronger than ever.

JUPITER TRINE MOON

This is not a particularly earth-shattering transit in any direction, but you're likely to feel good, positive, and in harmony with the universe.

JUPITER OPPOSITION MOON

You'll either feel kind and benevolent toward others or turn these feelings on yourself and be self-indulgent and demanding. Observe which species of bird you are, especially in close relationships, and you can make positive and creative changes in yourself, if necessary.

JUPITER CONJUNCT MERCURY

Your interest in spiritual or philosophical areas may be intensified, though you'll probably be more concerned with the practical aspect, rather than the mystical.

JUPITER TRINE MERCURY

This is a time of positive feelings and optimism. Take the initiative in looking for opportunities, making plans for the future, and attempting to actualize your ideas and ideals.

JUPITER CONJUNCT VENUS

You're feeling friendly and sociable. You may also be in a self-indulgent mood, so take care not to overdo. Surround yourself with beauty. Visit a museum, beautify your home, listen to beautiful music, go to a park—whatever. And take your friends.

JUPITER SEXTILE VENUS

You're feeling pleasant, unambitious, generally friendly, and possibly flirtatious. You want to surround yourself with beauty and may overspend on "trinkets."

JUPITER SQUARE VENUS

You'll probably feel sociable and friendly, possibly a little bit lazy. Your appreciation of beauty is accentuated, and you should try to surround yourself with it—a good day to go to the park or museum and relax.

JUPITER TRINE VENUS

You feel very much like being with friends and having a good time. You're probably tending toward self-indulgence, too, so be careful at those social gatherings you're inclined to attend now.

JUPITER SEXTILE MARS

Your energy, self-confidence, and health are good now. You feel great and are able to take advantage of opportunities as they arise.

JUPITER SQUARE MARS

Exuberance, energy, self-confidence, and impulsiveness characterize this transit. With discipline and caution, you can put this energy to very good use and accomplish a great deal. As with all Jupiter transits, though, be careful not to go overboard.

JUPITER TRINE MARS

You are ambitious and want very much to succeed. This is an excellent transit under which to initiate anything, including a program of self-development and growth. Don't neglect outlets for your physical energy, though.

JUPITER OPPOSITION MARS

You're incredibly full of energy and exuberance. Be aware of your limitations and don't overdo. Try to keep your cool.

JUPITER CONJUNCT JUPITER

This transit comes every 11 or 12 years and signifies a new cycle of growth and maturation. This may be a time of new opportunities, but it should also be a period of taking stock of yourself.

JUPITER SEXTILE JUPITER

This is an extraordinary time when everything, including growth, seems to happen as if by magic, without your having to do much of anything. Don't relax totally, though. You can be objective now and should use this opportunity to take stock of yourself and set goals. You can implement the necessary actions later.

JUPITER SQUARE JUPITER

Life is likely to be pretty hectic for you now, especially if you spread yourself too thin among duties and commitments. Be aware of yourself and your limitations though—both materially and spiritually— and things will run more smoothly.

JUPITER TRINE JUPITER

You're feeling content, confident, and relaxed at this point. Self-examination would be beneficial, as would seeking experiences that expand your horizons and understanding.

JUPITER OPPOSITION JUPITER

You're probably feeling so confident and optimistic you think you can take on the world single-handedly. A little restraint and caution might be advisable.

JUPITER CONJUNCT SATURN

This transit has to do with restriction—self-imposed or otherwise—and freedom. Either you'll find new freedom within your existing structures, or you'll break away from them entirely. This applies to either your inner or your outer world, and nothing will be quite the same after this transit.

JUPITER SEXTILE SATURN

Expansion and growth are balanced with practical caution. You'll begin to see how to actualize your ideals and work toward your goals with the patience of Job.

JUPITER SQUARE SATURN

This is a time of change, growth, and uncertainty. It would be good to try to sort things out alone. Take your time, there is no rush. Snap decisions will not work for you now.

JUPITER TRINE SATURN

You're concerned with the practical now, and you'll handle it very well, working patiently and carefully toward an eventual goal. This is a good time to be by yourself and sort things out, make plans, decide what you want. Don't overcommit yourself.

JUPITER OPPOSITION SATURN

You may feel pulled in two directions at once—toward total freedom or toward the security of your tried and true routines. You don't know whether to expand or retreat. You may make sweeping changes in your life, especially if you feel burdened by your obligations and responsibilities.

JUPITER CONJUNCT URANUS

You're torn between the needs of others and your own. You may suddenly gain new perspectives and see everything in a new light. You may kick over all traces and make a break for freedom—or you may not. Expect the unexpected.

JUPITER SEXTILE URANUS

You're tired of the same old routines and want to transform your life for the better. Your perspective is changing. Sudden occurrences may afford opportunity for growth.

JUPITER SQUARE URANUS

You urgently and impatiently want freedom now, and you'll probably get your opportunity one way or another. It will little benefit you, though, if you're in such a turmoil you can't recognize it or take advantage of it. Try to keep your cool, be patient, and exercise a little restraint.

JUPITER OPPOSITION URANUS

You want change and freedom from anything you perceive as limiting your growth, and you may very well get your chance when this opposition is exact. This will no doubt be a great relief to you, but consider carefully at this point. You don't want to toss out the computer with the damaged disc.

JUPITER CONJUNCT NEPTUNE

You're much more aware of your idealistic nature at this time, and you'll be inclined to turn more to your inner world, toward the spiritual and mystical, to find what the outer one cannot give you. Beware the illusion that all is right with the world when, in fact, it may not be. Keep your eyes open, in other words, even in a spiritual milieu.

JUPITER SEXTILE NEPTUNE

You're very aware of, and involved with, your ideals at this time. You're compassion is high as well, and you're seeking spiritual enlightenment. You needn't expect a turbaned guru (though that's possible); insight may come from the daily life around you.

JUPITER SQUARE NEPTUNE

Neptune has a way of creating beautiful, but impractical, illusions. The practical application of your ideals will be tested. Keep trying, but keep your eyes open—both about the people you'll be trying to help (some just won't be helped) and about the spiritual teachers you choose to follow now (remember about Neptune).

JUPITER TRINE NEPTUNE

Your idealism is awakened, and you desire to help one and all.

You may also be seeking deep spiritual truths, and someone who can help you in this quest may enter your life now. Or, you may act as guide for another. Either way, be wary of over-idealization.

JUPITER OPPOSITION NEPTUNE

Your quest is toward the spiritual now, and you may seek a utopian world to which you can escape from everyday reality. Do not for a moment think that drugs or alcohol can provide it. Insights may come to you, but it will be difficult to tell, until this transit is passed, whether they were real or not.

JUPITER CONJUNCT PLUTO

Here, the issue is power—how you get it and how you use it. Use it to improve yourself while adhering to the highest of ideals, and you'll greatly enhance your life.

JUPITER SEXTILE PLUTO

This is a time of change, regeneration, and transformation in your life. This can be on either a spiritual or material level, but one influences the other. You'll seek to better express the real, inner you. If power comes to you, maintain a high degree of integrity and work toward the good of all.

JUPITER SQUARE PLUTO

Be completely aboveboard in all your efforts now. You should closely examine your spiritual or metaphysical convictions and contemplate the ethics of trying to foist them on others. Obsessiveness is a possibility under this transit and should be guarded against.

JUPITER TRINE PLUTO

You can wield quite a force for effecting change in your life now. You must be careful, however, not to do so for entirely selfish reasons, but for the benefit of everyone in your sphere.

JUPITER OPPOSITION PLUTO

You must keep the goals of the group in mind and work toward them while maintaining integrity of the highest order if you're to achieve your own goals now.

JUPITER CONJUNCT MIDHEAVEN

Recognition is likely to come to you, and your entire life will broaden from new experiences, people, and places. The only caveat is not to overexpand or to let all this attention go to your head.

JUPITER SEXTILE MIDHEAVEN

Now is a good time to tune in to your inner self and gain greater self-knowledge. You're confident of your ability to mature and grow, and the opportunities to do so will probably come to you.

JUPITER SQUARE MIDHEAVEN

You have great ambition and confidence in yourself now and feel that you can accomplish near wonders. And you can, if you are careful not to overestimate your abilities or let your ego take over. Don't neglect any area of your life now; each is important.

JUPITER TRINE MIDHEAVEN

You feel confident, optimistic, peaceful, and serene. Don't get overconfident and overdo in any area. Despite what you're feeling now, a person can only do so much.

JUPITER OPPOSITION MIDHEAVEN

Now is a time to look to your inner self and toward personal growth, to tie up any loose ends from the past and establish a secure home base. You'll feel good about doing this and will learn a great deal.

JUPITER CONJUNCT ASCENDANT

You're growing and maturing, and your sphere of experience is expanding. You feel positive, optimistic and self-confident, and these attitudes will be reciprocated by the world at large. Make an effort to avoid feeling and acting superior to others, and this can be a very positive period of personal growth.

JUPITER TRINE ASCENDANT

You are ready now to grow in spiritual awareness and development. Someone may come along who will help you in this area. Your relationships, whether old or new, will be catalysts for this consciousness expansion.

JUPITER OPPOSITION ASCENDANT

You are seeking personal growth and will find relationships, new or old, to be mutually beneficial in this area. This is a good time to turn to someone for counseling of any sort.

SATURN IN FIRST HOUSE

Now and for the next several years you're going to have to look within, and if the outer world interferes with this process in any way, complications with it will ensue. You must devote time to your own introspection; inner development always precedes the outer.

SATURN IN SECOND HOUSE

Now you will learn more about yourself through the medium of whatever you cherish, whether material or spiritual. You'll have to learn what it is you really value, and this may not necessarily be what others (or you) think you should. If you have trouble with your possessions—either handling or keeping them—take a close look to see if you really value them all that much. Are you in charge or are they?

SATURN IN THIRD HOUSE

Now Saturn directs you to observe your thinking and your method of communicating. This is important, because as you think, so you and your environment are. This will be a time of introspection and evaluation. There will be some changes made, whether you're conscious of them or not.

SATURN IN FOURTH HOUSE

After years of relative quiet and introspection, you'll begin to turn your attention more to the outer world. Specifically, now you must take care of any problems in your personal and domestic life. This is a good time for psychotherapy, meditation, yoga, or other self-knowledge techniques to help you cope with possibly unresolved problems from the past.

SATURN IN FIFTH HOUSE

You are going to be making discoveries about yourself through the way you work or create and through encounters or confrontations with others. You will work harder and with greater discipline than usual. You're giving outer form to the inner restructuring you've been doing these last several years. Be organized, be observant, be patient.

SATURN IN EIGHTH HOUSE

During this time you are to learn more about yourself through your interdependence with others, or through their values and resources. Changes may occur in your life which precipitate these lessons. Also, you may become more interested in the mysteries of death and of life after death.

SATURN IN NINTH HOUSE

Very likely you're feeling comfortable with who you are now and think you know yourself very well. And probably you do. But you must guard against being rigid and thinking you have all the answers. Remain open to new ideas and insights to get the most out of this transit and the next one to come. You'll be interested in the practical aspects of attaining higher consciousness, as you should be now.

SATURN IN TENTH HOUSE

You'll feel as if you've finally grown up and really know who you are. You'll feel confident, in control, and perhaps revel in the sense of power that self-knowledge can bring. If you've worked hard and ethically, you'll feel that who you are now is a complete and satisfactory expression of your inner reality; and, in the outer world, you'll be able to shine as an individual star not lost in the masses of the Milky Way.

SATURN IN ELEVENTH HOUSE

You've had your chance to be an individual supernova; now you must learn to use your sparkling personality and abilities to work with others. Also, the ideals you've been trying to implement should begin to manifest if you've prepared and worked well for them.

SATURN IN TWELFTH HOUSE

A 29-year cycle is ending in preparation for a new one that will begin when Saturn enters your first house. Old ways, circumstances, projects, perhaps even persons and philosophies are fading from your life. Don't berate yourself or feel guilty about any of this. Such is life. Some things work, some don't. Look back over the last several years without evaluating, to see what you have or have not accomplished. Merely note your progress and prepare to go on, perhaps in new directions or areas.

SATURN SQUARE SUN

You may experience downheartedness in the face of various tests now. The best advice is to be patient and hang in there. Things will improve.

SATURN TRINE SUN

This can be a time of preparation for challenges that will come later on. Establishing a secure inner base through meditation or other self-knowledge techniques at this time will pay off later.

SATURN OPPOSITION SUN

This is the end of a 29-year cycle, and there are apt to be many endings or culminations in your life. Your energies are low and you feel discouraged, incapable of coping. Others may oppose you. Be patient and don't struggle and flail about too much. This, too, shall pass.

SATURN CONJUNCT MOON

Self-examination and self-doubt are likely to be the order of the day. Just remember you are human and that's OK, because that's what you're supposed to be now. Don't be so hard on yourself. You may feel discouraged and depressed, want to withdraw from others, and tend to make mountains out of molehills. This is no time for major life decisions. Things appear gloomier now than they really are.

SATURN SEXTILE MOON

You can observe and deal with difficult problems without letting your emotions dominate you. Now is a perfect time to initiate changes in your life, because you can be objective and detached.

SATURN SQUARE MOON

You may feel lonely, depressed, neglected, frustrated, even guilty. The underlying problem is likely to be conflict between your responsibilities and your emotional self, your need to be that self. You must make an effort to balance these two areas in order to achieve inner harmony, from which all else flows.

SATURN TRINE MOON

Your life is likely to be well-balanced and running smoothly for you. Seeking advice from someone older than you, especially a woman, is favored now; you may gain greatly in self-understanding.

SATURN OPPOSITION MOON

This can be a very difficult and emotionally stressing time. The problem, as in Saturn's square of the Moon, is likely to be an imbalance between your emotional self and your work-related responsibilities. You've favored one over the other. Though it may be difficult, you must make the effort to bring these two into harmony; you'll be a happier, more complete person as a result.

SATURN CONJUNCT MERCURY

Your attitude is more serious than usual; you may even feel a little depressed. However, you can thoroughly concentrate on details now and can use this time for a self "review." Do you really subscribe to all the beliefs you've been taking for granted for years?

SATURN SEXTILE MERCURY

You're of a serious turn of mind now and are not interested in the frivolous. A good time to make detailed plans, but stick to logic and reason—your intuition is in neutral.

SATURN SQUARE MERCURY

You may be feeling depressed and alienated. The basic problem may well be that you've allowed your attitudes and beliefs (and consequently yourself) to solidify into a rut that's no longer viable. Reexamine and change them if necessary. If you rigidly refuse to do so now, you'll face more difficult challenges and confusion in approximately seven years.

SATURN OPPOSITION MERCURY

Don't give in to negative thinking; that way leads to depression. Concentrate on responding positively to challenges and on improving your plans or ideas, and proceed.

SATURN CONJUNCT VENUS

This is a time of introspection and evaluation, especially concerning true identity and your relationship to people and possessions. Spend some time alone to do this.

SATURN SQUARE MARS

Try to be as self-aware as possible to help avert conflicts with others. Meditation or other awareness techniques will help. This is a time of testing and it will pass eventually. Learning to handle and vent anger properly will greatly improve your life.

SATURN OPPOSITION MARS

It may seem that the whole world is against you, and you may be smoldering with anger and frustration. Vigorous physical activity would be one way to ameliorate it. Learning to properly vent anger is another. Think back to actions you inaugurated about 14 years ago, and the real reasons for your difficulty may become apparent and thus solvable.

SATURN CONJUNCT JUPITER

You may be tense and restless during this transit or just the opposite—calm and steady. There are apt to be many changes in your life now, and your reactions will be determined by your inherent nature, which will be intensified.

SATURN SEXTILE JUPITER

You now have the chance to enhance your spiritual maturation, for you can look at your self more realistically than usual and can effectively use this insight. Don't let this opportunity for constructive change and growth pass unheeded.

SATURN TRINE JUPITER

The help or advice of older people may be of great help to your growth now.

SATURN OPPOSITION JUPITER

This is a time both for examining your life to see if you're still on the path you've set for yourself and for absorbing and consolidating the progress you've made to date—a time to evaluate and learn. This is not a time of dramatic new growth or for beginning new programs.

SATURN CONJUNCT SATURN

This happens about every 29 years—at ages 28 to 30 and 58 to 60. You may begin feeling the effects of this transit as much as a year ahead of the exact conjunction. It's a very important time in your life—a time of major changes and maturation. There may be a dramatic shift of direction as you strive to get on with what you came into this life to accomplish. It will be easier for you if you consciously go along with what is happening, of course.

SATURN SEXTILE SATURN

Things are probably running along fairly smoothly, but if you're unhappy in any area of your life, look within to see if you may be reacting to unconscious drives or patterns rather than consciously directing your life. You're in a practical frame of mind, so it's a good time to do this and plan for the future.

SATURN SQUARE SATURN

This may be a time when you seriously question your life and what you're doing with it. You may go through trials of self-doubt, even guilt; or you may simply experience this time as a period of reappraisal, with little or no difficulty. It depends on your self-awareness and how you've been living your life up to this point.

SATURN TRINE SATURN

You feel calm, stable, self-assured. You've matured, you're experienced, and you have confidence in yourself and your ideals. You're working steadily toward your goals, laying down a foundation for the future. Don't get cocky, though, thinking you know it all now. Stay open and keep in touch with your inner self.

SATURN OPPOSITION SATURN

Several years ago when Saturn squared your natal Saturn, the projects or new phases of development you'd begun at Saturn's return to its natal position were tested to see if they were appropriate for you and your progression. If you stubbornly held on by your fingernails to anything that wasn't working for you then, this can be a difficult transit for you. A change is necessary; you must begin restructuring and find the right path. If you *have* been on the right path these last years, you'll experience a very satisfying time. You can reap the rewards of your efforts.

SATURN CONJUNCT URANUS

You're probably feeling repressed, suppressed, and possibly oppressed by people or circumstances. You want change, freedom, excitement, while all around you may seem to be conspiring against your having it. Whatever your reaction—sudden shifts or controlled, sustained effort—some sort of change at this time is necessary and will occur.

SATURN SEXTILE URANUS

At this time you can readily accept the fresh and innovative and incorporate it patiently into your old, existing structures. All seems steady and secure now, giving you the courage to experiment.

SATURN SQUARE URANUS

If you've become too rigid and fear change, you may find this transit upsetting many of your applecarts. If you're flexible, however, you can make positive changes in your life and will be able to enjoy the new experiences and opportunites that may come to you now.

SATURN TRINE URANUS

You're able to approach change in a patient, disciplined manner. And this is what you should do—make changes, incorporating the new into the old. Avoid falling into rigid routines that will be hard to modify during the more difficult transits of these two planets.

SATURN OPPOSITION URANUS

You may feel that everything and everyone is keeping you from truly being yourself, and you want to get away from it or them. Actually what is happening is that you feel a prisoner of the ruts you've fallen into. You want to burst, break, or explode free! There must be change to accommodate your growth, but it's best to make the necessary readjustments and improvements coolly, consciously, and intelligently. Do this, and your frustrations will vanish.

SATURN CONJUNCT NEPTUNE

Pessimistic moods, self-doubt, and confusion are some of the things you may have to contend with during this transit. Try to hang on to the thought that things are not really as bad as they seem. If you are well-grounded and in touch with your inner strength, these effects will not be as troublesome, and you may be able to advance spiritually.

SATURN SEXTILE NEPTUNE

This is a good time for some serious introspection and self-examination. You may be operating on a more spiritual level than usual. Don't take yourself too seriously and slip into self-righteousness, though. Neptune and ego are like oil and water. They don't mix well, and if you try to combine them, Neptune will sooner or later find a way to zap you.

SATURN SQUARE NEPTUNE

The effects of this transit are similar to the conjunction. Doubt, confusion, and negativism want to dominate your thinking and your life. Try to take these emotions and yourself as if seen from hyperspace. Your view of reality is a bit warped at the moment.

SATURN TRINE NEPTUNE

You would greatly benefit now from studies designed to put you more in touch with your inner self. You'll be able to reach a new depth of self-knowledge. This is also one of the times when you can act out of truly humane and selfless motives; you'll very much enjoy it, too.

SATURN OPPOSITION NEPTUNE

You feel confused now, possibly pulled in first one direction and then another by guilt, doubt, pessimism—a feeling that you're losing your grip on self and reality. Going off alone for a while would be worthwhile. Keep yourself well-grounded in physical reality. This is not a time to delve into the occult; you'd only increase your confusion. Know that all is not as bad as it seems, and that when this is all over you'll have deepened your wisdom.

SATURN CONJUNCT PLUTO

Old orders of all sorts may be overthrown in preparation for new ones to come. Don't recoil from this prospect, but turn your efforts toward effecting new growth and transformation.

SATURN SEXTILE PLUTO

This is a time of great inner and outer strength and power. You can overcome formidable trials and tribulations at this time if necessary. The "force" is with you.

SATURN SQUARE PLUTO

You may find yourself confronted with obstacles on every hand. It's best not to flail against them like a fish in a net, but to take stock and clear away those things in your life which are not working. Try to remain calm and detached and to conserve your resources.

SATURN TRINE PLUTO

You can peer into the deep inner resources of yourself as if looking into a crystal ball at this time. Studies designed to bring about more self-knowledge would be beneficial now.

SATURN CONJUNCT MIDHEAVEN

Now you will reap what you've sown over the past 14 years or so. If you've operated with integrity, all will suddenly bear fruit. If not, if you've stepped on others, or taken unethical shortcuts, you'll likely lose what you've worked so hard to gain. The older you are, the more important this transit will be for you.

SATURN SQUARE MIDHEAVEN

This may be a time of self-questioning and doubt. You may feel alone, yet unable to relate. The problem is likely to involve personal relationships. Either you've been overlooking their importance or you feel one is holding you back. In any case, it will be better to make changes now rather than later.

SATURN TRINE MIDHEAVEN

You feel self-confident and adequate to any task. This is a good time to pursue self-knowledge. Examine your attitudes and beliefs to see if they're really yours or the product of your training and upbringing. Now is the time to make necessary changes.

SATURN OPPOSITION MIDHEAVEN

You've just completed a fallow time of five to eight years when you possibly felt as if you were in limbo. Actually it was a time of preparation, and now your "star" is beginning to rise toward a pinnacle of success that will be reached in about 14 years. Concentrate now on making sure your domestic life is in order so it will be a support as you turn more and more toward the outer world.

SATURN CONJUNCT ASCENDANT

A period of preparation, which will last about five to eight years, is beginning. You'll be preparing for new beginnings at Saturn opposition your midheaven, at which time your "star" will begin to rise again. Now is the time to finish off old projects and eliminate the unnecessary in your life. Though busy, perhaps with many responsibilities, don't withdraw from others. Older persons, especially, may prove helpful to you at this time.

SATURN SEXTILE ASCENDANT

This is an important and significant transit. What you do now will establish models and routines that will define your relationships for a number of years. Be aware and don't act or react mindlessly. Older persons are excellent sources in trying to learn more about yourself now. Take their opinions of you into consideration, but not as law.

URANUS IN FIRST HOUSE

The big thing with Uranus is freedom, and right now you'll be seeking more of it. You'll be making changes in your life, including how you look at and manage the world around you. This is an excellent time to study consciousness-raising subjects or techniques.

URANUS IN SECOND HOUSE

Your inner needs, and consequently your values, are changing, particularly as they relate to possessions. If you are conscious of the necessity for change and are implementing it, this transit may pass with little or no upheaval in your life; otherwise there may be significant, possibly sudden, changes in your material resources or possessions—all for the purpose of facilitating your growth.

URANUS IN THIRD HOUSE

You'll be changing many things in your life now, and if you can remain flexible and be willing to accept the unexpected, this can be a very exciting time. We all must change, or we become rigid and stagnant.

URANUS IN EIGHTH HOUSE

All about you you'll find old structures passing away and new ones beginning. Suddenly. You are trying to break free of old restrictions or limitations, whether you realize it or not. You have to be free in order to grow.

URANUS IN NINTH HOUSE

Your interest in the mystical, spiritual, and occult is heightened, and if you can maintain a flexible, open mind, you will gain a great deal from the experiences you'll have under this transit.

URANUS IN ELEVENTH HOUSE

You're likely to change many of your goals and ideals—perhaps radically, as compared to what you might have thought possible in the past. As always with Uranus, be willing to roll with the punches.

URANUS IN TWELFTH HOUSE

You have the opportunity to confront the hidden aspects of yourself that have been buried perhaps for years. Techniques such as psychotherapy or meditation will help, for unconscious memories or behavior patterns are emerging now and you need to understand them. Refusing to face secrets or hidden aspects of yourself will precipitate sudden difficulties. Face them now, and they'll cease to haunt you.

URANUS CONJUNCT SUN

This may be a time of rebellion, a time of defining the parameters of one's true self and overthrowing restrictions and limitations. It can be a most productive time of personal growth; or, if one resists change tooth and nail, it may be a time of disturbing chaos. Change will come into your life at any rate, and when this transit is over, you'll be a freer, different, more real you.

URANUS SEXTILE SUN

New things are occurring in your life now, though they may not be incredibly dramatic. Nevertheless, new vistas and opportunities are opening up to you, and you'll be discovering that you can have more say about your life and its direction. You can be more free and have more potential than you ever imagined.

URANUS SQUARE SUN

Sudden occurrences will test your ability to remain true to yourself and stick to your guns. If you are on the correct courses already, you'll be able to survive the tests successfully and emerge strengthened in purpose. If your life becomes totally disrupted, it's time for a rethinking of goals and directions.

URANUS TRINE SUN

You're looking for change, the new and exciting. You'll grow into new insights if you'll open up and allow it. Groups or studies that expand your consciousness would be beneficial now; don't be afraid to reach out and enrich your Self. Changes are easily made under this transit.

URANUS OPPOSITION SUN

One cannot forever repress the expression of the true self, and if you've been doing that, sudden events are, one way or another, going to force that true self to crack out of its rut or shell or stifling security and to stand up and be counted.

URANUS CONJUNCT MOON

There are likely to be sudden events or psychological changes that stir up emotional turbulence. You may become moody, with sudden swings from one emotion to another. Whether happy or sad, you'll be feeling again. This is a necessary condition for a complete human being; you are not a robot.

URANUS SEXTILE MOON

Your emotions are quickened, and you can experience yourself and the world through them. You're subjective, yes, but it's a wonderful experience. You'll give and demand more emotional support and expression from all around you.

URANUS SQUARE MOON

Emotional freedom is a very pressing need for you right now, and you avidly and actively seek it. This may lead to emotional turmoil and upsets, but when this period has passed, you'll have a better understanding of yourself and your emotions.

URANUS TRINE MOON

Now is a prime time to make changes in your life. They will be easy to make now—even altering old habits, such as smoking. Examine your attitudes, too, especially "knee-jerk" responses. One habit you should probably change is the taking of friends and loved ones for granted. Show a little sensitivity and appreciation!

URANUS OPPOSITION MOON

You're undergoing some emotional changes, either by choice or through the force of sudden events. You are being induced to become an independent person. This growth will affect all areas of your life, but relationships in particular, and you'll feel freer than ever before. You are no longer a child and must put away old behavior patterns.

URANUS CONJUNCT MERCURY

New insights and ideas may be coming to you now. If you're flexible enough to allow the changes in your thinking or your environment, you'll greatly benefit. Be prepared for your life to be hectic for a while. Make conscious efforts to be flexible and relaxed.

URANUS SEXTILE MERCURY

You'll feel restless, mentally stimulated, lively, eager, curious, open to new ideas, and perhaps puckish. Just don't expect everyone to be as open and flexible as you are right now.

URANUS SQUARE MERCURY

Events and ideas may be bombarding you so quickly that you become confused and nervous. Try to put off important decisions until later. Avoid being authoritarian and rigid in the face of challenges to your beliefs; here is an opportunity to find out what you really think.

URANUS TRINE MERCURY

Your routine, daily life, and encounters take on new excitement. Get out of your ruts and learn something new about the world and yourself.

URANUS OPPOSITION MERCURY

The pace of your life is stepped up. Try to remain calm and keep things in hand. Mental exhaustion could result otherwise. On the whole this can be an exciting time of discovery and change. Remain open to it and enjoy.

URANUS SEXTILE VENUS

You're willing to try new things, meet new people, go new places—anything to get out of your old ruts. Doing so will afford you the opportunity to evaluate just what sort of social life and relationships you really want and need.

URANUS CONJUNCT MARS

The tremendous and potentially explosive combination of these two planets is trying to work through you now, and you absolutely must not suppress them in any way. Your true self is struggling to affirm itself and won't stand for any interference. Restrictions you've found onerous will become unbearable now. All this may disrupt your life, but if you're aware of what's going on and make an effort to direct and moderate these energies, changes and events need not be destructive.

URANUS SEXTILE MARS

You'll find yourself confronted with more and more opportunities for freedom now. Take advantage of them—you'll find out what you can do.

URANUS SQUARE MARS

Your insecurities may be showing, and you may feel compelled to prove yourself in some way. Trouble is, this may take the form of sudden, rash actions that could have unwelcome consequences later. To avoid this, try to exercise a little control and be aware of your motives. Better still, come to terms with your insecurity.

URANUS TRINE MARS

Your self-confidence is high, and you're more willing to try new things. You'll have opportunities to show yourself and others your real self and what you can do. Take hold of opportunities that come your way now, and you can assert greater control over your life.

URANUS OPPOSITION MARS

You'll now rebel against any restrictions you can. You want to show yourself and others what you can do. This is good if you can exert at least some control over your "damn the torpedoes" mood and avoid foolish risks. Changes are needed, but do try to manage a little moderation and caution.

URANUS CONJUNCT JUPITER

Your appetite for a better understanding of yourself and the cosmos heightens your desire to learn more, do new things, take chances, and seek new freedom. There may be a sudden change of "luck," one way or another. Enjoy, if appropriate, but don't worry too much if it isn't. Things are likely to be changing rapidly.

URANUS SEXTILE JUPITER

Many "lucky" breaks or other opportunities may come your way under this transit. Consider everything that happens as another chance for personal growth. What are you being told? Are you, perhaps, not as limited as you thought?

URANUS SQUARE JUPITER

You are feeling great, optimistic, almost invulnerable. Be careful, though; with Uranus, you can't tell which way those risks you're thinking of might go. They may fizzle out, or it may be that you really are hearing a different drummer.

URANUS TRINE JUPITER

You'll feel freer and more confident than usual. Or, the effects may be more subtle, being in the form of slow and satisfying growth of your understanding of the universe and your place in it. You'll be more spiritually inclined and will want to share this knowledge with others.

URANUS OPPOSITION JUPITER

Personal freedom is important to you now, and you'll probably take steps to get it. Careful consideration is recommended, though, before doing anything.

URANUS CONJUNCT SATURN

The freedom-loving, often disruptive Uranus may suddenly overthrow the seemingly concrete structures that Saturn has helped you build in your life, causing all sorts of mayhem. Any area of your life that has been restricting your growth, whether you realize it or not, will be subject to this disruption. Do not suppress this energy. You'll be better for the change in the long run.

URANUS SEXTILE SATURN

Now is a good time to make sure the structures of your life, in whatever area, don't eventually become too rigid and confining. You'll probably be amply rewarded for your efforts at constructive change, whether they concern your inner or outer world.

URANUS SQUARE SATURN

Circumstances will force you to reexamine the structures in your life to see if they are facilitating your personal growth. Any that are not in your best interest will become intolerable, and you'll want to escape them no matter what. Sudden disruptions may occur. It will help to find someone you can talk with and confide in as you decide on an appropriate course of action. It would also help to take up, or keep up, meditation or other relaxation techniques.

URANUS TRINE SATURN

You'll be able to see that there can be freedom and achievement even within a structured system or prescribed set of guidelines. A sonnet is not just another pretty poem. You may receive very clear and well-deserved rewards.

URANUS OPPOSITION SATURN

Events may suddenly happen that force you to reevaluate your thinking about almost any structure of your life. Uranus doesn't let anyone grow smug, reminding us there is always room for change and growth. No one ever just "arrives" and stays there, if Uranus can help it. Accept what happens and try to learn from it. Resisting will turn the tensions inward, causing bodily harm.

URANUS CONJUNCT URANUS

This transit occurs every 84 years. When it occurs in childhood, it often brings upsets that leave you wary of surprises, as you'll connect them with disruption. Or, it may implant a strong need for personal freedom. When it occurs later in life, you experience spiritual awakening and insight. You develop a broader outlook: There is more to life than this Earth and its trivialities. *This* is the wisdom of old age.

URANUS SEXTILE URANUS

This transit brings you exciting new thoughts, ideas, and information—from without and within. It first occurs when you are about 14 and again at about 70. It signifies growing, but from two different perspectives. At 14, you question and learn from your experiences outside yourself. At 70, you look back and inward to see what you've learned.

URANUS SQUARE URANUS

This transit has to do with taking responsibility, and it occurs around age 21 and again at about 62 or 63. The first transit generally coincides with breaking away from parental authority, learning to be responsible for your own actions. Rebellion is often necessary at this time to "justify" taking the big step of leaving the safety of the family. When in your 60's, it begins to dawn on you that you're growing old, and you start questioning the value of what you've been doing these last few decades. Now, if you don't know it already, you have to learn that you're responsible for your own happiness and spiritual worth— that your true value comes from within, not from job or status—and you must learn to take that responsibility.

URANUS TRINE URANUS

This transit occurs when you're about 28 and again at about 56. During the first one, you realize you are truly an adult and no longer need to "follow the herd." You'll do things your way and may radically change your life in some way. At age 56, almost the same thing occurs. You may change your mode of living or life direction to express your true self more accurately, and, once again, to "do it your way."

URANUS OPPOSITION URANUS

This is the transit commonly associated with "mid-life crisis." You'll feel that time is passing you by and that you'd better get up and get busy if you ever want to accomplish what you set out to do years ago. You may make radical changes in your life, possibly leaving a marriage or career. Or, none of this may happen at all. If you've been on the right track all along, this will not be a crisis time, but a time when you begin to look more inward and become concerned with how your accomplishments relate to the real meaning of your life.

URANUS CONJUNCT NEPTUNE

New philosophies or beliefs will interest you now, and they may well bring you enlightening experiences or insights. Be aware, though, that it will be difficult to sort the positive influences from the negative right now, so it's best not to make any definite commitments until this transit is over. Do not take *any* drugs.

URANUS SEXTILE NEPTUNE

Your interest in the occult or spiritual matters as a whole will be heightened. You may have psychic experiences and become associated with a group or new friends who have the same interests. You'll see yourself and the universe in a whole new light, and this may cause you to reevaluate and change your goals in life.

URANUS SQUARE NEPTUNE

Unless you have a very firm grounding in reality, confusion and delusion, including self-delusion, are apt to be rampant under this transit, especially concerning psychic, occult, or drug experiences. If you're sure that you *are* firmly grounded in the real world, it is, however, possible to have truly enlightening experiences under this transit.

URANUS TRINE NEPTUNE

Psychic and spiritual insights are likely under this transit, and you'll grow in your understanding of yourself and the universe. Your compassion for others will increase or surface, and you'll want to do something about the lot of those less fortunate than you.

URANUS OPPOSITION NEPTUNE

Upsetting or confusing experiences, possibly of a psychic or spiritual nature, may be your lot now, especially if you've been one to deny the existence of such things in the past. If, however, you've been aware of and have accepted the higher dimensions of life, you'll possibly be further enlightened and party to even deeper insights.

URANUS CONJUNCT PLUTO

The key word of this transit is change; changes of all sorts will occur as you grow and adapt to rapidly shifting situations around you. Be flexible and nothing will stand in the way of your growth.

URANUS SEXTILE PLUTO

Your intuition and insight may be enhanced under this transit. It's a good time to study subjects that lead to greater self-knowledge; you are concerned with the deeper reaches of your psyche. True to the symbolism of Pluto, this transit may signal changes radical enough to be dubbed personal rebirth.

URANUS SQUARE PLUTO

This is likely to be a time of upheaval in your life and in the lives of others of your generation. Dramatic changes will be taking place, and you'll be challenged to adjust to them. Though seemingly sudden, these changes have been in the works for quite some time. The old is being torn down to make way for the new.

URANUS TRINE PLUTO

Your interest in areas of higher consciousness, occult studies, or philosophy will deepen, and you'll have a chance to easily make changes in your life to bring it toward the higher plane you've glimpsed. Look within to increase your self-understanding.

URANUS OPPOSITION PLUTO

Pluto is at work once again to eliminate the useless and out-moded from your life. And Uranus is stepping in to make these changes which have been building up for a long time seem sudden and upsetting. If you can be flexible now and not resist these energies, you have the opportunity to effect change both in your inner awareness and in your outer circumstances.

URANUS SEXTILE MIDHEAVEN

You can make positive changes in your life now, especially in your profession and close relationships. You're looking for greater personal freedom. Don't waste this opportunity; change will be more difficult later.

URANUS SQUARE MIDHEAVEN

This should be a time of new opportunity for expanded personal freedom and creative changes in your life. You need to be free to be your true self, and consciously or unconsciously, voluntarily or involuntarily, it will happen, one way or another. You might as well make it easier on yourself and go along with it.

URANUS TRINE MIDHEAVEN

Your interest in the occult, particularly astrology, may be aroused. At any rate, you'll be creative and original in any area of interest now. Now is a good time to make changes you feel are necessary in your life.

URANUS CONJUNCT ASCENDANT

You'll probably be impatient with restrictions or limitations in any area of your life. Anywhere you feel dissatisfied, there may be disruptions requiring change or adjustment. You may take up astrology or other occult subjects, seeking truths you believe will set you free.

URANUS SEXTILE ASCENDANT

You're undergoing inner changes, and many areas of your life heretofore taken for granted may suddenly seem outdated or too conservative for your present tastes. You're growing and attempting to express your real individuality. New and unusual people whom you'll find stimulating may enter your life, and you may learn a great deal from them.

URANUS SQUARE ASCENDANT

Change, in the form of overthrowing old, outworn aspects of your life, will suddenly enter the picture now. You may do all sorts of new things, as well as change or adjust relationships. You're seeking new freedom of personal expression and won't be satisfied until you get it.

URANUS TRINE ASCENDANT

New, possibly brief, relationships may occur that prove to be valuable to your growth and development, though you may not realize it until later. You'll feel invigorated and stimulated during this transit, and you shouldn't resist changes that occur now.

NEPTUNE IN FIRST HOUSE

You're likely to go through some confusion about who you really are—the image or images you project to others versus your real identity. The search for the real you may be discouraging at times, but you mustn't give up. Meditation or other self-knowledge techniques would be very helpful.

NEPTUNE IN SECOND HOUSE

The issue here is your attitude toward your possessions. The goal is to develop a detached point of view regarding material wealth. The more your ego is defined by or identified with what you do or do not own, the more difficulty you'll have with this transit. There may be some losses. Basically, your value system is undergoing change; you're being taught that you are not your possessions, nor are they you.

NEPTUNE IN THIRD HOUSE

Your interest in the spiritual and metaphysical will increase. Psychic or intuitive insights may occur, which, if you are rigid and inflexible in your thinking, may cause you to be upset or confused. It's best to be open to learning new things and ideas in new ways. If you do experience confusion, don't make any important decisions until later if you can.

NEPTUNE IN FOURTH HOUSE

You are undergoing considerable inner change, and this can be reflected in your domestic and personal life, perhaps making you moodier than usual. Your interest in the metaphysical may increase, and you may begin meditating now, possibly about your home life, which may be causing some confusion for you now.

NEPTUNE IN EIGHTH HOUSE

Your interest in the metaphysical, spiritual, or occult will intensify as you try to learn more and more about yourself. There are changes going on within you, though you may not be fully aware of them for a while.

NEPTUNE IN NINTH HOUSE

Your interest in the metaphysical will become even greater than ever. This can also be a time of confusion so that after a while you don't know *what* to believe for sure. Be wary of joining any groups that will do your thinking for you. The best thing to do is to proceed much as a writer doing research—just soak up information; and, in time, all *will* coalesce and come together for you. Do try not to become insufferably self-righteous at that point, though.

NEPTUNE IN TENTH HOUSE

You may be confused, possibly fearful—but observe: You are not your job, nor is it you. This can be an important lesson of this transit. Also, at this time your interest in the occult or psychic may increase.

NEPTUNE IN ELEVENTH HOUSE

You'll be concerned with your ideals and how to implement them. Remember, however, that Neptune is famous for making illusion seem real. Be careful to see people and ideals as they really are, not as you'd like them to be.

NEPTUNE IN TWELFTH HOUSE

During this transit, you'll be concerned with the deeper levels of existence and the meaning of life. You'll want to slow down, retreat, and meditate, and this is good, for it will help you to get in touch with your deeper, hidden self, higher consciousness, and the spiritual values of life. You may find your psychic abilities enhanced, and this, too, will help you.

NEPTUNE CONJUNCT SUN

Neptune can bring contact with the higher aspects of consciousness, if you're ready and can handle them. Your interest in the spiritual side of life will be increased, as will your idealism in general. If you are still mainly based in your ego and the material world, you may experience weariness, confusion, and possibly depression. Drugs should be avoided, as should deception of any sort.

NEPTUNE SEXTILE SUN

You'll be more in tune with your intuitive nature—a good time to meditate and seek the meanings of your life. Your interest in the metaphysical and spiritual will be heightened. Psychic insights or events are possible. You can be truly selfless at this time.

NEPTUNE SQUARE SUN

You may be confused, unsure of what you're doing or where you're going. Your grasp of reality is not quite what it should be. Hence, this is not a good time for a number of things, such as joining a religious group or sect, getting involved with the occult, changing jobs, severing or committing to relationships, retreating from people, or using drugs or alcohol. Remember—this, too, shall pass.

NEPTUNE TRINE SUN

You're much more interested in your spiritual, intuitive self now. You'll be very idealistic, possibly given to daydreaming, but you'll be rewarded if you get out and work toward making your ideals a reality.

NEPTUNE OPPOSITION SUN

You're more susceptible than usual to delusions—involving yourself or otherwise—as well as subject to misunderstandings with others. Be very specific and clear in all your communications. Don't commit to anything, especially spiritual cults or movements, until this transit is over. Deeper insights can be yours now, but let them stand the test of time before entrusting yourself to them.

NEPTUNE CONJUNCT MOON

You may receive so much information from your unconscious or on the psychic level that you become confused as to what is real and what isn't. It will help to be aware that your subconscious often communicates in symbols. Don't necessarily take everything at face value. Be receptive to psychic insights, but don't forget that you live in the real world and that your insights have to live in it, too. Be wary of making emotional commitments, also. You may find your feelings have changed when this transit is over.

NEPTUNE SEXTILE MOON

You'll be highly intuitive, creative, imaginative, and empathetic now. You'll be able to sense the moods and possibly the thoughts of others with ease, though if you're not awake to this possibility, you may not realize what's going on. Other types of psychic phenomena may also occur.

NEPTUNE SQUARE MOON

You'll be unusually moody and sensitive to others' feelings. Therefore, avoid negative persons and try mightily to curb any negative thoughts of your own. Be very clear and specific with communications. Don't rely too heavily on intuition now.

NEPTUNE TRINE MOON

Your intuitive, psychic, and empathetic abilities are enhanced and mostly on target. You'll feel for others and want to help them, but be sure your help is really wanted before jumping in with both feet. Your interest in learning more about occult or psychic subjects is also increased, and you can do so safely now.

NEPTUNE OPPOSITION MOON

Be careful—you are seeing only what you want to see. Your view and interpretation of reality is not up to par. This is obviously not a good time to make permanent decisions about anything, nor to become involved in occult or spiritual experiments. Wait awhile; let this transit pass.

NEPTUNE CONJUNCT MERCURY

Forget about finally getting yourself organized or making important decisions until this transit is over. Your rational mind has shifted into neutral. There is a possibility of deception, involving yourself or others. You may be more intuitive or psychic than usual but have trouble communicating your insights.

NEPTUNE SEXTILE MERCURY

Your intuitive, psychic, and creative abilities are enhanced, as is your ability to communicate your experiences. Be careful not to get lost in your imagination, though; you can appreciate and gain insight from the ordinary world around you at this time.

NEPTUNE SQUARE MERCURY

Try to keep your mind focused as much in reality as you can at this time. Avoid going off the deep end on anything, especially religious, spiritual, or occult tangents. Wait until this transit has passed to make important decisions. Do not attempt to use deception with anyone, but be aware that someone may try it on you. Under this transit, your grasp of reality is not what it should be, nor even what it usually is. You'll find daydreaming extremely alluring.

NEPTUNE TRINE MERCURY

Your left brain and right brain are totally in sync now. You intuitively and intellectually understand almost any subject or aspect of your life and are able to communicate it effectively. Your interest in the spiritual and metaphysical is high, and you'll gain enormously from studying these subjects.

NEPTUNE OPPOSITION MERCURY

Mental confusion, poor communications, perhaps actual deceit may cause you problems at this time. Don't make any important decisions until later. Do not try to deceive others, and take precautions against its happening to you. Be very specific and clear in all communications.

NEPTUNE CONJUNCT MARS

The best course of action under this transit is to cultivate a detached, self-observant attitude and just wait this one out. Don't get discouraged. You're likely to be walking around in a Neptunian fog for the duration. Delusion is common.

NEPTUNE SEXTILE MARS

This transit allows you to slow down and smell the roses. In the process you may discover a great deal about yourself. You may discover psychic abilities, but certainly your intuitiveness will be enhanced. You'll discover there is an inner you, and if you'll just be still and listen to it, you'll find it knows and can teach you plenty. Your understanding of others will deepen, too.

NEPTUNE SQUARE MARS

You may suffer defeats of various kinds at this time. Events will occur that will force you to fall back on your own devices. Try not to get too discouraged. Things will look different when this transit is over. Remember, if a project or an effort fails, *it* is the failure, not you. During this transit, stay away from anything underhanded.

NEPTUNE TRINE MARS

Do not seek ego gratification or to advance yourself in the world during this transit, but work with and help others selflessly. Your interest in the metaphysical aspects of life will deepen and expand. You'll begin to see how you fit into a very grand scheme, and provincialism will fade away with the old you as you grow in consciousness.

NEPTUNE OPPOSITION MARS

Your energy, self-confidence, and possibly your health status may be low. You may find it hard to carry on, but don't give up necessarily; you'll perk up soon. Wait for this transit to pass before beginning grand new projects.

NEPTUNE CONJUNCT JUPITER

This is a time of intense idealism and feeling a need to help others. If you can control that idealism somewhat and manage to keep at least a toehold on reality, you may acquire valuable knowledge about yourself and your place in the universe.

NEPTUNE SEXTILE JUPITER

A time of increased spiritual awareness and interest, this transit may lead you into meaningful insights about yourself and how you fit into the larger scheme of things. You're optimistic and positive now, which will probably be reflected back to you from almost all areas of your life.

NEPTUNE SQUARE JUPITER

Your idealism may be so great that you lose all sense of reality and see everything through very rosy glasses. This, of course, can lead to problems. The reality we are in is the one we must deal with now, and attempting to escape from it by any means—religious cults, drugs, whatever—retards our growth. A little daydreaming now and again is a good thing, but when it begins to adversely affect your life, forget it and get busy. Try to remain grounded and focused in this plane. A positive thing to do would be to get out and be of genuine service to others.

NEPTUNE TRINE JUPITER

Optimism and idealism about yourself and the world at large is very likely your dominant feeling now. As long as you don't overdo this attitude and take foolish risks, you may be able to gain tremendous insight and understanding. This is a good time to study the metaphysical.

NEPTUNE OPPOSITION JUPITER

You are so optimistic and idealistic at this moment that you're not seeing reality as it is, and you may overlook something important. You want to help others, but be careful that they really want, need, and can benefit from your help. This is not a good time to join or commit to any religious, spiritual, occult, or metaphysical group.

NEPTUNE CONJUNCT SATURN

This may be a confusing, even depressing, time. You may find yourself vaguely fearful for no apparent reason. You are being shown new and different aspects of reality, which the well-structured Saturn side of you finds unsettling. Try to stay calm and avoid stress and negativity as much as you can. The old is being washed away to make room for new insights. Wait for them.

NEPTUNE SEXTILE SATURN

You're able to see yourself, your hopes and desires, and reality more clearly now and can intelligently plan for your future. This is a superb time for introspection. Helping others now is also an excellent use of this transit.

NEPTUNE SQUARE SATURN

You may experience self-doubt and insecurity, and may even have thoughts of giving everything up and withdrawing from the world—to become a hermit, maybe. You may be fearful for no particular reason. Be aware that all this is temporary. Seek out positive, upbeat friends; they're a real and necessary help when you're down.

NEPTUNE TRINE SATURN

You can work steadfastly to bring your ideals to fruition by not getting overbalanced in one direction or the other. You can be self-sacrificing if necessary and can handle problems in a calm, rational manner. This is an excellent time to begin studying psychic or occult subjects. You'll learn and understand without getting confused or unsettled.

NEPTUNE OPPOSITION SATURN

Once again Neptune is challenging the Saturnian structures in your life. This will cause confusion and possibly fear for a while. You're being prepared for even greater insights and understanding of yourself and the universe. If you can let the old structure go without replacing it with one just as rigid, this is an excellent opportunity for growth.

NEPTUNE SEXTILE URANUS

Your interest in the spiritual, metaphysical, or occult will be enhanced. You may even wish to seriously take up the study of astrology. Psychic experiences or insights may occur. At any rate, this will be a period of growth for you. You may also find yourself more willing to help others.

NEPTUNE SQUARE URANUS

There may be sudden changes in your life, your moods, and your ideas. You may be confused and upset, wondering what in the world is going on. There may be psychic experiences that force you to at least admit there is such a thing. This is not a good time for psychic or occult experimentation, however, or for deciding to join any such groups or cults. You're too confused to handle this now. Wait until later when you'll be more clearheaded. Accept change, let go of limitations, and let yourself grow.

NEPTUNE TRINE URANUS

Your intuitive and psychic abilities are enhanced now. Your interest in the abstract, metaphysical, or spiritual is also stimulated, and you may well have some meaningful experience.

NEPTUNE OPPOSITION URANUS

There are radical changes going on in your basic understanding of yourself and the universe. Your views and opinions are in a state of flux. All this may leave you a little confused, but don't be afraid. Try to remain calm and avoid taking on any long-term obligations right now. Things will stabilize when this transit is over. Your consciousness is undergoing tremendous change; a new you is emerging. Wait for it.

NEPTUNE SEXTILE NEPTUNE

Life, and your role in it, will take on a new, larger perspective, and you may decide to make radical changes of direction. This will result in a new sense of freedom and expectation for you. This transit generally occurs around the same time as your first Saturn return to its natal place in your chart, and they reinforce one another's maturing and reorienting effects.

NEPTUNE SQUARE NEPTUNE

This transit occurs at around age 42 and is partly responsible for, or at least indicative of, the "middle-age crisis." There may be emotional confusion, a feeling that changes need to be made and that, since you're a grown-up now, you know exactly what they are and how to make them. Guess again. This is not the best time to be making important life decisions or long-term commitments. Use this period for introspection, self-evaluation, and life-review, but don't take any precipitous actions yet. Just observe and wait and see. Recall that Neptune can be the planet of illusion.

NEPTUNE TRINE NEPTUNE

This time of spiritual harmony with yourself and with others usually occurs around age 55. Whether conscious of it or not, you've become more understanding and empathetic. You may experience spiritual or mystical insights or awakenings, and a sense of yourself in a larger universe may emerge. Also, your interest in religion may be revived.

NEPTUNE OPPOSITION NEPTUNE

This transit will occur in your mid-80's or thereabouts. You may find yourself achieving a spiritual serenity in which material goods and goals don't have nearly the significance they used to. If you've not become too inflexible in your views and ideas, you may yet learn a great deal, expanding your consciousness. Perhaps this is the wisdom of old age that should be imparted to all who will listen. You may find you wish to withdraw into your own inner peace, perhaps to prepare yourself to accept the insights of the next important phase of your life. If, however, you try to hold on to the old, you can find this time a period of confusion, and possibly fear.

NEPTUNE SEXTILE PLUTO

Your intuitive powers are enhanced now, and you'll be able to see into and understand your own subconscious extremely well if you try. Many things in your life will be falling away now in preparation for a new beginning. It's best to let them go and look forward to the next cycle.

NEPTUNE SQUARE PLUTO

You're undergoing tremendous changes, and part of the process may be the emergence of feelings or frustrations you've pushed down inside and never expressed. It's imperative that you try to understand and get in touch with these subconscious facets of yourself. Psychotherapy would be beneficial, as would directed meditations, perhaps with a trusted teacher or friend. If you're unaware of these negative energies within you, it may seem that everybody or somebody is working against you. This is a sign that you're projecting these energies, and you had better start looking into them.

NEPTUNE TRINE PLUTO

Your interest in the mystical, spiritual, and occult disciplines will increase, mainly because you want to find out more about yourself on the deepest level. Or, you might decide to get into psychotherapy. You may well have enlightening experiences that will significantly affect your life.

NEPTUNE OPPOSITION PLUTO

This can be a disturbing or an enlightening time, depending on your attitude toward the intangible aspects of life. This transit commonly occurs in your early 60's and can bring enhanced spiritual or intuitive awareness. You may have the opportunity to learn about hidden aspects of your psyche. If you generally pooh-pooh this type of information, you may be in for an upsetting period. The material aspects of your life may be changing, too, with some areas falling by the wayside.

NEPTUNE CONJUNCT MIDHEAVEN

You may suddenly feel confused, wondering if you've been heading in the wrong direction all this time. Maybe you have, but also maybe not. Wait until this transit is over to make any important decisions. Mystical philosophies may attract you, and you can learn a great deal under this transit if you stay open and quit being so hard on yourself. Again, make no hard and fast commitments at this time.

NEPTUNE SEXTILE MIDHEAVEN

If you allow it, you may find yourself being guided by intuitive insights and information. If you're not upset by this, you'll experience a sense of emotional well-being. You'll learn that the ego and the rational intellect are not the end-all and be-all of existence and also that you can find your Self through selflessness. Your interest in things spiritual or mystical will increase.

NEPTUNE SQUARE MIDHEAVEN

Feelings of insecurity or lack of confidence may lead you to avoid confrontations, submit to the wishes of others, or play the martyr to gain sympathy. You may even stoop to deception to get your way, and this can lead to further problems. On the other hand, you may become more interested in living spiritually, learning that the demands of your ego are not what's really important.

NEPTUNE TRINE MIDHEAVEN

Self-sacrifice for the needs of others may well be your guideline now. Don't totally neglect your own needs, which are also important, though. Also, your interest in the mystical or spiritual will be enhanced, and you may have psychic experiences.

NEPTUNE OPPOSITION MIDHEAVEN

There may now be upheavals in your life that leave you confused. Some areas of your life may be ending. Let them. It's time to start a new cycle of growth. This is a superb time to look within, to reevaluate your life and the direction you'd like it to take.

NEPTUNE CONJUNCT ASCENDANT

Your intuitive faculties may be enhanced, and so will your idealism to an extraordinary degree. Be wary of being deceived or deluded. Your interest in the spiritual or mystical will be increased under this transit.

NEPTUNE SEXTILE ASCENDANT

Your intuitive awareness of others will increase and so will your compassion. Old acquaintances will suddenly mean more to you, but you may over-idealize new ones, which, of course, is nonproductive for either of you. Your interest in the spiritual, metaphysical aspects of life will increase, and you can learn a great deal—even from aspects of your daily life—if you pay attention.

NEPTUNE SQUARE ASCENDANT

You may suffer some blows to the ego at this time. If so, try to determine what you can learn from the experience and get on with living. The less ego-involved you are, the less difficult this transit will be.

NEPTUNE TRINE ASCENDANT

You'll have much more compassion for others, but you may tend to over-idealize some of them. Your interest in the spiritual is enhanced, and you may especially idealize a spiritual-guide type. But don't forget that you, too, are of great worth. Hang in there—make no permanent commitments, and reassess what you've learned after this transit of about one year is over. Take some time off and meditate away from the clamor of the world if you can.

PLUTO IN FIRST HOUSE

You'll have a great desire for self-improvement and self-understanding, which you may seek through metaphysical or spiritual means. Meditation or psychotherapy would be beneficial in helping you to understand, and therefore control, your subconscious urges and drives. You may find yourself seeking more power and control over others, which could cause problems until you do reach more self-understanding.

PLUTO IN SECOND HOUSE

There is going to be quite a reorientation in your attitude toward possessions, a reshaping of your values as a whole. There may be some losses or material setbacks just to make you realize how really unimportant some values are. As always with Pluto, there is a tearing down before new construction can begin. Don't try to hang on, tooth and nail, if resources want to leave you now. It will only postpone the construction phase.

PLUTO IN THIRD HOUSE

Pluto always signals the death and regeneration of some aspect of your life. In this case, it's the death of old ideas, ways of thinking, and attitudes. You need to look at and question any and all your beliefs and thoughts and your manner of communicating with others. Overlook nothing. Probe deeply within. Great, gradual changes are taking place in you now, and you can assist by being observant and aware.

PLUTO IN FOURTH HOUSE

There are tremendous inner changes going on now. You may have to face and handle suppressed or "forgotten" problems from as far back as your childhood. Psychotherapy would be helpful now, although you'll undergo these changes anyway.

PLUTO IN EIGHTH HOUSE

There may be a death of someone of importance to you, which will profoundly affect your life and your thinking. Even if this doesn't happen, your interest in the subject of death, life after death, and the meaning of life will increase. You may seek answers through study of the occult or metaphysical. You will not be satisfied with platitudes or superficial answers.

PLUTO IN NINTH HOUSE

This is going to be a period when certain experiences will affect you profoundly, increasing your knowledge and (it is hoped) wisdom. In addition, you may become more interested in philosophical or metaphysical disciplines, and may also become involved in social reform groups. Remember, though, that as you've had to gain your insights through experience, so will others. Guard against becoming a zealot, trying to force-feed your hard-won knowledge to everyone else.

PLUTO IN TENTH HOUSE

If you've taken the time and opportunities to find out who you really are and what your life's goals are, you very likely will succeed now—if you don't resort to unethical, ruthless tactics. On the other hand, if you still aren't secure in your knowledge of yourself, you'll have the ability to find out now, though this may take a great deal of change in direction and searching. In either case, the efforts will be worth it.

PLUTO IN ELEVENTH HOUSE

There may be radical changes in your life direction and in your personal goals. Relationships will change, and you may meet someone who will profoundly affect your life. Beware of mixing with unsavory types.

PLUTO IN TWELFTH HOUSE

Unconscious memories, drives, motivations, or past actions that you've kept suppressed even from yourself are likely to surface now so that you can deal with them. And that is exactly what you should do: face them, confront them, acknowledge them, and they'll cease to plague you and run your life. Psychotherapy, meditation, or other self-knowledge techniques may be helpful, though not absolutely necessary.

PLUTO CONJUNCT SUN

You must now be consciously concerned with, and work hard toward, getting rid of old, outgrown aspects of your life to make room for the new. Bear in mind throughout that Pluto does not reward ego trips. What you do, you must do for the good of all, but do not attempt to dominate or ride over others for any reason whatsoever. Try to learn about yourself—who you are and what you want to be, and what is truly outgrown and needs to be discarded.

PLUTO SEXTILE SUN

If you take the initiative, you have the opportunity now to learn more than usual about yourself and your own inner workings. You're undergoing great changes, and this is a very good time to get in touch with your subconscious to meditate, to listen to your intuitive faculties.

PLUTO SQUARE SUN

This transit is about power, and your ability to know and control yourself in power struggles will be tested severely. You cannot ruthlessly walk over others, nor can you allow them to do it to you. You must develop a spirit of creative compromise, and if you can do this, you'll astound yourself with your accomplishments.

PLUTO TRINE SUN

You're in fine fettle, and this is an excellent time to begin any sort of self-improvement program. Positive changes will occur in your life, especially if you go after them.

PLUTO CONJUNCT MOON

Your intuitive and emotional faculties will be stimulated—probably powerfully, possibly explosively—and they will be a source of great change in your life. Subconscious reactions may be coming to the fore, and you must deal with them, no matter how upsetting and emotionally intense. You're being prepared for a new cycle in your life. If you can roll with the punches, you'll more easily cope with these changes.

PLUTO SEXTILE MOON

Your emotions are both heightened and deepened, as are your psychic abilities. You're better able to understand them and yourself now. You feel secure in your foundations and have a feeling of unity with the world that supports you in whatever you do.

PLUTO SQUARE MOON

Subconscious feelings or drives may be coming to the surface, forcing you to confront them if you are to grow. You may find yourself in deep, possibly subconsciously motivated, emotional conflicts with family members, probably women. There may be power plays or guilt trips. By paying attention to what comes out of you or by looking deep within, you can learn a great deal about yourself now. It won't be a stroll through a rose garden, but it will be worthwhile in the long run.

PLUTO TRINE MOON

This is a favorable time to deepen your self-understanding through any means and to make improvements you deem necessary. You may have profound psychic or emotional experiences at this time, which will also help to broaden your understanding.

PLUTO OPPOSITION MOON

This can be a time of emotional upset, as suppressed and outmoded habits or ways of thinking that you haven't dealt with come to the surface. You have to learn to handle them, accept them, or transform them. Psychotherapy, or other means to self-knowledge, may help you understand these seemingly compulsive actions that may appear to be running (or ruining) your life. They're habits from the past that are no longer appropriate for you.

PLUTO CONJUNCT MERCURY

You have opportunities to learn and understand more about yourself and life in general, if you can remain flexible enough to recognize and accept when your opinions or ideas need changing. You want to get at the truth, and you have to plow through much to do so. You may be in a position to teach others what you've learned, or you may be the student.

PLUTO SEXTILE MERCURY

You now have the opportunity to look deeply into your own mind and inner resources to see what makes you tick. Your mind is keen, probing, and perceptive now—well up to the task. Studying metaphysics or psychiatry would be good.

PLUTO SQUARE MERCURY

You may find that you have to change many of your ideas. You will at least have them challenged. Don't try to coerce others to think the way you do, nor let them do it to you. It doesn't have to be either-or, you know. You may be drawn to the occult or mysterious. Just don't get carried away with any power you may gain. New concepts you're exposed to can have very positive results on your growth.

PLUTO CONJUNCT MARS

This may be a time of success or tremendous struggle. Either way, you'll have the energy to handle it, especially if you work very hard and avoid the temptation to totally dominate others. You'll succeed best if your energy is used to work for the good of all, not just to gratify your ego.

PLUTO SEXTILE MARS

You'll be able to accomplish a great deal under this transit, as your energy level is very high. You'll succeed best if you use that energy to work for the good of all, not just yourself. Your interest in the spiritual and occult may be deepened.

PLUTO SQUARE MARS

You may find yourself impatient, egotistical, frustrated, easily angered, aggressive—or the object of the same from someone else. Do at least try to be patient, considerate, and cooperative with others and not to do anything just for your own ego gratification.

PLUTO TRINE MARS

Your self-confidence is up. You may make great progress in self-growth and regeneration, and may gain from occult studies.

PLUTO OPPOSITION MARS

Your ego energies and ambition are high, and if you can avoid using them to step on others on your way, you can succeed and accomplish a great deal. Do not suppress this energy but control it, and a new you can emerge.

PLUTO CONJUNCT JUPITER

You'll experience a surge of optimism and positive feelings that may well create the atmosphere for personal success, especially if you're working toward something beneficial to society as a whole, or at least not for yourself alone. Your interest in spiritual matters may be kindled or rekindled, and you'll probably feel like converting others to your viewpoint.

PLUTO SEXTILE JUPITER

This transit is likely to stimulate your idealism more than usual. You'll be willing and able to effect reform in almost any area of your life, though you may lean toward social reform. In addition, your interest in your own spiritual growth will increase. Opportunities for advancement in almost any area are likely.

PLUTO SQUARE JUPITER

This can be a time of buoyant optimism and personal success and achievement—if you're careful not to take on more than you can handle and don't become so self-righteous and arrogant that you turn people against you. Your interest in higher consciousness is heightened, but care must be taken that you don't become downright fanatic about some spiritual or religious movement.

PLUTO TRINE JUPITER

You're interested in reforming society on almost any level—from the family to the world—in order to bring it to a more ideal state. You're generous, kind, and helpful. Your interest in philosophy, metaphysics, religion, or law is stimulated, and you may have a desire to attain power through the study of such subjects, but only so you'll be better able to help others. Your interest in occult subjects is also increased, and you'll benefit from such study.

PLUTO OPPOSITION JUPITER

You'll have the opportunity for real spiritual growth and development as a human being under this transit, if you don't allow your very strong will to succeed in making you act holier-than-thou. If you do, you'll not only excite severe opposition but will also waste an excellent opportunity for growth.

PLUTO CONJUNCT SATURN

Change at fundamental levels is upon you, and it's best to let it happen. Old ideas, beliefs, relationships, or possibly possessions may pass away to make way for a new cycle—all of which may be distressing but, nevertheless, affords opportunity for spiritual growth and self-improvement. Occult and metaphysical studies may be beneficial.

PLUTO SEXTILE SATURN

Like the turtle, you'll find that you can patiently and effectively plod along toward your goal until you eventually reach it. Slow, steady change is going on within you. You begin to feel on more solid ground. At the same time, your intuitiveness will be boosted.

PLUTO SQUARE SATURN

Serious obstacles and oppositions may enter your life, forcing you to determine what really is important to you. What isn't must go by the wayside, and if you don't voluntarily make changes in the basic structures of your life, you'll later be forced to do so. Whatever is sound will survive the struggle, and you'll be able to progress as a human being, without useless, excess baggage.

PLUTO TRINE SATURN

During this transit you're disciplined, meticulous, orderly, patient, and can work with great endurance. You're not in some mad rush to accomplish now; you realize you're building for the future. This applies to the world within, as well as without.

PLUTO OPPOSITION SATURN

You're undergoing changes from within, and this will be reflected in your outer world as well. Some relationships or circumstances may have to fall away, and you must let them. They belong to another cycle, another era of your life. Don't suppress your emotional responses at this time, but exercise discipline in other areas of your life.

PLUTO SEXTILE URANUS

You'll experience deeper insights into yourself and your goals. Latent psychic abilities may surface; your intuitive grasp of things will deepen or be enhanced. You may make profound changes in your life direction. Interest in occult, spiritual, and possibly scientific disciplines will increase, and you'll benefit from their study.

PLUTO SQUARE URANUS

Your world is changing, and this will trigger change within you. Basically, though, your charge at this time is to adjust to changes around you. The need to be flexible is paramount. Change only what has become inappropriate in your life, though—not everything willy-nilly. Also, do not overlook or become insensitive to the emotional needs of yourself and others.

PLUTO TRINE URANUS

New awareness and insight will be yours now as you evolve into a new stage of life. Old structures and relationships will fall away to make way for the new you. New friends, experiences, and ideas will expand your life. You may set new goals. Interest in the occult will be stimulated, and you'll gain from it. You'll experience a sense of liberation and excitement at the discovery that you can do more than you ever thought you could.

PLUTO OPPOSITION URANUS

This transit signals great changes in your life and in the lives of everyone else about your age. Do not resist these changes, this overthrowing or releasing of the old and outworn structures of your life, but try instead to assist in making these changes, in building and starting anew. Flexibility is of paramount importance at this time.

PLUTO CONJUNCT NEPTUNE

You may find old ideas and beliefs invalidated. New insights are coming to you now, and you may be confused for a while, but you're not alone. This transit affects a whole generation at the same time. Your views are changing and so are you. Many areas of your life may fall away now. You may be experiencing psychic phenomena that may confuse or enlighten you. This is a good time to begin studying anything that will increase self-understanding.

PLUTO SEXTILE NEPTUNE

Your interest in the spiritual or occult and mystical will be stimulated, and you may even experience spiritual enlightenment or advancement. It will begin to be clear to you that there is more to existence than the material world. You'll find yourself interested in life after death and the deeper meanings of life.

PLUTO SQUARE NEPTUNE

You'll find many old aspects of your life falling away, old orders changing. This may leave you upset or confused for a while, especially if you fight to retain them. It's best to accept changes and prepare for a new order evolving in your life. Your interest in the spiritual or metaphysical side of life may be heightened, and you may gain immensely from their study. Hidden or suppressed facets of yourself may emerge; facing them now is best.

PLUTO SEXTILE PLUTO

You're entering a period of greater self-awareness and stability. There may be change, but not of a rapid, disruptive nature. Your interest in the meaning of life may deepen. Goals may stabilize or change gradually.

PLUTO SQUARE PLUTO

Many changes are going to be occurring, in keeping with Pluto's reputation of death and regeneration—death of the old, outworn, and useless so that the new can be born. It may not be completely pleasant, especially if you rigidly resist. Look within for the root of any changes or difficulties in your life now. It's best to avoid the practice of occult powers at this time; they may be overwhelming.

PLUTO CONJUNCT MIDHEAVEN

Some circumstances or relationships may end or fade from your life. If so, let them go as part of a necessary evolutionary process. This is an excellent time for self-examination and a reevaluation of your goals and the manner in which you're achieving them. Don't think you can get away with believing that ends justify the means; Pluto won't allow such nonsense.

PLUTO SEXTILE MIDHEAVEN

This is a good time to work through, and thus eliminate or overcome, subconscious habits or buried drives or emotions from the past. You'll be able to handle them effectively now, thereby getting rid of the drain they have been on your life. Look within, also, and see where you stand spiritually.

PLUTO SQUARE MIDHEAVEN

You may have to face challenges from others during this transit, which may force you to become aware of how you really stand on any issue. As you closely examine yourself in this light, your ideas and goals may change radically. There are also likely to be changes in your family or professional life that will reflect changes within yourself.

PLUTO TRINE MIDHEAVEN

You'll gain insight into yourself under this transit. Psychotherapy, meditation, or other disciplines of self-knowledge would be beneficial. You may gain power, either from authorities or from within. In either case, you must not misuse it.

PLUTO OPPOSITION MIDHEAVEN

The past or its effects may be coming to the fore, forcing you to deal with it and liberate yourself from it. If you try, you can gain great self-understanding during this transit. Important changes will be going on in your life, and you'll fare better if you flow with them and not resist.

PLUTO CONJUNCT ASCENDANT

Aspects of yourself that you may have attempted to keep hidden are emerging. Whether you're aware of these surfacing aspects or not, others will begin to behave differently toward you, causing you to react. And change. Do not ignore or resist these energies, or you'll be forced to acknowledge them in possibly unpleasant ways. Face up to all aspects of yourself and to the changes within you, and you'll emerge a stronger, better person when this is all over. Techniques for greater self-knowledge will help immensely.

PLUTO SEXTILE ASCENDANT

You have many opportunities to change your life at this time, especially through your relationships. Your goals may change, your life may take on a new direction, and you can grow as a human being. You may achieve some position of power or authority; be careful not to abuse it.

PLUTO TRINE ASCENDANT

You'll have experiences and encounters that will widen and deepen your self-understanding. Both you and your relationships are likely to change and grow. Superficialities will hold no interest whatsoever for you now. As always, Pluto impels you to dig beneath the surface, and deeply. Sometimes this is painful, but always necessary and rewarding.

Chapter 19

Travel

It used to be that traveling 30 miles was at least a two-day journey. Travel was a big event, not taken lightly. Today, we're so casual about it we often overlook the fact that it does have an effect on us, having to do, if nothing else, with the different set of vibrations we insert ourselves into. That, coupled with our own resonating vibrations and the transits in effect at the time, can determine the type and outcome of the trip. Some times are better for business trips, some for pleasure, some for actual change of locale in the physical plane, some for mental excursions. Take a trip in conjunction with an appropriate set of planetary vibrations, and you may never take travel so lightly again.

Transit Descriptions

SUN IN THIRD HOUSE

This is a good time for short trips in conjunction with your daily life. You won't be able to relax and properly enjoy a "get-away-from-it-all" journey.

SUN IN NINTH HOUSE

This is a good time for travel, especially if you can combine learning with pleasure.

SUN TRINE SUN

This is a great time to take a vacation. Your energy level is high, and all seems right with the world.

SUN CONJUNCT MERCURY

You really don't want to sit still today anyway, so get out and go somewhere. Experience all you can; today you can handle it.

SUN SEXTILE MERCURY

This is an excellent time for traveling, but you'll especially enjoy a trip that excites your intellect. A trip to a museum would be perfect.

SUN TRINE MERCURY

This is a good time to begin a trip, especially to conduct business.

SUN OPPOSITION MERCURY

You may find yourself having to travel a fair amount, especially for business.

SUN TRINE JUPITER

Travel today! You're optimistic, enthusiastic, and energetic, and you can expect all to go well.

SUN TRINE ASCENDANT

This is a favorable time for an outing or vacation. You're more in the mood to enjoy yourself than to work—unless you really enjoy your work.

MERCURY IN FIRST HOUSE
You'll find yourself taking, or wanting to take, short trips for various reasons.

MERCURY IN NINTH HOUSE
Travel is favored, particularly to countries, regions, or cultures foreign to your own.

MERCURY CONJUNCT SUN
You're eager for new experiences and have an itch to move around. Go ahead and take a trip if you can. You'll enjoy yourself and probably learn a great deal to boot.

MERCURY SEXTILE SUN
You're likely to do more traveling around than usual in the course of your daily life, though you may not go long distances.

MERCURY CONJUNCT MERCURY
Your normal business may require some travel today, usually not far—unless that *is* your normal business.

MERCURY SEXTILE MERCURY
You may do more running around today pursuant to your daily life, though long distances are not too likely.

MERCURY TRINE MERCURY
Local travel to see something new and different is your cup of tea today—say, to a museum or antique car show. This is also a good time to begin a longer trip.

MERCURY OPPOSITION MERCURY
You may tend to be rash and impulsive today, so be extremely careful while traveling. Don't put your mind on automatic.

MERCURY SEXTILE VENUS
This is one of those days when you'll really enjoy a leisurely drive into the country, or anywhere that will impress you with its beauty

and serenity.

MERCURY SQUARE MARS

If you've suppressed your emotions, you may be an accident waiting to happen today. Be especially careful while walking or driving; there is possible danger to arms and legs.

MERCURY OPPOSITION MARS

Suppressed anger or hostility may make you accident prone, due to a tendency toward impulsive behavior. Pay attention and be careful while traveling. Arms and legs are especially vulnerable at this time.

MERCURY SEXTILE JUPITER

Barring powerful influences to the contrary, this is a good time to take a trip. You're intellectually curious and more than usually broadminded.

MERCURY CONJUNCT URANUS

Be especially careful if you're in control of a vehicle today. Fast-paced thinking and impulsiveness may lead to an accident.

MERCURY SQUARE URANUS

Uranus, the impulsive one, and Mercury, the quicksilvered one, warn you in this configuration to be very cautious while driving today. Rash movements and ill-considered judgment can prove dangerous in a vehicle.

MERCURY TRINE URANUS

Traveling to new and different and, especially, foreign places will appeal to you today. Do try to go somewhere you find unusual if at all possible. You're interested in and stimulated by everything, and if you're open to all you encounter, this can be a useful and truly exciting day.

MERCURY CONJUNCT ASCENDANT

You may find yourself scurrying around familiar territory more than usual today. Necessary chores in first one place and then another may keep you hopping.

MERCURY SEXTILE ASCENDANT

There may be many short hops all around the town today, or

perhaps a longer drive to a neighboring area. Beginning an extensive trip is also favored.

MERCURY TRINE ASCENDANT
You may travel a little more than you usually do today, though this probably won't entail long trips.

VENUS IN FIRST HOUSE
You're in a sociable and fun-loving mood—a perfect time to begin and enjoy a vacation.

VENUS IN NINTH HOUSE
This is an excellent time for a vacation, particularly to someplace new to you.

VENUS CONJUNCT MERCURY
This is an excellent day for an enjoyable trip to visit friends and to revel in being surrounded by beautiful scenery.

VENUS SEXTILE MERCURY
This is a good day to take a relaxing drive or to go somewhere purely for the fun of it, especially if it also piques your mind.

VENUS TRINE MERCURY
This is a good day to take a pleasant drive or to start a vacation. Such a trip now will be very beneficial to you. And, you just might make new friends who will become old friends.

VENUS SEXTILE VENUS
This is a wonderful time to take a short trip just for fun and relaxation. A picnic in the country, perhaps?

VENUS TRINE VENUS
Your appreciation of beauty is enhanced, so you'll greatly enjoy and benefit from attending a concert, museum, art gallery, or simply putting yourself into some beautiful scenery.

VENUS TRINE JUPITER
This is a good time to begin a vacation or any other trip for purely fun and recreational purposes.

MARS IN NINTH HOUSE

Travel would be very pleasant and mind-expanding for you now, unless there are severe afflictions in this house.

MARS SEXTILE MERCURY

This is a favorable time for all kinds of travel, but especially for business purposes. Your high energy level—both mental and physical—would make it hard for you to simply sit still and relax on a vacation, unless it involved some sport you find relaxing, such as swimming, tennis, or golf.

MARS TRINE MERCURY

This is an excellent time for going somewhere, especially if it involves effort, such as hiking, jogging, bicycling, rowing, or whatever. You have so much energy, you can hardly sit still and do nothing.

MARS SEXTILE MARS

This is a great time for doing something new and different. Take a vacation if you can, or at least take a short trip in your area to some place or event you find intellectually stimulating.

JUPITER IN THIRD HOUSE

You may find yourself traveling for some reason or another, and it's likely to prove beneficial to your self-understanding.

JUPITER IN NINTH HOUSE

There is a possibility of travel to other countries or cultures under this transit. If you do travel now, you will learn a great deal and be a different person when it's all over, as far as your beliefs and prejudices are concerned.

JUPITER TRINE SUN

You may very well take a trip today, either physically or mentally, that will expand your knowledge and understanding.

JUPITER CONJUNCT MOON

This is a transit that says you *can* go home again, and it encourages you to do so to see old friends and relatives. You'll see now how your home environment and the people in it contributed to the person you currently are. You'll want to reminisce about the past and be surrounded by it.

JUPITER SEXTILE VENUS

You don't really feel very ambitious and would greatly enjoy a vacation. You're feeling sociable and will also appreciate beautiful surroundings. Be careful, though; you'll tend to overspend.

JUPITER SQUARE VENUS

Now is a good time to take a vacation or short trip just to have fun. You really don't feel like working anyway.

JUPITER TRINE VENUS

You feel relaxed, unambitious, rather mellow—a very good mood in which to enjoy a vacation.

JUPITER SEXTILE JUPITER

This is an excellent time to expand your outlook through travel—and to take stock of yourself as you go along.

JUPITER TRINE JUPITER

This is one of those rare times of physical and mental balance. Trips for educational or relaxation purposes, or which combine the two, would be beneficial to you now.

JUPITER CONJUNCT URANUS

A sudden travel opportunity may arise, possibly to distant and exotic places.

JUPITER CONJUNCT ASCENDANT

Travel sometimes occurs under this transit, and if so, it's for the purpose of maturing your viewpoint and enhancing your tolerance of the world's diversity. You'll meet new and fascinating people. Enjoy.

JUPITER SEXTILE ASCENDANT

Travel is sometimes indicated by this transit; but even if you don't travel, you're likely to meet interesting and different people.

SATURN IN NINTH HOUSE

You may travel a long distance for your business or other obligations or for educational pursuits.

URANUS IN THIRD HOUSE

Short, even seemingly routine, trips may result in unexpected incidents. This does not necessarily imply an accident, unless you are resisting change in your life so arduously that the suppressed energy must burst out in this way.

URANUS IN NINTH HOUSE

You may travel to distant places, and if you keep an open, flexible mind, the experience will be very enlightening for you.

URANUS CONJUNCT MERCURY

This is not one of your better times to travel. There are likely to be frustrating delays or other problems. A situation may come up suddenly, forcing you to travel to take care of it.

URANUS SEXTILE MERCURY

You're restless and curious, and you may very well want to travel and explore, particularly in your own bailiwick.

URANUS SQUARE MERCURY

Upsetting delays or other problems are apt to plague travel under this transit. Travel only if really necessary and then very carefully. Accidents are a possibility.

URANUS TRINE MERCURY

Travel undertaken now will be exciting and invigorating, rather than relaxing and restful.

URANUS OPPOSITION MERCURY

This is not a good time to travel for either business or pleasure. Too many unexpected, disruptive, upsetting things may very well happen.

URANUS SEXTILE JUPITER

A chance to travel may come your way under this transit. If so, you'll have an opportunity to broaden your viewpoints and opinions. The experience will be more exhilarating than restful.

URANUS TRINE NEPTUNE

This is a favorable time for travel, especially for increasing your knowledge of the world and its peoples, and consequently, of yourself.

NEPTUNE SEXTILE JUPITER

Your interest in travel may be increased, and, indeed, you would greatly benefit from journeys to strange and distant places at this time.

NEPTUNE TRINE JUPITER

Travel at this time, especially long, unstructured trips, can be an extremely valuable learning experience. You're seeking understanding of the world and your place in it.

PLUTO IN THIRD HOUSE

Any traveling you do now, if you are observant and self-aware, will help to give you a new perspective on yourself, your ideas, and your attitudes. Be very careful, though, if Pluto is afflicted in or passing through this house.

PLUTO IN NINTH HOUSE

If afflicted, Pluto could cause problems during extended or foreign trips. Take care. In any case, profound experiences could occur that change your life.

BIBLIOGRAPHY

Arroyo, Stephen. *Astrology, Karma, and Transformation*. Davis, California: CRCS Publications, 1978.

Arroyo, Stephen. *Astrology, Psychology, and the Four Elements*. Reno, Nevada: CRCS Publications, 1975.

Filbey, John, and Peter Filbey. *Astronomy for Astrologers*. Wellingborough, Great Britain: The Aquarian Press, 1984.

Hand, Robert. *Planets in Transit, Life Cycles for Living*. Rockport, Massachusetts: Para Research, 1976.

Hickey, Isabel M. *Astrology, a Cosmic Science*. Watertown, Massachusetts: Fellowship House, 1970.

Lewi, Grant. *Astrology for the Millions*. St. Paul, Minnesota: Llewellyn Publications, 1978.

Lunstead, Betty. *Transits, the Time of Your Life*. York Beach, Maine: Samuel Weiser, Inc., 1980.

Luntz, Charles, E. *Vocational Guidance by Astrology*. St. Paul, Minnesota: Llewellyn Publications, 1978.

Luxton, Leonora. *Astrology, Key to Self Understanding*. St. Paul, Minnesota: Llewellyn Publications, 1978.

Meyer, Michael R. *A Handbook for the Humanistic Astrologer*. Garden City, New York: Anchor Press/Doubleday, 1974.

Parker, Derek and Julia. *The Compleat Astrologer*. New York: Bantam Books, 1975.

Rudhyar, Dane. *Astrology and the Modern Psyche*. Vancouver, Washington: CRCS Publications, 1976.

Ruperti, Alexander. *Cycles of Becoming.* Vancouver, Washington: CRCS Publications, 1978.

Sakoian, Frances, and Louis Acker. *Transits Simplified.* Weston, Massachusetts: ACA, Inc., 1976.

Tyl, Noel. *Integrated Transits.* St. Paul, Minnesota: Llewellyn Publications, 1976.

GENERAL INDEX

Air signs, 10
Ascendant, definition of, 10
Aspects, definition of, names of,
    degrees of, symbols, 5
Astrology, qualifying language of, 3–4

Birth chart, 5

Cross of Matter, 10

Degrees of aspects, 5
Descendant, definition of, 10
Direct planet turns, use in timing, 15
Doppler Effect, 14

Ephemeris, definition of, 1; how to
    use, 1; where to obtain, 1

Four Angles, 10

Glyphs, 6

Horoscope, 5
How to use this book, 2–3

Imum Coeli, 10
Inner planets, 7

Midheaven, 10, 17

Nadir, 10, 17
Natal chart, how to obtain, 1

Orb, definition of, 13; allowances,
    general guideline, 14
Outer Planets, 7

Planets, direct, making a station,
    retrograde, 15; locations, 7; orbits,
    length of, 7

Quadruplicities, 10

Retrograde, planet turns, use in
    timing, 15

Signs, zodiacal, 6; air, earth, fire,
    water, 10; cardinal, fixed, mutable,
    10–11
Solar system, heliocentric, 7;
    geocentric, 8

Station, planet making a, 15; use in
    timing, 15
Strengths, Doppler Effect, 14; relative,
    of angles, aspects, planets, transits,
    16–17
Symbols of aspects, 5

Timing, 15–16
Transiting aspect, definition of, 2
Transits, cross-checking, 3; definition
    of, 1; how to find, 1
Triplicities, 10–11

Yogananda, Paramahansa, 4

TRANSIT INDEX

STAY IN TOUCH

On the following pages you will find listed, with their current prices, some of the books and tapes now available on related subjects. Your book dealer stocks most of these, and will stock new titles in the Llewellyn series as they become available. We urge your patronage.

However, to obtain our full catalog, to keep informed of new titles as they are released and to benefit from informative articles and helpful news, you are invited to write for our bi-monthly news magazine/catalog. A sample copy is free, and it will continue coming to you at no cost as long as you are an active mail customer. Or you may keep it coming for a full year with a donation of just $2.00 in U.S.A. ($7.00 for Canada & Mexico, $20.00 overseas, first class mail). Many bookstores also have *The Llewellyn New Times* available to their customers. Ask for it.

Stay in touch! In *The Llewellyn New Times'* pages you will find news and reviews of new books, tapes and services, announcements of meetings and seminars, articles helpful to our readers, news of authors, advertising of products and services, special money-making opportunities, and much more.

The Llewellyn New Times
P.O. Box 64383-Dept. 674, St. Paul, MN 55164-0383, U.S.A.

• • •

TO ORDER BOOKS AND TAPES

If your book dealer does not have the books and tapes described on the following pages readily available, you may order them direct from the publisher by sending full price in U.S. funds, plus $2.00 for postage and handling for orders of $10 and under. Orders over $10 will require $3.50 postage and handling. There are no postage and handling charges for orders over $100. UPS Delivery: We ship UPS whenever possible. Delivery guaranteed. Provide your street address, as UPS does not deliver to P.O. Boxes. UPS to Canada requires a $50 minimum order. Allow 4-6 weeks for delivery. Orders outside the USA and Canada: Airmail—add $5 per book; add $3 for each non-book item (tapes, etc.); add $1 per item for surface mail.

FOR GROUP STUDY AND PURCHASE

Because there is a great deal of interest in group discussion and study of the subject matter of this book, we feel that we should encourage the adoption and use of this particular book by such groups by offering a special "quantity" price to group leaders or "agents".

Our Special Quantity Price for a minimum order of five copies of *Transits in Reverse* is $38.85 Cash-With-Order. This price includes postage and handling within the United States. Minnesota residents must add 6% sales tax. For additional quantities, please order in multiples of five. For Canadian and foreign orders, add postage and handling charges as above. Credit Card (VISA, MasterCard, American Express) Orders are accepted. Charge Card Orders only may be phoned free ($15.00 minimum order) within the U.S.A. by dialing 1-800-THE MOON (in Canada call: 1-800-FOR-SELF). Customer Service calls dial 1-612-291-1970. Mail Orders to:

LLEWELLYN PUBLICATIONS
P.O. Box 64383-Dept. 674 / St. Paul, MN 55164-0383, U.S.A.

SIGNS OF THE TIMES
by Stan Barker

With remarkable accuracy, Barker predicts political and social events from now until the next century, based on Neptune's current transit through Capricorn.

In this book the author predicted:
- The popularity of Ronald Reagan
- The popularity of the Bill Cosby Show
- The U.S. involvement in Central America
- The Space Shuttle disaster

And you can too!

Stan Barker discovered that the planet Neptune astrologically indicates the direction of America. Here, he shows how the position of Neptune against the Zodiac has always indicated U.S. involvement in wars, depressions and politics. More than that, the *Neptune Factor* also shows very clearly how the transits of Neptune indicate: our morals; architecture; fashion, popular music, movies, and books; and our economic trends.

While this book is valuable for astrologers, it is not just for experts in that field— *even if you know nothing about astrology, you will fully understand this book!*. This is because everything is fully and clearly explained. Explanations show how the Neptune Factor has affected America since Columbus, and how Neptune affects our country when it is in any particular sign. From this, the future is easy to determine.

Neptune entered a new sign in 1984, and will be in that sign until 1998. Will you be ready for this period and beyond? Get *The Signs of the Times* and be prepared!

0-87542-030-3, 320 pages $9.95

PLANETS IN LOCALITY
by Steve Cozzi

DIRECTION . . . it's what we all need, what we all seek. Is there a method that is clear, simple, concise and logical that will bring this needed direction to our lives? Yes. It's called Locational Astrology, a comprehensive system on the cutting edge of contemporary astrological thought and practice. Steve Cozzi, an expert in locality charts, computers, and the creator of this system of Locational Astrology, has put together a book that will show the average student of astrology as well as the professional how to use this innovative system to help not only themselves, but also their clients.

This is not only a historical analysis of Local Space Astrology—it is also a practical guide for the individual reader, applicable to most aspects of everyday activities. Did you know that your route to work each day could actually shape the way you perform or how others perceive you? That where your home is located in your town could affect your state of mind? That where you decide to relocate could change your whole sense of self or your ability to create what you desire? This is all proven fact. Cozzi shows you how to determine your own planetary lines and how to best use them to further your ideals. *Planets in Locality* has over 50 figures and maps, geomantic compasses and other illustrations to help you find and plot planetary lines within your home, town, region and on out to the country and the world. It is an essential astrological volume.

0-87542-098-2, 308 pages, 6 x 9, illus., $12.95

URANUS: Freedom From the Known
by Jeff Green

This book deals primarily with the archetypal correlations of the planet Uranus to human psychology and behavior to anatomy/physiology and the chakra system, and to metaphysical and cosmic laws. Uranus' relationship to Saturn, from an individual and collective point of view, is also discussed.

The text of this book comes intact in style and tone from an intensive workshop held in Toronto. You will feel as if you are a part of that workshop.

In reading *Uranus* you will discover how to naturally liberate yourself from all of your conditioning patterns, patterns that were determined by the "internal" and "external" environment. Every person has a natural way to actualize this liberation. This natural way is examined by use of the natal chart and from a developmental point of view.

The 48-year sociopolitical cycle of Uranus and Saturn is discussed extensively, as is the relationship between Uranus, Saturn and Neptune. With this historical perspective, you can see what lies ahead in 1988, a very important year.

0-87542-297-7, 192 pages, 5¼ x 8, softcover $7.95

HEAVEN KNOWS WHAT
by Grant Lewi

Heaven Knows What contains everything you need to cast and interpret complete natal charts without learning any symbols, without confusion from tricky calculations, without previous experience or training.

How does the system work? Simply look up the positions of the planets in the tables at the back of the book. Plot these positions on the handy tear-out horoscope blanks. Use the aspect wheel provided to determine the planetary aspects and then read the relevant paragraphs describing their influence.

It's easy, fast, and amazingly accurate! Grant Lewi interpets the influence of the Sun and Moon positions at birth, and describes the effects of every possible planetary aspect in language designed for the modern reader. The tables have been updated so that you can cast a chart for any birth from 1890 through 1999.

Heaven Knows What forms an excellent astrological background for the beginner, yet Lewi's interpretations are so relevant that even long-practicing astrologers gain new psychological insight into the characteristics of the signs and the meanings of the aspects.

0-87542-444-9, 300 pages, softcover. $9.95

THE NEW A TO Z HOROSCOPE MAKER AND DELINEATOR
by Llewellyn George

This is a new and totally revised edition of the text used by more American astrologers than any other—135,000 copies sold. Every detail of: How to Cast the Birth Chart—time changes, calculations, aspects & orbs, signs & planetary rulers, parts of fortune, etc.; The Progressed Chart—all the techniques and the major delineations; Transits—how to use them in prediction, also lunations and solar days; Rectification; Locality Charts, a comprehensive Astrological Dictionary and a complete index for easy use. It's an encyclopedia, a textbook, a self-study course and and a dictionary all-in-one!

0-87542-264-0, 600 pages, 6 x 9, softcover. $12.95

THE LLEWELLYN ANNUALS

Llewellyn's MOON SIGN BOOK: Approximately 400 pages of valuable information on gardening, fishing, weather, stock market forecasts, personal horoscopes, good planting dates, and general instructions for finding the best date to do just about anything! Articles by prominent forecasters and writers in the fields of gardening, astrology, politics, economics and cycles. This special almanac, different from any other, has been published annually since 1906. It's fun, informative and has been a great help to millions in their daily planning.   **State year $3.95**

Llewellyn's SUN SIGN BOOK: Your personal horoscope for the entire year! All 12 signs are included in one handy book. Also included are forecasts, special feature articles, and an action guide for each sign. Monthly horoscopes are written by Gloria Star, author of *The Optimum Child*, for your personal Sun Sign. Articles on a variety of subjects written by well-known astrologers from around the country. Much more than just a horoscope guide! Entertaining and fun the year round.
State year $3.95

Llewellyn's DAILY PLANETARY GUIDE and ASTROLOGER'S DATEBOOK: Includes all of the major daily aspects plus their exact times in Eastern and Pacific time zones, lunar phases, signs and voids plus their times, planetary motion, a monthly ephemeris, sunrise and sunset tables, special articles on the planets, signs, aspects, a business guide, planetary hours, rulerships, and much more. Large 5¼ X 8 format for more writing space, spiral bound to lay flat, address and phone listings, time zone conversion chart and blank horoscope chart.   **State year $6.95**

Llewellyn's MAGICKAL ALMANAC
Edited by Ray Buckland
The Magickal Almanac examines some of the many forms that Magick can take, allowing the reader a peek behind a veil of secrecy into Egyptian, Enochian, Shamanic, Wiccan and other traditions. The almanac pages for each month provide information important in the many aspects of working Magick: sunrise and sunset, phases of the Moon, and festival dates, as well as the tarot card, herb, incense, mineral, color, and name of power (god/goddess/entity) associated with the particular day.

Each month, following the almanac pages, are articles addressing one form of Magick with rituals the reader can easily follow. An indispensable guide for all interested in the Magickal arts, *The Magickal Almanac* features writing by some of the most prominent authors in the field.   **State year $9.95**

Llewellyn's ASTROLOGICAL CALENDAR: Large wall calendar of 52 pages. Beautiful full color cover and color inside. Includes special feature articles by famous astrologers, introductory information on astrology. Lunar Gardening Guide, celestial phenomena for the year, a blank horoscope chart for your own chart data, and monthly date pages which include aspects, lunar information, planetary motion, ephemeris, personal forecasts, lucky dates, planting and fishing dates, and more. 10 x 13 size. Set in Central time, with conversion table for other time zones worldwide.
State year $7.95